What People Ar
Lessons Lived and Learned

MW01615485

"For anyone who has an even passing interest in how judges gain their experience before they take the bench, *Lessons Lived and Learned: My Life On and Off the Bench* is a treasure trove of wonderful information and stories! Judge Platt's storytelling in this memoir makes you feel like you're having a conversation with him in the family room of his home. It's warm and undeniably interesting, and you leave truly feeling enriched for having read it. I had the pleasure of appearing before Judge Platt many times, and his memoir superbly captures his self-deprecating, comical, yet always insightful and intelligent way of looking at a situation and rendering a meaningful solution. I highly recommend it!"

Steven B. Vinick, attorney, Stein Sperling, Bennett, De Jong, Driscoll, PC

"Having had the pleasure of appearing before Judge Platt and becoming his friend once he retired, he is an engaging story teller. Inasmuch as this story is his own, he tells it in his own captivating and enthralling manner. His war time exploits in the 'Battle of College Park' truly capture the spirit of the National Guard in the Vietnam War era. *Lessons Lived and Learned: My Life On and Off the Bench* is a worthy read."

Alvin I. Frederick, principal, Eccleston & Wolf

"Judge Platt has written a book not just about a great life in law and politics, but how law and politics have changed profoundly in our lifetime. *Lessons Lived and Learned* is insightful, fun, and full of important history. Anyone who cares about politics or our legal system should read this."

Timothy F. Maloney, attorney, Joseph Greenwald & Laake, PA

"It is not enough to describe Judge Platt as having an excellent mind, sound judgment, compassion, a keen sense of justice, and a compelling sense of humor. Nor is it adequate to call him scholarly or loyal, or possessed of the highest integrity and discretion. He is all of this. The key to understanding him is to know that at every moment he is gathering information of every kind to understand what individuals and groups have done, are doing, will do and why. This level of curiosity and analysis has imbued him with the wisdom that made him an effective politician, a great judge and a masterful, effective mediator. It also makes him a wonderful and compelling storyteller as you will see when you read his memoir. I am proud of him and grateful that we are friends."

William H. "Billy" Murphy, Jr., partner, Murphy Falcon & Murphy

"Judge Steve Platt is a unique combination—historian, jurist, commentator, scholar, politician, teacher, and mediator. It is that last skill that I appreciate most. He settled every single case he mediated for me. All of his skills, and his rich life, are reflected in *Lessons Lived and Learned: My Life On and Off the Bench*."

Laurence W.B. Cumberland, founding member, Cumberland & Erly, LLC

"In his characteristically inspiring and entertaining way, Judge Platt shares the story of his remarkable life and accomplishments. From humble beginnings, but imbued with the awareness that he had something special to offer the world, Judge Platt forged an impactful life and career that ranged from his start as a young and energetic operative in Maryland's O'Malley-Hoyer political machine of the 1970s and 1980s to become an esteemed practicing lawyer, a distinguished judge in three levels of Maryland's court system, and ultimately a highly respected and sought-after mediator/arbitrator of legal and business disputes. Could anyone have predicted that this grandson of a Jewish immigrant from Russia who came to America in 1913, with only $17 in his pocket, could reach such heights? Indeed, Judge Platt has provided something special to the world— his basic decency and a career distinguished by his courage, scholarship, diligence, good humor, integrity, and passion for justice. I highly recommend *Lessons Lived and Learned: My Life On and Off the Bench* to anyone looking to enjoy a true American success story or to discover a roadmap for living a meaningful life."

Wayne M. Willoughby, past president, Maryland Association for Justice/Maryland Trial Lawyers Association; partner, Gershon, Willoughby & Getz, LLC

"Judge Platt is an amazing storyteller. He captivates you from the beginning with intrigue and laughter; but there is always a lesson to be learned, and *Lessons Lived and Learned: My Life On and Off the Bench* does not disappoint. Through the many experiences in his life as a lawyer and a judge, he reminds us to laugh and live; but he also reminds us about humanity and how we all have a part in making the lives of others just a little bit better."

Lisa A. Johnson, attorney and supervisory program analyst, Bureau of Information Resource Management

"Judge Platt's chronicle leads the reader to conclude that he is truly the 'Forrest Gump' of the Free State. From tales of the Holocaust to the rural rolling hills of Virginia, with stops into local politics, *Lessons Lived and Learned: My Life On and Off the Bench* takes us on a trip from the shtetls of Poland to the hallowed halls of Annapolis. A good read."

Bruce L. Marcus, partner, MarcusBonsib, LLC

"Judge Steven I. Platt is an insightful and irreverent raconteur who knows how to tell a story. Mark Twain would like this book. Even though it's all true!"

Douglas Furlong, attorney, Furlong ADR, LLC

"With this fascinating memoir of his incredible career, Judge Steven Platt brilliantly illustrates the connection between law and politics in Maryland. For those who engage in or have any interest in Maryland politics, in particular Prince George's County political history, *Lessons Lived and Learned: My Life On and Off the Bench* is a must read. For those who may think otherwise, Judge Platt shows that 'the game' hasn't changed; only the players have."

Gregory K. Wells, partner, Shadoan, Michael & Wells LLP

"Judge Platt is the kind of person who always made time for a chat, whether light-hearted laughter or a deep heart-to-heart. This memoir literally tastes like a cup of coffee with a rare mentor. As an openly gay, first generation Indian American and woman of color, I never had an easy time finding mentors—professionals who could understand what I might be experiencing or seeking in my journey. The stories in *Lessons Lived and Learned: My Life On and Off the Bench* help me to see what experiences led Judge Platt to be the most down-to-earth, approachable, and inclusive leader I've ever met. Whether you know him or not, this book will move you to pursue your dreams with a bit more confidence and focus."

Mala Malhotra-Ortiz, attorney, former director of Court of Special Appeals ADR Program, and past chair of MSBA ADR section

"*Lessons Lived and Learned: My Life On and Off the Bench* is a riveting journey through Maryland politics, full of stories, universal truths, and insights into recent Maryland political history. Judge Platt's reflections on his career as an attorney, judge, and professional mediator provide insightful, captivating, and often humorous legal lessons. Just the cogent collection one would expect from such an exceptional legal mind."

Stephen Reichert, attorney, Law Office of Stephen J. Reichert, LLC, and founder and editor of *Smartish Pace*

"Two decades of hearings, chats, and whimsical stories with Judge Steve Platt are not enough. With a keen eye for intricate details of a case or events of our time, he was a step ahead of everyone in the room with his legal analysis and thought-provoking insight, typically layered with a hilarious anecdote lightening the mood for everyone within earshot. A jurist like none other, a person you always wanted to hang out and shoot the stuff with ..., Steve Platt made me laugh out loud more than anyone I know. And he's still at it with his new memoir!"

John P. Lynch, principal, McNamee Hosea

"For litigants, there are times when the judicial process—and the judges tasked to oversee it—seem removed from the disputes that courts are tasked to address. *Lessons Lived and Learned: My Life On and Off the Bench* provides an intimate behind-the-scenes look at the courtroom, cases, and heart behind the conflict from the vantage point of senior Judge Steven I. Platt. For lawyers, Judge Platt's book is a candid and inspirational account of how hard work, determination, and community pave the way from rural beginnings in Strasburg, Virginia, to high-tech innovations with Maryland's Business and Technology Case Management Program and beyond. For mediators and arbitrators that question whether a balance between zealous advocacy and calculated compromise can be achieved, *Lessons Lived and Learned* delivers."

Shelly M. Ingram, attorney, Law Office of Shelly M. Ingram, LLC

"Judge Platt was an outstanding judge on the Circuit Court for Prince George's County, Maryland. When I served as his law clerk, attorneys frequently pulled me aside to say, 'You know he's an excellent judge, right?' He is a great mentor and quite the comedian, always recounting stories with hysterical punch lines. *Lessons Lived and Learned: My Life On and Off the Bench* is sure to reveal all these qualities and more."

Rose Crunkleton, attorney, Law Offices of Rose C. Crunkleton, LLC

"Having lived in the courthouse during many of the years that Judge Platt presided in the District Court and Circuit Court in Prince George's County, I particularly enjoyed the judicial history recounted in his book. It provides an entertaining and informative judicial history from the perspective of a judge who has presided over a wide variety of interesting and challenging cases. The judicial history in this book also reveals a judge who did not just preside over cases but devoted his time and expertise to improving the judicial system with new programs that benefited from the insight of a lawyer, a judge, and one who truly invested the time and effort to make the justice system work. I have always appreciated Judge Platt's legal acumen and the respect he showed for the litigants and attorneys who appeared before him. Win or lose, one always felt that they had benefited from a fair, compassionate, and caring jurist. If one could clone a great judge, Judge Platt's DNA would be the foundation for success."

Robert Bonsib, partner, MarcusBonsib LLC

"Twenty-five years after clerking for Judge Platt, I still reflect on the legal lessons he impressed upon me, as expressed in his memoir, *Lessons Lived and Learned: My Life On and Off the Bench*. His mentorship is only exceeded by his caring, sincere friendship, and desire to help others succeed."

Michael J. Winkelman, partner, McCarthy, Winkelman, Mester & Offutt, LLP

LESSONS

Lived and Learned

LESSONS
Lived and Learned

My Life On and Off the Bench

Steven I. Platt

With a foreword written by Ron Bergman

RAMSES HOUSE PUBLISHING LLC
BALTIMORE, MD

Published by Ramses House Publishing LLC, Baltimore, MD
www.publishingforlawyers.com

First Printing, 2023
ISBN 978-1-7351462-6-3 paperback; 10-digit: 1-7351462-6-9
ISBN 978-1-7351462-7-0 eBook; 10-digit: 1-7351462-7-7
ISBN 978-1-7351462-8-7 hard cover; 10-digit: 1-7351462-8-5

Library of Congress Control No.: 2022923043

Cover image: Beverly Funkhouser Photography

Notice: The book is written for attorneys, scholars, and laypeople who are interested in historical accounts, opinion, and analysis of economics, law, and politics on a local, state, and federal level.

Printed and bound in the United States of America

The Platt Group Inc.
P.O. Box 6604
Annapolis, MD 21401

*With my deepest love, appreciation, and affection to
my expanded family; each of you has enriched
my life more than you will ever know
in your own unique ways.*

*To my son, Jason Benjamin Platt, and his wife, Anne
Fleetwood Platt; my daughter, Sarah Edan Carter, her
husband, Kevin Carter; and my cherished grandchildren, Dylan Emerson Carter, Benjamin Graham Platt,
and Charlie Robert Platt.*

*To my partner and "Significant Other" going on 22
years, Frances Hughes Glendening.*

*To my ex-wife, Patti Hartlove Platt, for the years she
partnered with me, raised our children, and gave me
the time to live these stories.*

*To the memory of my parents, Nathan Platt and Adele
Lober Platt, as well as my grandparents, Charlie Platt
and Rose Berliner Platt, whose voyage on stowage
from Russia to Ellis Island in 1913 laid the foundation
for me to live out my dreams, which were their dreams
for me.*

*My parents raised me to believe I could do anything
that I wanted, limited only by my own capabilities.
This book is the evidence that I believed them and was
guided by their faith in my abilities and the freedom,
education, and finances that enabled me to make my
dreams a reality.*

Symmetry

*"Lawyers and judges enjoy being story tellers, and
Judge Platt has done a masterful job in combining
such wonderfully selected lore, history, and
perception into a fine read."*

ABOUT TWO YEARS ago, Judge Platt and I met for lunch in Annapolis, a number of months after I had very happily served a two-year stint on the Maryland State Bar Association Committee on Laws. Of course, Steve already had participated (for about 20 years) with this quite interesting group; and it was my pleasure to have reconnected with him. To my delight, there was far more life symmetry for us to share, as we told stories and laughed in the open air and fine weather.

Though we had enjoyed our briefer, mostly legal-related courthouse encounters in earlier years, there had always been an element of mirth, sociability, and interest in our shared experiences. Not surprisingly, I had started as a law clerk for a mid-sized firm in the county around the same time he had begun his legal career.

As it turned out, our heritage was also basically the same for our forebears. My father's side started in Germany, ending up in what is now Belarus before leaving the Czar's Army from the Sino-Japanese front in 1905 with some town mates who all ended up in Ellis Island. My mother's family consisted of shopkeepers who hailed from Lithuania and settled in Flemington, New Jersey. My mom was an identical twin, and the twins as teenagers were drawn to the Lindbergh kidnapping trial. While Steve's family went to the Blue Ridge Mountains of Virginia, mine went to New Jersey and to Massachusetts, and then spent about 35 years at the chemical plant next to the Delaware Memorial Bridge.

My wife and I loved the Blue Ridge Mountains. We had a house and land near the Appalachian Trail at 3,500 feet for 20 years. It was fully covered with wild rhododendron and mountain laurel.

That's enough about me; suffice to say, the similarities in our paths continued.

Judge Platt and I were both politically sensitive and completely intrigued with how things were handled and accomplished by the illustrious lawyers, politicians, power brokers, influencers, and others who dominated the scene for many years.

To say that Steve had a well-rounded, comprehensive approach to everything he touched would be an understatement. It was these same qualities that served him well with the varied matters he handled.

To read Steve's carefully constructed and organized material set forth in his memoir, *Lessons Lived and Learned: My Life On and Off the Bench*, brought back all the tales and insights of the era. Now well-conceived and fleshed out, not only for the consumption of those tangentially connected to those days but as a well-written guide to almost anything in Prince George's County. Not surprisingly, I had a trial with Steny Hoyer after his first election and many cases over the years with Peter O'Malley's fine firm of defense attorneys. I even had a hiring interview with Abe Pollin to handle a rent control case in northwest D.C. and Chevy Chase, Maryland, in the mid-1970s.

Lawyers and judges enjoy being story tellers, and Judge Platt has done a masterful job in combining such wonderfully selected lore, history, and perception into a fine read. His ability to tell a tale is well nuanced throughout the book.

Of course, my mindset, when we lunched two years ago, was geared toward crafting screenplays like *The John Wick Trilogy* with "the Adjudicators" brightening our moods. In his inimical way, Steve only laughed and stated he was not heading in that direction at all.

Now, his well-crafted prose and honed perspective will finally reach the minds and interests of his varied readers and stimulate their senses of humor and passion, all from a highly plugged-in viewer of the scene.

Ron Bergman, attorney and president, Rb Companies

Chapters

PART FIVE: The State of Criminal Justice in Maryland

PART SIX: The Civil Docket

PART SEVEN: Thriving as a Professional Mediator and Arbitrator

---

PART EIGHT: Comic Relief

CONCLUSION

APPENDICES

Acknowledgments

I THANK THE persons who have made this book possible by working with me to edit, print, and publish these stories. They include my selfless, trusted, and dependable Administrative Assistant, Penny M. Simpson; Dr. Marilyn Smith—"The Wordsmith" whose Vince Lombardi–like coaching saved you, my readers, from having to endure too many very long sentences and paragraphs; and my confidence-building editor and publisher, Tatia Gordon-Troy, Esquire, and her publishing company, Ramses House Publishing, LLC.

I also want to thank those who, with me, were players in the case histories that are recreated in the pages of this book. They are my Courtroom Clerk during most of my time on the Prince George's County Circuit Court bench, Barbara Patterson, who partnered with me in the courtroom for over a decade and whose friendship I have valued ever since; and my two invaluable Executive Administrative Assistants while I was a full-time judge, Martha Folea and Sara Baldwin.

My law clerks, who became a second family, also deserve my thanks for making me a better judge than I would have been without them. They are Gigi Matthews, Michelle Hansen, Esther Anne Alpert, Connie R. Lynch, Rose Crunkleton, Anne P. Depman, Tara Rutley, Lisa Johnson, Sarah Qureshi, Effi Rife, Julia Langston, Michael Winkelman, Christopher Montgomery, Stephen Reichert, Shelly Ingram, Allison Sayers, Jessica Rizer, and Allison Byers.

Finally, I want to remember and thank the deceased friends and mentors who shaped me and these stories. The person who left the greatest impression on me was the first Maryland District Court Chief Judge, Robert F. Sweeney, whose style, history, and career served as an inspiration and a role model for me; Ernest A. Loveless, Jr., Chief Judge for the Maryland 7th Judicial Circuit, for whom I clerked and whose observed political, diplomatic, and interpersonal skills instructed my conduct for the rest of my life; my friend, retired Judge Howard S. Chasanow of the Maryland Court of Appeals, whose intellect and scholarship set an example that I always sought to emulate and whose trailblazing in the field of alternative dispute resolution (ADR) inspired my own; and Judge Joseph S. Casula, whose friendship, nurtured by his combination of intelligence and humility, made my life more fun and fulfilling than it would have been without being his pal.

Finally, my friend and counselor, Peter Francis O'Malley, Esquire, who showed me through his example that friendship, honesty, and integrity, can be successfully reconciled with being an effective political and business operative.

I also thank my judicial colleagues (now "retired" and "sitting") and more importantly good friends, including but not limited to Judge James P. Salmon, Judge Glenn T. Harrell, Jr., Judge William B. Spellbring, Jr., Judge C. Philip Nichols, Jr., Judges Jim and Debbie Eyler, Chief Magistrate Judge William Connelly, Judge Irma Raker, Judge Diane Leasure, Judge Ronald D. Schiff, Judge Tim Meredith, Judge Larnzell Martin, Jr., Judge Sean D. Wallace, Judge Leo E. Green, Judge Theresa Nolan, Judge Paul Bowman, and Judge Julia Weatherly.

Finally, my unexpectedly deceased younger brother, Howard, who put up with my well-placed barbs and advice for more than 70 years; my pal Patricia Hincken, who was always there over and over as a friend to talk to; and my friends, attorneys Al Frederick, Tim Maloney, William F. Edwards, Robert Zarbin (deceased), Maryland Senate President Thomas V. Mike Miller (deceased), Kathy Meredith,

John Lynch, and Wayne Willoughby. Your advice and counsel have enriched my personal and professional life immeasurably.

Thanks to all!

About the Author

FOR NEARLY THREE decades, Senior Judge Steven I. Platt presided over the following courts in Prince George's County, Maryland: Orphans' Court (1978–86); District Court (1986–90); and Circuit Court (1990–2007).

Senior Judge Platt is a Neutral and member of the Maryland Board of Directors of The National Academy of Distinguished Neutrals, which after a thorough peer review by the board of directors of that "invitation only" organization, selects only the top 10 percent of Neutrals in the country. He also serves on the Judicial, Commercial, Employment, Large Complex Case, and Construction Panels of the American Arbitration Association, the International Institute for Conflict Prevention and Resolution, the International Mediation Institute, the Association for International Arbitration, and Resolute Systems.

Senior Judge Platt has taught the use of mediation and arbitration in resolving business disputes to judges and lawyers in Maryland and nationally through the Judicial Education Program of the American Enterprise Institute Brookings Joint Center for Regulatory Studies (serving on the Judicial Advisory Board), and through the American College of Business Court Judges (past-president).

Upon "retirement" from the bench in early 2007, Senior Judge Platt founded and now manages The Platt Group, Inc., and is currently engaged in mediation, arbitration, and neutral case evaluation of complex civil litigation, including legal malpractice cases, medical malpractice cases, product liability cases, business disputes, real estate matters, and other civil cases.

Senior Judge Platt is a Fellow of the American Bar Foundation and a Life Fellow of the Maryland Bar Foundation. He has been a member of the Prince George's County Bar Association since 1976 and is a past president. In addition, he has been a member of the Maryland State Bar Association (MSBA) since 1976 and served on its board of directors for four years. He also served as faculty member for its course on professionalism.

Senior Judge Platt has served as a consultant to the Court of Appeals of Maryland Standing Committee on Rules of Practice and Procedure, Special Subcommittees on Alternative Dispute Resolution, General Administration, and Electronic Discovery. Since 1986, he has been a member of the MSBA Litigation Section and served on the MSBA Committee on Laws for more than 30 years.

From 1977 to 1978, Senior Judge Platt served as chair of the Prince George's County Human Relations Commission and was a mentor for its Leadership Development Forum, which he helped develop while chairing the commission.

Other books written by Senior Judge Platt:

- *Black Robe Fever: The Role of the Judge in American Society*;

- *Of Politics and Economics: The School of Hard Knocks and Gentle Persuasion*; and

- *The Winding Road: Criminal Courts, Civil Matters, and the Ongoing Quest for Access to Justice*.

Detailed Contents

PART TWO: Maryland Politics: Establishing a Foothold
A Mystery Deposit and the 'Road to Nowhere'

PART THREE: Hanging Out a Shingle: My Days as an Attorney
A Female Grifter, a 'Company' Culture, and a Bail-Skipping Client

---

PART FOUR: Donning the Robe: My Days on the Bench

PART FIVE: The State of Criminal Justice in Maryland

PART SIX: The Civil Docket
Multiple Personalities, a Half-Million-Dollar Penalty, the Making of the Drug Court, a Model for the Nation, and Judicial Job Performance

---

PART SEVEN: Thriving as a Professional Mediator and Arbitrator
An Incarcerated Politician, a Thankful Mayor, and a Record-Setting Settlement

---

PART EIGHT: Comic Relief

CONCLUSION

APPENDICES

Introduction

Dragnet Still Has Its Place

"I think I have brought these stories into the realm of my readers' worlds. I hope you, the readers, agree."

I AM PLEASED to report my life has been largely the interesting experience I imagined and hoped it would be. Moreover, I have found joy in the journey I have traveled. Equally important, I am still enjoying the ride. In fact, my collective experience is what has motivated me to write my story. As I said over 12 years ago upon my retirement from the full-time judicial bench, I have been lucky in my life—not too many people can look back and say, "I have no regrets about the course I took personally and professionally."

I certainly am not vain enough to compare myself to Winston Churchill, yet I cannot help but share a very befitting statement Churchill shared with his American mother, Jennie Jerome, as he wrote to her from India:

> *"I have had faith in my star—that I am intended to do something in the world. If I am mistaken, what does it matter? My life has been a pleasant one ..."*

This book recounts the various stages of my adult life with plenty of humor thrown in:

- PART ONE: My Foray into the World of Politics

- PART TWO: Maryland Politics: Establishing a Foothold

- PART THREE: Hanging Out a Shingle: My Days as an Attorney

- PART FOUR: Donning the Robe: My Days on the Bench

- PART FIVE: The State of Criminal Justice in Maryland

- PART SIX: The Civil Docket

- PART SEVEN: Thriving as a Professional Mediator and Arbitrator

- PART EIGHT: Comic Relief

A few words are in order about the storytelling that will unfold in this book. I grew up in the 1950s and 1960s with television shows such as *Dragnet* starring Jack Webb as Sergeant Joe Friday. Every episode began with this:

> *This is The City—Los Angeles, California, I work here—I carry a badge.*

> *Dum Dah Dum Dum, Dum Dah Dum Dum Dum.*

> *The story you are about to see is true. The names have been changed to protect the innocent.*

In contrast to *Dragnet's* opening theme, I carry a robe instead of a badge. The stories you are about to read are true, but only some of the names mentioned have been changed; and where they have been changed, it is to protect both "the innocent and the guilty."

Also, in a few of the cases cited where I simply could not recall the names of the cast of characters, I reached the self-serving conclusion that the names of the persons who are not identified are not essential to the story being told.

Some of these stories are largely based on court records or printed judicial opinions in an effort to recount precisely what happened in a particular case or event. This is mostly true throughout the sections that discuss my time in private practice and the time I spent serving on the bench.

Where that is not the case, the facts cited are based on my memory of the events and the individuals involved in the cases. In those instances, I have clearly stated that I am relying on memory, which is particularly true in the part of the book that focuses on my days as a mediator and arbitrator where I provide an accurate account but with the creative license of a fiction writer conveying the feel, tone, and mood of a situation. This license is necessary to preserve the inherent confidentiality, which is legally required in all mediation processes, while assisting the reader to step into the shoes of the people in the story. It is the only way to bring these stories to life for an audience beyond other mediators, the parties, and their respective counsel.

I think I have brought these stories into the realm of my readers' worlds. I hope you, the readers, agree.

PART ONE

My Foray into the World of Politics

Chapter 1

A Democrat at Heart
Mountain Republicans, Two Assassinations, and a Thing Called the "Byrd Machine"

> *"[Robert F. Kennedy] could play with rogues and scoundrels and still maintain his principles. His sudden death robbed me of my hopes for the country and left me feeling unsure of the future. I firmly believe that history would've been different had he won; and today, this would be a different country."*

I WAS BORN on New Year's Day in 1947 and grew up in a little town called Strasburg in the heart of Virginia's Shenandoah Valley.

My grandfather, Charles Platt, at the age of 19, immigrated to the United States in 1913 from the Russian partition of Poland. Accompanying him was his 17-year-old wife, Rose. With a burning ambition for a different and better life, they traveled by stowage on a passenger ship from Rotterdam.

After a long and arduous voyage, my grandparents landed at Ellis Island with only $17 in my grandfather's pocket and very little knowledge of English. The immigration officials in charge of processing at Ellis Island kept moving my grandparents to the back of the line because they couldn't correctly pronounce my grandfather's last name.

Quick-witted and resourceful, my grandfather changed his last name from Plachta to Platt to get through the processing line and off the boat. This began a pattern for my grandfather—he would do what he needed to do to get where he needed to go.

Charles and Rose Platt initially settled on the Lower East Side of New York City where most immigrants from Europe lived when they first arrived in this country in the early 20th century. Theodore Roosevelt, a Republican, was president of the United States.

My grandparents became naturalized citizens in 1914. Upon registering to vote, they chose Republican on the theory that they owed their loyalty to the Grand Old Party (GOP) after having attained their citizenship under a Republican administration.

My grandparents maintained their loyalty to the Republican party as they continued to build their lives in America as entrepreneurs, eventually relocating from New York to Patterson, New Jersey, and then to their final destination, Strasburg, Virginia—population 2,500. It was 1933.

My family moved to Strasburg to own and operate a textile mill that manufactured silk. My father, Nathan, was a single 18-year-old. He registered to vote as Republican alongside his parents, Charles and Rose, primarily out of respect for Grandpa Charles's history (which Grandpa described as his heritage, some of which he made up on the fly, with a grin on his face) and a natural affinity for the perceived philosophy of the then–Republican Party. The philosophy at the time was pro-business and anti-labor with an emphasis on individual responsibility and limited government.

In the 1950s and into the 1960s, Virginia's politics and the government at all levels were under the control of what was known as the "Byrd Machine," which dominated the Democratic Party and exercised almost absolute control over access and entry to every elected and appointed position in state government.

Run by the undisputed leader or "Boss," Harry F. Byrd, Sr.—a former Democratic governor of Virginia who later became a senior U.S. senator—the Byrd Machine was mostly white, male, and in most cases, racist. Having been the architect of a policy labeled "massive resistance" was its claim to fame. This policy essentially amounted to closing the public schools in Virginia in response to the 1954 ruling in *Brown v. Board of Education* in which the U.S. Supreme Court ordered the integration of schools with "all due deliberate speed."

In the Shenandoah Valley of Virginia, where our family settled, Republicans were known as "Mountain Republicans" because of their concentration in the Blue Ridge Mountains in the western part of the state. Mountain Republicans, however, were to the left as they were not particularly racist and they opposed "massive resistance."

This made for interesting dinner conversations when, at the age of 13 in 1960, I announced that I was a Democrat supporting John F. Kennedy for president instead of my family's choice of Richard M. Nixon. To their credit, my family accepted my decision with a degree of equanimity, probably viewing my choice as a product of my youthful naiveté and lack of real-life experience.

I think they also instinctively understood that the structure and culture of politics in Virginia at that time and for the foreseeable future would severely restrict my ability to pursue a political or judicial career—my desire for which, even then, was manifesting itself. Neither party in Virginia seemed to be the appropriate place—the Democratic Party was not inclusive and not likely to welcome a Jewish kid from a Republican family into its protective wings, while the small and minority Republican Party would not be an effective vehicle for me to progress toward my goals.

The realities of Virginia politics would lead me to leave Strasburg sooner rather than later. Even before I graduated from Massanutten Military Academy, a college-prep high school in Woodstock, Virginia, my parents facilitated my desire to escape the geographic and cultural confines of Strasburg by sending me at my request to live and work in New York City.

CONGRESSMAN JOHN V. LINDSAY
FOR MAYOR OF NEW YORK

While in high school, following my 16th birthday, I began working summers in a law firm in Manhattan and again while I attended the University of Virginia (UVA) in Charlottesville. The lawyers in my family were partners in the Law Firm of Becker, Ross & Stone located at 42nd Street and Madison Avenue.

Part of my work was detailed to the mayoral campaign of U.S. Congressman John V. Lindsay, a "Silk Stocking Republican"[1] (before he became a Democrat). Lindsay represented the borough of Manhattan in Congress. He ran for mayor as a reformer—a Fusion Party[2] candidate—against the Democratic Party's Tammany Hall Machine[3] and the Republicans. He won!

I learned a great deal about politics from that campaign: about "reform movements," "how to fight City Hall," and the inner workings of a "political machine." I had been bitten by the political bug and there was no turning back.

ROBERT F. KENNEDY (RFK)
FOR U.S. SENATOR FROM NEW YORK

My next political campaign involvement was in Robert F. Kennedy's (RFK) run for a U.S. Senate seat for New York. Essentially, the same group of volunteers from "The Lindsay for Mayor" campaign transferred their considerable skills, energy, and time to RFK's campaign. Essentially, we were up against the same people and organizations—Tammany Hall Democrats, who would later be more than accommodating to the Kennedy Campaign, and subsequently the New

---

[1] "Silk Stocking Republicans" were part of the aristocratic or wealthy class in New Yok City who were politically influential or active.

[2] The Fusion Party comprised minor political parties coming together to back one candidate. New York's Fusion Party comprised the Independence Party of New York, the Working Families Party, and the Conservative Party of New York State.

[3] The Tammany Hall Machine was the name given to a powerful political machine that ran New York City throughout much of the 19th and 20th centuries.

York State Republican Party, known as "Rockefeller Republicans," whose candidate was incumbent U.S. Senator Kenneth Keating, a "liberal Republican."

I came to admire RFK for his ability to work with the rogues and scoundrels of politics to achieve his ends while maintaining his ideals and later his growth as a politician and as a human being. The former was part of the reason he was clearly labeled "ruthless." That "ruthlessness," which I admired, was perhaps illustrated colorfully by RFK's response to the chairman of the New York Democratic State Central Committee's description of him as a "Carpetbagger from Massachusetts":

> *"Well, if they (the central committee) were any good, I wouldn't be here. The train is rolling; they can be on it or under it."*

Kennedy won! And I was lucky to be a passenger on his proverbial train.

ROBERT F. KENNEDY FOR PRESIDENT

My experiences prepared me to return to UVA in the winter and summer of 1968. There, I volunteered to work in the "Robert F. Kennedy for President" campaign during the academic year and the summer. RFK had attended law school at UVA. He, therefore, had a coterie of law school professors and law students devoted to his cause and his campaign for president in 1968.

His honorary state chairman was a courageous state senator from Arlington, Virginia, named Armstead Booth. The campaign was managed by law professor Mason Wilrich and law student John Milliken. Milliken later served as Virginia secretary of transportation and in other cabinet and political offices under a number of Democratic Virginia governors.

I was given the title of "Virginia Student Coordinator for the Robert Kennedy for President" campaign, and the authority to recruit one other person to assist me in organizing the campaign. What more could an aspiring, idealistic, young man looking for political action, experience, and interesting fun times along the way ask for?

None of us suffered any illusions that RFK would win the state of Virginia—which was then solidly Red (Republican)—in the general election against any Republican and certainly not against Richard Nixon, who was popular there in 1968. Nor did we believe he could win the support of the Democratic Party, then still at least partially controlled by the Byrd Machine, and governed by soon-to-be-converted Republican, Mills Godwin. The local party caucus of "Insiders" selected the delegates to the Virginia Democratic Convention, which, in turn, would select the delegates to the Democratic National Convention in Chicago during summer 1968.

The Kennedy campaign did, however, want to demonstrate pockets of support in Virginia where expected and to show our loyalty and faith that justice would prevail nationally. We expected that RFK would be nominated as the Democratic Party's candidate and ultimately be elected to the Office of President of the United States. I was given directions to use my skills and my Kennedy campaign American Express card to organize African American communities (then referred to as "Black communities") and college campuses.

My "assistant" was one of my college roommates, Bob Gartley. He and I, with smiles on our faces, chose as our first foray out of Charlottesville the African American community in Lynchburg, Virginia. Our reason was that Lynchburg, home of Liberty University and Moral Majority leader Reverend Jerry Falwell, was perhaps the least likely place in the state to produce any visible support for RFK. That tactic suited our purpose and served our alternative motive.

Upon our arrival in Lynchburg, we proceeded to check in at the local Holiday Inn. At the registration desk, we were handed an envelope with the warm greeting scrawled in all caps:

"YOU ARE NOT WELCOME HERE. GO HOME!"

We ignored this lack of southern hospitality and proceeded with our work (which also could have been described as mischief). That work consisted of contacting the chairman of the Lynchburg Democratic Committee—whom our sources advised was a "functioning alcoholic"—and inviting him to dinner using our American Express card, then after a sufficient evening of good cheer, procuring his midnight endorsement of our candidate. Our plan was coming together.

We then had him send out a "notice" to the registered Democrats in Lynchburg in the African American neighborhoods using flyers and limited knocking on doors. Incidentally, the total number of Democrats in Lynchburg in 1968 easily could have met in a telephone booth.

As a result, the predominantly African American and college student "caucus" consisting of Democrats met around midnight one night to select delegates to the Virginia Democratic Convention in Richmond, Virginia. Viewed as the "Lynchburg Delegation," it miraculously endorsed RFK for president and pledged its support to his delegates. The local newspaper known for publishing "all the news that's fit to print," dutifully headlined the event probably because there was no other news. The next day, the still hung-over Democratic Party chairman sent us packing as he expressed his concern:

"You boys are getting me in serious trouble!"

We next selected the colleges we should attempt to organize for RFK in accordance with our direction from Campaign Central in Charlottesville. Lynchburg, in whose African American community we had initially rested our weary feet and allocated our energy, was surrounded by a number of women's colleges including Sweet Briar College, Mary Baldwin College, Mary Washington College, Madison (then a women's college), Hollins College (in Roanoke), and Radford College.

Bob Gartley and I, being red-blooded, heterosexual males, decided that it was our "patriotic duty" to organize the "bobby soxers" on these campuses for their favorite candidate, RFK. We recognized that it was a "dirty, filthy job, but someone had to do it." As a result, the delegates from each of these college-dominated areas attended the Virginia Democratic Convention pledging to support RFK for president.

Tragically, our symbolic efforts went for naught. On June 6, 1968, Senator Robert F. Kennedy was assassinated. I watched it over and over on television. I was devastated. He was a figure I could compare any politician to. He could play with rogues and scoundrels and still maintain his principles. His sudden death robbed me of my hopes for the country and left me feeling unsure of the future.

I firmly believe that history would've been different had he won; and today, this would be a different country.

WILLIAM C. BATTLE FOR GOVERNOR OF VIRGINIA

My next political exercise, while still a student at UVA, was to support and work for the "William C. Battle for Governor of Virginia" campaign. This was a natural transition from the tragically aborted "Robert F. Kennedy for President" campaign. Ironically, former Ambassador William C. Battle had been aboard PT 109 with John F. Kennedy. He was considered an ally and a friend of the deceased president—not so (at least publicly) with RFK, who was considered toxic for any campaign for a statewide Virginia office, particularly governor, due to RFK's record, work, and advocacy of civil rights causes while serving as U.S. attorney general and U.S. senator.

William C. Battle was the son of John S. Battle, a former Virginia governor and full-fledged, active leader of The Byrd Machine. But in 1969, after a history of working in his father's law firm and supporting him and other candidates of the Byrd Machine, William Battle ran for governor as a reformer. He positioned himself as one who could transition between the "old" and "new" Democratic Party and who could, in that process, dismantle the policy of "massive resistance."

His two opponents in the Democratic Party primary were Lieutenant Governor Fred G. Pollard, the standard bearer of the "Old Guard" Byrd Machine who ran on a platform of maintaining the status quo, including the policy of "massive resistance; and State Senator Henry Howell, a populist who promised to dramatically challenge the political, legal, and economic establishment, particularly the electric power company's influence in the Commonwealth.

Interestingly, the infrastructures and staffs of two previous 1968 national campaigns for president of the United States—RFK and Senator Eugene McCarthy—transitioned predictably into the separate campaigns of William Battle and State Senator Henry Howell. The practical pols, including me, who were more concerned with immediately sending the Byrd Machine into the history books than in sending a message on issues, moved into the Battle campaign; while the more liberal and idealistic volunteers, whom I and others posthumously labeled "Latte Liberals," were attracted to Howell.

My memory of that split in the Virginia Democratic Party eerily parallels the Biden-Sanders match-up in 2020 with "Bernie" wanting to "take on the political and economic establishment" and Biden focusing on "beating Donald Trump now"!

William Battle won the Democratic Party nomination for governor in 1969, thereby taking control of the Party from the captains of the Byrd Machine and sending its racial legacy of "massive resistance" into the dustbin of history. However, the moderate Mountain Republican, Linwood Holton, won the general election and became Virginia's first Republican governor in a generation (and if I may say so, one of the best governors the Commonwealth has ever seen).

The Battle candidacy was my last campaign and political involvement in the state in which I was born and raised.

Chapter 2

The Political Scene in Maryland (1966–1986)
A User's Manual

"This need to maintain self-esteem and the esteem of others (i.e., the political and professional network they develop) explains why people who are egotistical enough to believe (including this writer) they have something 'special' to offer others will oftentimes seek the ability to do so through political involvement."

IN 1966, WHILE an undergraduate student at the University of Virginia studying "very conscientiously" in my major of Government and Political Science, the State of Maryland was undergoing a change in its politics, particularly within the Democratic Party. These changes would have national implications two years later.

Three different factions of the Maryland Democratic Party emerged from the loss of control suffered by different political machines throughout the state in the mid-1960s. Before that time, the political machines and leaders got their way policy-wise—through patronage and financial support from the business community (particularly in Baltimore City and the suburban counties around Baltimore and Washington, D.C.)—and elected their favored candidates.

The three emergent factions of Democratic Party leadership in Maryland were the "liberal" reformers led by Congressman Carlton Sickles; the more "moderate" pro-business Democrats led by Thomas Finan, the incumbent attorney general of Maryland; and the right-wing "conservative" Democrats led by George P. Mahoney, the candidate favored by the rural population, whose slogan was "Your Home Is Your Castle." This became Mahoney's calling card and euphemism, indeed a metaphor for even less benign positions on racial issues. The result of the three-way split in the Maryland Democratic Party in 1966 was the choice of Mahoney as the Democratic Party's nominee for governor of Maryland.

As a result of a bitter primary election, many of the otherwise loyal Democratic state and local elected officials, civic and community leaders, and opinion-makers, as well as a significant portion of the business community and Democratic donors, shifted their support to Mahoney's Republican opponent for governor, Spiro T. Agnew, the county executive of Baltimore County.

Agnew branded himself a "moderate" while serving as county executive and then as the Republican candidate for governor in comparison to Mahoney. As a result, Agnew won and became governor of Maryland succeeding J. Millard Tawes. A mere two years later, in 1968, Agnew was selected by Richard Nixon as his running-mate for Vice President of the United States—an office Agnew ultimately disgraced.

When Agnew resigned as governor of Maryland to take the oath of office as vice president, the constitution of Maryland required the General Assembly to act, in effect, as a committee of the whole to select Agnew's replacement for governor. They selected Democrat Marvin Mandel, then Speaker of the Maryland House of Delegates.

Governor Mandel was a product of one of the Democratic Party organizations in Baltimore City. This organization (or machine if you were one of its detractors), was managed by his ally Irvin Kovens, a Democratic power broker. Mandel's political acumen, people skills, and patience were renowned. In other words, he suffered fools exceedingly well! Political insiders who had observed Mandel would joke that no matter how silly any person or any proposal might be when presented to him, he would simply (but intently) deadpan, engage the person and their idea, puff on his pipe, and reply, "We can certainly look at that; we might be able to do it." More often than not, the supplicant would then leave thinking he or she had some sort of commitment.

Those skills, as well as Mandel's almost encyclopedic knowledge of every legislator's needs and wants at every level, accounted, at least in part, for his selection by the Maryland General Assembly as governor. Among his many accomplishments in that position, was, most critically, his complete reorganization of state government and creation of the District Court of Maryland to replace the hodgepodge of corrupt and inefficient municipal courts and commissioner systems.

Mandel made it immediately clear after his selection that he would run for a full term as governor in 1970. Most state and local elected officials, political and civic leaders, and other opinion-makers in Maryland queued up to come on board. Most, but not all.

Later, Mandel would be convicted and imprisoned on charges of corruption that were eventually reversed and his conviction vacated. His legacy was, thereafter, largely restored; in later years, he was repeatedly called upon by governors who succeeded him for advice and counsel.

THE DOMINANT DEMOCRATIC PARTY ORGANIZATION

Steny Hamilton Hoyer and Peter Francis O'Malley

Two men who later would play a large role in my life and career, State Senator Steny Hoyer and attorney Peter O'Malley, brought vastly different but complementary skillsets and strengths to their friendship and political alliance. The Hoyer-O'Malley dynamic ultimately evolved into leadership of the Prince George's County and Maryland Democratic Parties.

In 1966, O'Malley captained then–Attorney General Thomas Finan's campaign[4] for governor in Prince George's County against local popular rival candidate, Congressman Carlton Sickles, and George ("Your Home Is Your Castle") Mahoney. Although Sickles won Prince George's County in the Democratic primary, his margin was not anywhere near what he had expected or needed. Mahoney ended up winning the Democratic Party nomination for governor of Maryland.

Nevertheless, the Finan campaign was universally viewed as extremely well-run, well-staffed, and well-financed. Much of the credit was attributed to O'Malley. This would be the beginning of a pattern that would emerge and then be maintained over the next 25 years. O'Malley's candidate(s) might occasionally lose election(s), but he personally would never lose. In fact, O'Malley's reputation as a political strategist was enhanced in each successive campaign.

The unequaled energy and smart organization of Hoyer and O'Malley rapidly expanded following the 1966 statewide election. Their rise to power was aided by supporters recruited with the promise of a new era with new leadership—many from D.C. and Maryland law schools, Andrews Air Force Base, and college campuses. They sequentially took over the Prince George's County Young Democrats (1967), the Maryland Young Democrats (1968), and the Prince George's Democratic Party (1970) from the "Old Guard."

In doing so, they took steps to make sure that no one could do to them what they did via the Young Democrats by developing a successor generation of leaders. These were persons whom Hoyer and O'Malley as well as others around them like Tom Farrington, a lawyer and the Maryland Democratic National Committee man, had identified as capable and loyal.

I was among the successor generation of capable and loyal leaders. (*It was never clear which was and would be more important— capability or loyalty. I, for one, saw no need to find out.*)

---

[4] Thomas Finan was the incumbent attorney general of Maryland.

By 1970, the political organization led by Hoyer and O'Malley had the ability and the clout to develop a financial network. Hoyer had the retail political skills and charisma to convince others that if they joined with him on "his ticket," he could carry them to victory. The organizational skills, political contacts, and respect of the "business community of donors" as well as the county and state were brought to the organization by O'Malley.

THE CLEAR VISION OF PETER O'MALLEY

The management skills, work ethic, attention to detail, and clear vision of Peter O'Malley drove his control and influence. In his 20s, O'Malley, from a suburb of Boston, Massachusetts, moved his family to Maryland and Prince George's County to attend law school at Georgetown University. He worked on Capitol Hill while a law student where he met many of the law students and young professionals who would be with him throughout his many political and business activities going forward. He also developed a relationship with, among others, Tip O'Neill, then– speaker of the U.S. House of Representatives. After graduating law school, he worked in the Office of the Maryland Attorney General. His formal title was "Assistant Attorney General." His formal responsibility was to staff the Maryland Subversive Activities Control Board.

O'Malley's skillset was unique and unparalleled and his ambition and desire to attain power and influence was actually unlimited, although it did not manifest itself in a conventional manner. As our mentor-mentee relationship and friendship evolved, I had the opportunity to observe him from the time I first met him until the time he stepped back to "retire" from politics in the mid-1980s.

He had absolutely no interest in elective office. Therefore, no one with such ambitions saw him as a potential direct threat. That enabled him to assemble coalitions of candidates and elected officials with vastly different and, at times, conflicting constituencies, philosophies, and followers who shared a single common interest that O'Malley recognized and ultimately utilized to maximize his influence—their personal election, reelection, and perpetuation in power.

He was able to coalesce folks by convincing them to ally themselves with other candidates and officials with whom they disagreed politically, professionally, and even at times, personally, to accomplish their common interests. It helped that, as is almost always the case, at the level of state and local politics many of these people were not well-known and psychologically dependent on holding onto their elected or appointed positions to maintain their self-respect, identity, and, in whole or in part, their livelihoods.

In the meantime, O'Malley was carrying out his actual responsibility rather than his formal job assignment. His real responsibility, almost full time, was as Attorney General Thomas Finan's political advisor, strategist, and operative. Although comparatively young to play this role, even then his intelligence, political vision, and strategic capabilities were recognized; and, in the case of Attorney General Finan, utilized on a daily basis.

By 1970, O'Malley had risen in Maryland Democratic Party politics as well as in the legal world both in Prince George's County and the State of Maryland. He now headed the largest law firm in the county and one of the most influential in the state. The practice of the firm during this period was continually expanding thanks to his ability to strategically identify and then develop emerging areas of practice by recruiting lateral transfers of respected lawyers and litigators with established client bases.

A large part of that expanding practice was administrative law, which meant the firm represented business and corporate clients in need of licenses and services from county and state government. This included builders, developers, restaurant and bar owners, liquor stores, real estate brokers, lawyers, doctors, engineers, and other professionals.

O'Malley's firm, in its heyday, was one of the go-to law firms for people and businesses needing the goodwill, fair administration, and efficiency of those in elected and appointed offices who provided these services, licenses, and economic support. Unquestionably, folks were aware that many of these elected and appointed officials credited their positions to the Democratic Party organization led by

O'Malley and Hoyer. So, they were naturally inclined to support and contribute to their recommended candidates and tickets.

While he was engaged in the management of the party, O'Malley was able to largely control the flow of campaign contributions, and, more significantly, he could limit or even cut them off completely if he so desired.

Steny Hoyer and Peter O'Malley were justifiably confident about their ability to accomplish their personal and political goals, as well as to bring others along for that ride by meeting their lesser needs and wants along the way.

Based on my observations of the operations of this political organization between 1970 and 1990 and my interactions with the various personalities involved—in their official and unofficial capacities—the strategic vision of Hoyer and O'Malley was unmatched because of their combination of leadership and personal and political skills.

Other partners and occasional rivals appeared on the scene during those years, most notably, Parris N. Glendening, who later became governor of Maryland; Thomas V. Mike Miller, Jr., who became the longest-serving president of any state senate in the history of the United States; and Winfield M. Kelly, Jr. and Wayne K. Curry, two county executives who sometimes partnered with and sometimes rivaled the dominant Democratic Party organization led by Hoyer and O'Malley during those years.

Those strategic partners and rivals, however, were exclusively concerned with their personal and political careers, ambitions, power, and influence. Therefore, they dealt with the Democratic organization through Hoyer and O'Malley to accomplish their personal and political goals.

These capable political players were content to live with the Hoyer-O'Malley–led party and its influence and control over the political and economic life of Prince George's County, as well as the leverage that influence and control gave Hoyer and O'Malley over politics and economics in the rest of the state—as long as their personal and political interests were accommodated.

Besides superior interpersonal and political skills, which were different but complementary, Hoyer and O'Malley brought an ability to visualize and, therefore, predict and strategically address long-term political issues—while dealing tactically with those same issues in the short term.

They were consistently able to inspire confidence in their judgment by the exponentially expanding numbers of political players in Prince George's County and around Maryland. These players viewed their ability to fulfill their own personal and political ambitions and the timing of when to try to do so as dependent upon the judgment of Hoyer and O'Malley and the ability of the organization to finance their political campaigns and ambitions.

By its perceived electoral successes at the state and local levels in 1970, 1974, and 1978, the Hoyer-O'Malley–led party's deference increased year after year as the organization increased its ability to control and coordinate the ambitions of the many otherwise obscure public office holders who depended on the organization for electoral survival. Hoyer and O'Malley accomplished this through constant attention to detail on a day-to-day basis during the peak years of its operation—1970 to 1982.

I cannot overstate the significance of this phenomenon and the lessons in life, law, politics, and microeconomics I learned by observing and participating in it. The phenomenon is that many people get involved in politics for social reasons or to develop social circles that will accept them especially if they can't find a social network that they want to be a part of.

I am reminded of the quote attributed to Groucho Marx:

> *"I wouldn't want to be a member of a country club that would have me as a member."*

I'm also reminded of my grandfather's and my father's similar attitude toward any country club that turned them down for membership because of their Jewish faith. Their attitude was:

"I don't care, and I don't want to be a member if they don't want me. I don't go where I'm not wanted—I'll build my own goddamn club and it will be nicer than theirs."

To those individuals who engage in politics seeking to find a comfortable social network and life, politics is a natural habitat. Politicians and the people who promote them (including staff) will talk to *anyone* who can potentially vote or contribute support in the form of time, energy, and/or money.

Political players do not discriminate and will pretend to respect anyone and everyone who meets the minimal criteria—no matter what else they may think about them. In turn, once involved, the political players remain loyal because social acceptance is extremely important to them to sustain their self-esteem—indeed their core identity.

To glance into the future briefly, I firmly believe that, more than any other theory, this reality better explains the loyalty to Donald Trump and the social networks, including Fox News, which are devoted to him.

This need to maintain self-esteem and the esteem of others (*i.e.*, the political and professional network they develop) explains why people who are egotistical enough to believe (including this writer) they have something "special" to offer others will oftentimes seek the ability to do so through political involvement.

Political involvement takes the form of seeking elective or appointive public office, or seeking and accumulating power and influence by organizing, strategizing, fundraising, and networking for those who actually seek elective or appointive office.

Those who seek elective office, particularly those who are successful, will usually stay loyal to those who helped them (or did not hurt them) to keep their positions. My observation is that their self-esteem and their view of the esteem of others becomes, in their minds, inextricably intertwined with their public positions.

This explains the ability of political or party organizations (yes, later individual political figures such as Donald Trump) to retain their following and loyalty even when they do not deserve it, and why arguably "bad" policy and political decisions as well as bad behavior often appear to be blindly enabled by loyal followers.

Finally, I learned that there is an economic component in the ability of a political organization, or, in some cases, an individual leader to generate and maintain a loyal following. Particularly, at the state and local levels, many people who run for elective office come from civic and community backgrounds or become involved, at least initially, because they are dedicated to a cause, issue, or ideology.

Therefore, unless these individuals are independently wealthy, they do not have a network that is capable of fully financing their political ambition or any campaign they have undertaken.

Into that breach steps a political organization and/or leader(s) with that political and/or financial network. In the case of Prince George's County and the State of Maryland from 1966 to 1982, the premiere Democratic power brokers were my friends and mentors, Peter O'Malley and Steny Hoyer.

Chapter 3

The Battle of College Park

"My instinct for verbal survival, something I inherited from my grandfather, provided me with an escape from further sanction simply because the Career National Guard Staff could not determine whether I was credible and serious—or not."

MY TIME SERVING in the National Guard, at least partially, prepared me for my move to Maryland. After graduating from the University of Virginia (UVA) in 1969, and having been admitted to the American University School of Law, I took up residence in Prince George's County and was poised to begin my involvement in Maryland politics. But the Vietnam War was raging and the military draft was ongoing. In the fall of 1969, with the aid of Congressman John O. Marsh, Jr. (D) of the 7th District of Virginia, I was sworn into the Virginia National Guard.

The push from the congressman was necessary because there were waiting lists a mile long to get into the reserves and/or ROTC as a means of avoiding active duty in the Vietnam War. Marsh later switched to the Republican Party and became President Gerald

Ford's secretary of the U.S. Army; fortunately for me, his wife had been my kindergarten teacher.

Without Congressman Marsh's assistance, I would have had to report for active duty as ordered; furthermore, I would have been deployed fairly quickly to Vietnam, a war that was increasingly unpopular. More relevant to this narrative was my longstanding and ongoing opposition to fighting and risking life and limb in a war that I thought was morally and politically indefensible for both political and personal reasons.

At that time, I could not help but reflect on my grandfather's reason for leaving Poland and coming to the United States in 1913. As he noted to my son and daughter when they interviewed him over 75 years later:

> *"I didn't want to give the Russian Army seven years of my life."*

Similarly, in 1969–1970, I did not want to give the U.S. Army even two years of my life and expose myself to the risk of being killed or injured in a war that I, and an emerging majority in this country, did not believe in.

The National Guard was a safe haven for me and many others. It required four months of Basic Training and Advanced Infantry Training (AIT), six years of monthly meetings, and annual two-week summer exercises at a military base.

As it turned out in the early 1970s, my National Guard service also included being "called out" to quell the feared "riots" resulting from student protests of the Vietnam War at the University of Maryland in College Park for three springs in a row. One of those Tours of Duty, which my friends labeled the "Battle of College Park," resulted in an experience that stuck with me for years after the event and was publicly recounted for laughs at my investiture as a district court judge.

At the pinnacle of my comparatively brief and totally undistinguished military career, I was designated the "Acting Battalion Supply Sergeant" for my National Guard Unit. When we were called out to serve in the "Battle of College Park," I was detailed as the highest-ranking non-commissioned officer (NCO) on the scene to be in charge of security in neighboring Greenbelt Park where hundreds of troops were camped out. My orders were simple:

> *"No one who is not in uniform is to be admitted into Greenbelt Park."*

Shortly thereafter, I had my first important decision to make while stationed at the main entrance to the park. On a horribly hot, humid, 90-degree day, the troops were sweltering, hungry, and tired. Suddenly, the Good Humor Man approaches the entrance in his Good Humor truck filled with ice cream and cold drinks. Notably, he is wearing the signature white Good Humor uniform.

Some of the troops spotted him and no doubt viewed him as relief sent from on high, *manna* from heaven. The difficult decision I faced was clear—let the Good Humor Man into the park and please the troops or turn him away and please the permanent Command Staff of the Maryland National Guard.

Being a man of the people and seeking approval from the troops, a true sign of a politician in the making, I did the only thing that made sense at the time—I let the Good Humor Man into the park. Within minutes of his entry, Good Humor ice cream bars were spread upon the earth, satisfying the hunger and thirst of the masses.

The troops voiced their vociferous approval. The brass, however, were not happy. I was almost immediately summoned to the Battalion Commander's tent and interrogated (fortunately not with "enhanced" interrogation techniques!). My instinct for verbal survival, something I inherited from my grandfather, provided me with an escape from further sanction simply because the career Command Staff could not determine whether I was credible and serious—or not.

I attempted to explain that I did not intend to disobey orders—after all, my orders specifically stated that "no one who is *not* in uniform is to be admitted into Greenbelt Park." I argued that my orders never specified that the uniform had to be a specific color. Thus, the Good Humor Man was dressed in uniform; the color of which was not a reason to keep him from entering the park.

The National Guard Command Staff's dilemma was to decide if I was "really that stupid as a result of being a book smart law student with no common sense," or if I was a "smart ass" trying to avoid responsibility for breaking the security order.

Luckily, they gave me the benefit of the doubt; I guess I persuaded them that I, in fact, was book smart but lacked common sense. One of my better performances if I say so myself!

I escaped with a tongue lashing for undermining the health and safety of my fellow National Guard troops and a lecture about the potential threat of a conspiring-rogue-college student, anti-Vietnam War protester masquerading as the Good Humor Man.

Chapter 4

Idealists, Rogues, and Scoundrels in Maryland Politics

"Clearly, when [Conroy] felt he needed sympathy or support from an audience who would not naturally be attracted to him, [he] would wear the more severe-looking metal hook as opposed to the more unobtrusive prosthetic."

I PARTICIPATED IN Basic Training and Advanced Infantry Training (AIT) at Fort Ord, California, where the climate was great, the women were good looking, and I enjoyed the weekends with friends in a unit populated completely with reservists. Why they would send a member of the Maryland National Guard to train in California, I have no clue. Nevertheless, as I quickly grasped, "If you gotta go, Fort Ord was where you wanna go."

When it was time to return to Maryland, I moved into an apartment in Adelphi located in Prince George's County. It was the most affordable suburban jurisdiction for me to live in at the time. Unfortunately, it was too late to get "a real job" for the summer before returning to law school in the fall, so I acted on my developing addiction to politics and checked with one of my law school friends who was somewhat wired into the political and legal scene in suburban Maryland.

I thought it would be fairly easy to land an internship with a law firm or political campaign. But he explained that politics in Maryland was quite different from Virginia; and even within Maryland, situations vastly differed from region to region and even county to county. That turned out to be an understatement!

My friend recommended that with my background and experience, I should focus my energy and involvement in Prince George's County where politics was, at the time, "unsettled." From the late 1930s to about 1962, a political machine run by a lawyer and political "Boss" named Lansdale Sasscer, Sr. controlled the Democratic Party. Except in a few instances, the Democrats controlled county and state elected and appointed officials.

By 1962, however, Mr. Sasscer was aging, as were his friends and allies. In addition, the demographics and the generations in the county were changing. As a result, the Sasscer Machine's hold on the Party began to weaken. This ebbing of power manifested itself in the election of certain reform candidates over Party regulars in 1962.

This trend intensified when a "ticket" of reformers made substantial inroads into the Sasscer Machine's electoral control, to the point where the regulars lost several important offices to reformers including the Office of State's Attorney for Prince George's County and several legislative seats.

Eight years later, in 1970, three competing factions formed tickets, which contained Democratic primary candidates for every state and local office from governor to the members of the Democratic Party central committee. Each ticket had a candidate for each one of the 76 state and local offices to be filled. This meant 228 candidates were running for 76 mostly obscure state and local offices.

Most voters had never heard of any of these candidates. Nevertheless, the citizens voted. They chose whom to vote for by which ticket they supported. They chose their ticket by the candidates they "knew" by way of advertising—usually in the form of brochures and/or tabloid newspapers. Unfortunately, only those tickets with the money to pay for printing and mailing were the ones getting through to the voters. This campaign was vastly different from my experiences in Virginia—and totally different from the data-driven, digital, television, and social media campaigns of today.

I did not know any of the elected officials, candidates, or campaign staffers. I asked my wired-in law school friend whom I should see or volunteer with to begin developing a political and legal network. He suggested I volunteer to work for a ticket called "the Alliance 4 Action."

I said, "They are what?" reflecting my cynicism about "grown-up" politicians giving their alliance for electoral reasons a made-up name.

"Who are they?" I asked.

He said, "That's the ticket that's going to win."

"How do you know that?" I responded.

"These guys are a lot smarter, better funded, staffed, and organized because of their leaders than the ad hoc groups of candidates and elected officials who fill out the tickets running against them," he added.

He went on to explain that the Alliance 4 Action was created by the four incumbent state senators from Prince George's County and part of Southern Maryland—hence the "4" stood for the four incumbent state senators with different political views and constituencies uniting "4 Action."

As I became more enthralled with the political scene in Maryland, I was finding it not only interesting, but personally and professionally rewarding. It had everything a budding political junkie could ask for—a diverse cast of characters encompassing a sufficient quota of well-meaning idealists, as well as rogues and scoundrels.

In order to stay involved in politics, I attended American University Law School (AU) at night as a part-time student. I graduated AU in December 1974, passed the Maryland Bar exam, and waived into the D.C. Bar. I then ventured forth enthusiastically.

THE ALLIANCE 4 ACTION TICKET

The Alliance 4 Action was led by four incumbent state senators: Meyer M. (Manny) Emanuel, Jr.; Edward T. Conroy; Fred L. Wineland; and Steny H. Hoyer. Each of them represented a distinct and significant constituency within the county, the State of Maryland, and the country in 1970.

Based on the recommendation of my friend and fellow law student, Alan Bernstein (now deceased), I dutifully appeared at the headquarters of the Alliance 4 Action—a run-down house on Route 450 in Bladensburg, Maryland.

I arrived for my appointment to meet with campaign manager Bob Flynn and office manager Sue Pappas. I looked around. The furnishings were makeshift. I knew a little about the candidates from talking with State Senator Emanuel and my law school friends and reading some of their brochures. I remember wondering, *"If these are the people who are going to win, what must the other tickets' candidates be like?"*

I would later observe that although at times this campaign resembled "the gang that couldn't shoot straight," the other campaigns couldn't shoot at all and were no match for an organization led by Steny Hoyer and Peter O'Malley.

In May 1970, I served as "Deputy Campaign Manager" by day and "Assistant 2nd District Coordinator" by night for the Alliance 4 Action campaign. The campaign was giving out titles liberally with no compensation attached to them; hence my rapid rise in "The Campaign Organization." I never requested to be paid.

STATE SENATOR MEYER M. EMANUEL, JR.

Meyer "Manny" Emanuel was truly a "liberal" Democrat who was respected for his likable personality and honesty. In many cases, Emanuel was supported by people and organizations from other wings of the party and the community even if they strongly disagreed with him on issues. He was also a successful certified public accountant (CPA) by profession.

The dominant issue in the 1960s and 1970s in Prince George's County and other suburban areas in Maryland was "race." The third rail of that issue during those years was "busing to achieve racial balance" in the public schools. Emanuel supported "busing to achieve racial balance," which brought him emotional and political support from both the leadership and the rank-and-file of the African American community—including the clergy and civic and political activists.

Manny Emanuel's position also brought him opprobrium as well as political and personal attacks from those who vehemently disagreed with him, including threats of physical violence. His courage and determination in the face of this opposition guaranteed perpetual competition and conflict in both the Democratic primary and general elections. His steadfastness, however, spoke volumes about his character and explained my admiration for him personally and professionally, notwithstanding my differences with his position on certain political issues.

In both the short and long term, Emanuel's stance made him a valuable member of any electoral coalition, particularly in a county in which the racial demographics were rapidly changing, and which, in the not too distant future, would become the wealthiest majority-African American county in the country.

Fortunately for me, as time marched on, Emanuel figuratively "adopted" me. He liked my family and personal history and identified with my religious background and general views, which were similar to his. He also relied on my work habits and ethics and completely trusted me alone among campaign staff. We enjoyed many dinners and conversations together.

My loyalty to and friendship with him never wavered even as I went on to work for others. In turn, he never failed to make every effort to support my trajectory to achieve my personal and political goals. More importantly, I observed him as the voice or "conscience" of his more politically ambitious colleagues at the state and local levels.

STATE SENATOR EDWARD T. CONROY

Edward T. Conroy was a legitimate "war hero" having fought at the Battle of "Pork Chop Hill" where he was injured and lost the use of one hand. His role in the Alliance 4 Action was to solidify the support of veterans, where he had a substantial and loyal following both locally and nationally, as well as the voters in his district. He was a skillful politician at the local level, having been elected mayor of Bowie, Maryland, and to the Maryland House of Delegates before being elected to the state Senate.

The price for his support was tolerating his insecurities (bordering on paranoia) and fear of his running mates and campaign staff. The inside joke was that Conroy gave the cliché, "running scared," a new dimension. The more vicious among the campaign staff recounted anecdotes based on the observation that he had both a metal hook and a rubber prosthetic hand, either of which he could wear on appropriate occasions.

Clearly, when he felt he needed sympathy or support from an audience who would not naturally be attracted to him, Conroy would wear the more severe-looking metal hook as opposed to the more unobtrusive prosthetic. When Conroy expressed "concerns" about the lack of focus of our media campaign, sources who preferred to remain anonymous suggested changing his campaign's slogan to "Give Ed Conroy a Hand." We did! He triumphed!

STATE SENATOR FRED L. WINELAND

State Senator Wineland represented the remnant of the "Old Guard," *i.e.*, the Sasscer Machine. He was the senior Maryland state senator both in age and service representing the southernmost rural district in Prince George's County. He was also the most conservative of the four senators of the Alliance 4 Action. As such, his role was to hang on to the support of the most conservative, traditional, and mostly white Democrats in a demographically changing county.

In the process, Wineland became the magnet for the gun-rights advocates and anti-busers still in the party, as well as the fiscally conservative anti-welfare business class indigenous to the county.

STATE SENATOR STENY HAMILTON HOYER

The running mate with Wineland in that southernmost district (which elected two state senators) was the fourth of the state senators who provided the visual of the Alliance 4 Action. The youngest and most ambitious of the four—State Senator Hoyer—who would become Majority Leader Hoyer of the U.S. House of Representatives years later.

Hoyer had been elected to the Maryland Senate in 1966 at the age of 27, the year that the hold of the Sasscer Machine was finally obliterated. At that time, he was on a ticket of reformers led by then-Congressman Carlton Sickles. Soon his credentials and intentions as a reformer would draw considerable scrutiny.

Hoyer had been inspired, as were so many of his generation, by John F. Kennedy. I met him in the spring of 1970 when I joined the Alliance 4 Action campaign staff.

THE PRINCE GEORGE'S COUNTY YOUNG DEMOCRATS

In 1972, I became the first "Post–Hoyer-O'Malley" era president of the Prince George's County Young Democrats. My predecessor, John J. Garrity, who would later become a judge of Maryland's Intermediate Appellate Court, was 37 years old when he was elected president of the Prince George's County Young Democrats.

I was only 25 when I succeeded him with party support. My mandate was to keep the Young Democrats organization active and in line, although the latter part of the mandate was never expressly spoken. Nevertheless, I understood the expectation.

As part of keeping the organization visible, my team of 23- to 27-year-olds organized the Annual Jefferson Jackson Day Dinner. Tickets were $25 a plate. We did not anticipate problems because we viewed ourselves as the next generation of leadership of the Hoyer-O'Malley Democratic Party and assumed the base of the Prince George's County Democratic Party and its donors knew that. We were somewhat surprised when many of the donors whom I personally solicited responded with, "I'll get back to you!"

Fortunately, I was smart enough to realize that these donors were checking on me and my *bona fides* with Peter O'Malley, confirming that the "new" leadership of the Prince George's County Young Democrats was "ok." At that point, I knew that to meet our ticket sales goal, I had to eliminate the donors' perceived need for O'Malley's approval.

My mentor-mentee relationship with O'Malley was not yet fully developed but was enough of a work-in-progress that I felt comfortable calling to advise him of the current status. My proposed solution was to make Hoyer and him, as well as a couple of other well-known names, "co-honorary chairs" of the event.

O'Malley chuckled on the other end of the line as he complimented me on recognizing the problem and coming up with "a practical solution" that would work. This arrangement would save him valuable time from answering the same question 250 times—the record number of tickets we wanted to sell to declare the event a success in this "Transition Year." We exceeded our goal, selling over 280 tickets by ensuring they were "gift-wrapped" appropriately.

PART TWO

Maryland Politics:
Establishing a Foothold

A Mystery Deposit
and the 'Road to Nowhere'

Chapter 5

Establishing Human Relations Within the Human Relations Commission

*"By all accounts—including a cross-section of com-
missioners, the executive director, the county executive,
and the media—we succeeded on all fronts ..."*

I HAD BEEN a lawyer for about three years when I was appointed in 1976 to serve on the Prince George's County Human Relations Commission at a time when it was considered to be in chaos. After one year on the commission, I was appointed chairman. A local newspaper headline read:

"PLATT APPOINTED CHAIRMAN OF CHAOTIC COMMISSION— MANDATE TO CALM COMMISSION"

One year later, bestowing credit on me for "saving the Commission from itself" and the personality feuds and legal challenges destroying its credibility, the headline read:

"HUMAN RELATIONS COMMISSION BACK ON TRACK"

My year was spent successfully fending off attacks in the courts and in the media by the Prince George's County Council and the Maryland General Assembly, as well as the Prince George's County and Maryland Fraternal Orders of Police, regarding the commission's powers, jurisdiction, authority, and performance.

I was able to do so by establishing rules, policies, and protocols designed to either structure or eliminate personality conflicts, which masqueraded as policy debates between commissioners and, at times, with the executive director over conflicting views of the authority of the director, the commissioners, and the county executive.

By all accounts—including a cross-section of commissioners, the executive director, the county executive, and the media—we succeeded on all fronts, thereby paving the way for me to move on to my next role in 1979.

Chapter 6

Counsel to the Maryland Democratic Party

"This judgment was reinforced particularly in the face of Chairman Staten's resistance, which manifested itself in silly conversations during which he would tell me that he had raised money for the Democratic Party for 30 years without doing all this 'stuff.'"

IN 1979, I received a phone call from my friend and premier trial lawyer, Thomas A. Farrington, the Maryland Democratic Party's national committeeman. The conversation that ensued during that call would lead me to an experience that dramatically expanded my understanding of the relationship between law, politics, and economics. The conversation with Farrington went like this:

Farrington: "Steve, how would you like to be able to put on your résumé that you were counsel to the Maryland Democratic Party?"

Platt: "Tom, does that mean that I'm not going to be paid?"

Farrington: "Not exactly, but not to the extent as from some of your other clients. We'll work that out."

Platt: "You recommend it? Pete and Steny know about it? We're good to go!"

Truth be told, I was pleased that "the powers that be" had the confidence in my competence as a lawyer and my political and interpersonal skills to address the legal, political, and personal issues facing the party. They recommended my appointment to the governor, the state party chairman, the state party treasurer, and the entire state central committee.

This was the "Post-Watergate" era. Jimmy Carter was still president of the United States. Harry R. Hughes was governor of Maryland. Roy N. Staten, a Democratic Baltimore County state senator, was state party chair, a carry-over appointee from former Governor Marvin Mandel. Anne Baker of Howard County was state party treasurer.

The Post-Watergate Congress had passed a series of laws, including the creation of the Federal Election Commission, designed to regulate and police campaign finance laws and hold violators accountable. The Maryland General Assembly had also acted similarly. These legislative developments resulted in a volatile combination of "Old Guard" Democratic politicians, reformers, new laws, and resistance from all quarters interacting in our state on a daily basis.

Counsel for the Democratic Party would have to interpret the new federal and state laws; referee the personality conflicts between the players in the leadership of the parties; persuade the "Old Guard" wedded to the past that it was in their personal and political interests to comply with the new laws and regulations; and encourage the reformers to work with them to do so. My ability to succeed was tested daily!

STATE SENATOR ROY N. STATEN, MARYLAND DEMOCRATIC PARTY CHAIRMAN

Harry Hughes surprised the entire political establishment by being elected governor in 1978, defeating Lieutenant Governor Blair Lee III for governor and State Senator Steny Hoyer for lieutenant governor. State Senator Staten had become party chairman under former Governor Mandel and "carried Mandel's water" 100 percent of the time without any reservations or questions before and after Mandel got into trouble. He managed to remain party chairman for a time under the newly-elected Governor Hughes.

Hughes had priorities that preempted any immediate interest in who should serve as party chairman. Clearly, however, Staten was not and would never be Hughes's choice when the time came to focus on selecting a new person to fill that position.

Staten was a product of the old-line Baltimore County Democratic Party organization headed by Dale Anderson, a former county executive for Baltimore County. This was before Anderson and his friend Dale Hess went to jail for masterminding the decision to build an exit ramp off Route 695 leading to a hotel owned by Anderson and friends. This exit was dubbed, "the Road to Nowhere."

Staten was known by Annapolis,[5] Maryland, insiders as "the Senator from Bethlehem Steel," having worked as a midlevel employee of Bethlehem Steel— then–Baltimore County's largest employer—and for contributing to political campaigns of Anderson allies. Upon his election as state senator, Staten coincidentally was promoted to vice president of the company.

ANNE BAKER, MARYLAND DEMOCRATIC PARTY TREASURER

Anne Baker, of Howard County, a stalwart and dedicated member of the "Reform Wing" of the Maryland Democratic Party, was elected treasurer. A deal was struck to ensure that all the factions would be part of the leadership and their diverse views would be adequately represented and considered as party policy and appointments were developed and procured. Easier said than done! The relationship between Staten and Baker was, at best, volatile, and at worst, toxic!

---

[5] Annapolis is the capital of Maryland.

My weekly routine as counsel for the Democratic Party was to review the interactions and relationship between Staten and Baker. I reviewed correspondence, including formal written complaints to, among other entities: the Federal Election Commission, the Maryland Board of Elections, and various county and city boards of elections. I responded to various requests for formal and informal advisory opinions—usually from Baker—or one of the other members of the Maryland Democratic State Central Committee questioning an action or inaction of Staten.

I took it upon myself to issue weekly "Advisory Opinions" (some solicited, some not) with copies to the "world" declaring and perhaps warning the chairman that an action he had taken or proposed to take was or would be in violation of federal and/or state election law(s). In fairness, many of these federal and state statutes and regulations were comparatively new. For that reason, more enlightened and conscientious souls than Staten, as well as party and elected officials, did not have a detailed knowledge of their substance and the sanctions for violating them—intentionally or not.

My professional and ethical obligation to the party as counsel was to inform those covered and affected, including the party chairman, of their responsibilities and the criminal and civil liability for not discharging these responsibilities.

My duty was most compelling when I was faced with evidence of a potential violation and the filing of an official complaint referencing that evidence. The complaint I remember best was the $10,000 deposit that appeared in the Democratic Party bank account. No paperwork was to be found to explain from where that deposit came or from whom.

Faced with the fact that a written complaint with the Federal Election Commission and the Maryland Board of Election Supervisors already had been filed, my letter dutifully and diplomatically explained why contributions such as this $10,000 could not be accepted and deposited without documentation of its source and purpose. I wrote and delivered this advice and other much-needed counsel to Staten and Baker with copies everywhere for both professional and personal reasons.

The professional reasons for distribution of this advice were to address my role to protect the party and the chairman from incurring civil and criminal liability for violating both federal and state election laws even if unaware or oblivious to the new regulations. My personal reasons were grounded in my decision as the mid-1980s approached that I was not going to put my legal career and reputation, as well as my ambition for judicial office, at risk for the negotiated discounted attorney's fees I had accepted to represent the Maryland Democratic Party (and derivatively its chairman).

This judgment was reinforced particularly in the face of Staten's resistance, which manifested itself in silly conversations during which he would tell me that he had raised money for the Democratic Party for 30 years without doing all this "stuff."

"Why is this necessary?" Staten asked.

"Senator," I answered, "that's why they passed all these laws—so now you must act accordingly because of what you were not doing until now."

Staten finally, grudgingly, accepted the wisdom and need to follow my advice. In doing so, I could forego my constant weekly "CYA" letters. I received kudos from party leaders and elected officials for seeming to bring a degree of tranquility to the relations between the party treasurer and chair.

PART THREE

Hanging Out a Shingle: My Days as an Attorney

A Female Grifter, a 'Company' Culture, and a Bail-Skipping Client

Chapter 7

The Case of "You Always Get Your Way at Ourisman Chevrolet"

> *"One of the lessons you learn fairly quickly when you start practicing law, particularly criminal law, is not to presume your client's version of the 'facts' is true."*

I CHOSE TO be a lawyer through a process of elimination. First of all, I recognized that I had limited aptitude, knowledge, and skills in math and science. That eliminated the medical professions, architecture, and engineering as well as plumbing, carpentry, and landscaping as career options.

I also believed some of my teachers and mentors when they said that I did have some talent and skills as a writer and public speaker as well as organizational skills and analytic ability.

My high school typing teacher at Massanutten Military Academy in Woodstock, Virginia, contributed to my decision-making process by telling me to "make sure you attain an executive position because this typing class isn't going well for you."

I was inspired, as were many others, by some of the early television lawyers: Raymond Burr in *Perry Mason*, E.G. Marshall and Robert Reed in *The Defenders*, and Andy Griffith in *Matlock*. I was also personally motivated by a more eclectic group of television role models, including Jack Webb as Sergeant Joe Friday in *Dragnet* ("Just the Facts, ma'am—just the facts!").

Also making a memorable impression on my developing mind and ambition were Peter Falk as Lieutenant Columbo ("Just one more question") and perhaps, most uniquely, Shakespearean actor Richard Boone. Boone played Paladin, an upscale professional gunfighter who lived in a plush hotel in San Francisco in the later part of the 19th century. He would hire himself out for $2,000 per job to combat bullies and tyrants abusing their victims. Paladin fit my image of the lawyer as a "hired gun" who, nevertheless, fought for justice and made a nice living doing it. The name of the television show was *Have Gun Will Travel*, which provided perfect imagery for me as I searched for my role in the world.

Contained in this section are tales of some of the interesting cases that I handled as a lawyer from January 1976 when I was sworn in as a member of the bar in the State of Maryland until I became a district court judge in August 1986.

THE FEMALE GRIFTER

I had been practicing law for about three years when, in 1979–1980, a prospective client appeared in my law office with a story that sounded strange. At the time, Ourisman Chevrolet was one of the largest and most prominent retail automobile dealerships in the Washington metropolitan area. Its television and radio advertising was familiar to everyone: "You Always Get Your Way at Ourisman Chevrolet."

My prospective client was a topflight salesman at Ourisman. He came to my law office with papers charging him with various sexual offenses and assaults on a woman. His version of the facts differed dramatically from those set forth in the charging documents.

The charging documents described an incident that allegedly took place near closing time, about 9:45 pm, at the new car lot at Ourisman Chevrolet located on Branch Avenue in Camp Springs, Maryland. The alleged female "victim" appeared in the showroom expressing an interest in purchasing a new car and requesting a test drive in a vehicle she said she had viewed on the lot.

My future client, the dedicated "super salesman" that he was, volunteered to accompany her on a test drive. They went for a five-minute test drive and returned to the showroom in time for closing, he thought, without incident. Within 48 hours, the prospective female customer had gone to a district court commissioner and applied for and had charges issued against the salesman, including 3rd and 4th degree sex offenses.

In addition, her attorney had filed a civil lawsuit against both Ourisman Chevrolet, Inc., and the salesman claiming damages for a sexual assault that allegedly took place on the test drive. This was the narrative the salesman recounted for me in our initial interview.

One of the lessons you learn fairly quickly when you start practicing law, particularly criminal law, is not to presume your client's version of the "facts" is true. That wisdom gained from experience caused me to tell my client early on, in no uncertain terms:

> *"I am going to rely on what you tell me when I represent you. That means if you bullshit me, I will make big mistakes. When I do, two things will happen: I will be embarrassed, but I'll go home at the end of the day. You, on the other hand, will likely go to jail."*

As it turned out, what my client told me was "the whole truth and nothing but the truth," which enabled me to do my job and defend him against this effort to defraud both him and his deep-pocket employer, Ourisman Chevrolet. Fortunately, he had the means and resources to pay me sufficiently to zealously defend him and to find out what was going on, *i.e.*, the nature of the scam being perpetrated on him.

The Investigation

Enter a classic character: Ben Guiffre, Private Investigator. Guiffre looked, acted, and talked like the television character, Kojak, played by actor Telly Savalas. His physical appearance mirrored Kojak's look, he addressed everyone as "Pawdner," and frequently, as did Kojak, asked whomever he was talking to, "Who loves ya?" I had hired him before and, as a result of that experience, I concluded that I did not want to know how he found out, what he discovered, or who his sources were; but I knew his reports were absolutely correct and reliable.

Guiffre discovered that the so-called victim, a female prison guard at Lorton (Virginia) Correctional Institute, and her 5th Street lawyer, were running a scam operation. That operation, in a nutshell, was to report on a monthly basis the scenario described earlier—targeting a different car dealership each time. The female would approach the dealership near closing time and request a test drive, followed by action to obtain criminal charges the next day and the filing of a civil case against the salesman accompanying her on the test drive and his deep-pocket car dealership. The civil case would then be quickly settled for "nuisance value" with the corporate defendant, and the criminal charges would be dropped.

Guiffre dutifully discovered and reported this scam to me, handing me the documents to prove it. We were, at that point, "ready for bear!" I ruled out any plea bargaining, which required me to explain to the assistant state's attorney my reasons for refusing to even discuss his generous offer to accept a plea to minor charges with a guarantee of no jail time. I then chose an unconventional tactic.

Normally, the defense is not required to disclose its defenses to criminal charges except if the defense is that the defendant has an alibi; that is, he was not present when the crime was committed. Furthermore, that conventional wisdom calls for a criminal defense attorney to not tell the prosecutor anything he doesn't have to.

Nevertheless, ignoring the conventional wisdom, I laid out the entire defense of my client to the prosecutor—that meant copies of Guiffre's report, the documents proving the accuracy of the facts reported (including the lawsuits filed to extort the corporate defendants—all nine of them), and the record of the settlements reached in many of them. None of that was legally required. It was done under the perhaps naïve belief that the prosecutor's fundamental duty was to seek justice—not just a conviction—and that "facts matter."

Unfortunately, the facts did not matter in this case at that time because the assistant state's attorney's boss, the state's attorney himself, was running for reelection. The assistant state's attorney assigned to the case dutifully explained to me that "the complaining witness was a 'letter writer' and would complain to the media." So, the case had to be tried even if the state's chances of a conviction were, as I said to the assistant state's attorney, "slim and none and Slim is in Alabama."

Court and Judge Assignment

Onto the Upper Marlboro Courthouse stage where this case would be tried, there appeared the Honorable G.R. Hovey Johnson, an Associate Judge of the Circuit Court for Prince George's County. Judge Johnson in his prior life had been Colonel G.R. Hovey Johnson, a former Green Beret and JAG officer. He was a proud African American judge who had been appointed by Governor Harry Hughes a few years earlier under circumstances worth mentioning.

Hughes had pledged to diversify the judiciary of Maryland. Aware of that commitment, the Judicial Selection Commission of Prince George's County whose job it was, and is, to recommend only the most highly and professionally qualified lawyers for the position of judge, nevertheless sent the governor a list that included only three applicants—all of whom were white males.

Hughes sent the list back, requesting more nominees. However, the unspoken and underlying message was clear: Send me a list including the name of a qualified African American lawyer on it.

At that time, Retired Colonel G.R. Hovey Johnson was employed as a staff attorney for the Maryland Office of the Public Defender. His reputation for integrity, professionalism, and courtesy in the brief time he had served with the public defender was untouched. He was a zealous defender of his indigent clients without being an apologist for them. His candor and courtesy, indeed, his professionalism, were recognized by prosecutors, judges, and his fellow defense attorneys.

Therefore, it was clear to both the leadership of the political establishment and to G.R. Hovey Johnson, Esquire, himself, that his name should be sent forward by the judicial selection commission and that he would soon become Judge G.R. Hovey Johnson. He immediately completed the application form, was selected, and added to the commission's list. A short time later, he was appointed.

When this case was assigned to Judge Johnson, we were relieved. To say that he was a "No Nonsense judge" would be an understatement. His military manner and bearing, meaning firmness but fairness, were apparent to all.

All Rise!

The trial began on schedule. A jury was selected in short order. Obviously, the assigned prosecutor was simply going through the motions by presenting the case he had been handed and ordered to prosecute—a case that by his own confidential admission did not believe in.

The state's case essentially consisted of the testimony of the complaining witness. Some lawyers go through an entire career without catching a witness in a lie. In this case, I caught the complaining witness, who neither looked nor acted the part of a vulnerable victim, in a lie three times. Each time when asked:

Q. *"Then your testimony on direct examination was a lie?"*

A. *"Yes."*

At the end of the state's case, we approached the bench. I made a motion for judgment of acquittal while acknowledging that the complaining witness had testified to sufficient facts to make a *prima fa-*

cie[6] case, even though her story was not believable. Therefore, in this case, the court had to deny my motion while commenting gratuitously to the assistant state's attorney, the defendant, and me:

> *"I trust that you understand why I had to deny this Motion. But don't worry; if this jury doesn't do the right thing, I will! Mr. State's Attorney, why did you prosecute this case? She's trash!"*

The foundation for me to persuade my client not to testify had been established by the presiding judge. In a criminal case, the state has to prove the defendant is guilty. The defendant does not have to prove innocence. My client, the car salesman, desperately wanted to testify to explain to the jury what happened and, more importantly, what didn't happen in order to salvage his reputation.

However, weighing against his natural desire to defend his honor and reputation was my sound tactical decision as his attorney not to risk any harm. Judge Johnson had already said that he was going to find my client not guilty even if the jury didn't. One of the first rules of criminal defense lawyering is "Do No Harm," *i.e.*, do not take any unnecessary risks of hurting or adversely affecting your defense narrative. The defense was established. Any testimony would constitute "too much information" from my client.

Our defense case was the testimony of Private Investigator Guiffre exposing to the judge and jury the scam operation the complaining witness and her lawyer were operating on a large scale, enveloping my client. When we were quite confident of victory—acquittal on all charges—our case was fully presented.

Our confidence turned out to be justified. Judge Johnson instructed the jury on the law and their duties. After closing arguments, witnessed by the complaining witness sitting in the courtroom conspicuously holding a rosary, Judge Johnson asked the jury, "Do you need to leave the courtroom to deliberate?" The answer was "yes"; but not for long. In less than three minutes (a record by any standard), the jury returned with a unanimous verdict of not guilty.

---

[6] A prima facie case means sufficient facts have been testified about that if believed by the jury, the defendant could be found guilty.

That outcome proved to my client, and the observers in the courtroom, that if you seek justice and have the resources to hire effective counsel and a great private investigator, You Always Get Your Way at Ourisman Chevrolet!

Chapter 8

The Case of "the Vice President in Charge of Personnel—of a Drug Ring!"

"Only a lethal combination of hubris and hope could have led him to the mindset that he could credibly deny his involvement in the face of eyewitness testimony from the surviving victim, who knew him before identifying him in open court."

MY NEW CLIENT'S name was Robert Willie Young, and he was charged with first-degree murder and related counts. My assistant told me that Young was in the Prince George's County Detention Center in Upper Marlboro, Maryland, awaiting trial, and that $10,000 in cash had been brought to our law office to pay for his defense. I was to go to the jail to interview Young as soon as I finished my case in the courthouse.

It is 1979, and I've been a lawyer for three years, working for the Law Office of Howard L. Stern (not the radio personality). Actually, I was the trial lawyer for Stern who was both a CPA and a lawyer, primarily active in the area of business law and counseling.

Initially, I had visions of cash and an interesting case, which stayed in my mind until I arrived at the jail where I was immediately confronted with a dilemma. When I requested to see Robert Willie Young, the staff at the jail, who were then deputies of the Prince George's County Sheriff's Office, told me that two men named Robert Young were in the jail. I didn't know which one was my client because I had never met him, so I left it up to the jail personnel to bring me the right Robert Young. They failed in the first instance.

Back then, attorneys were given private cubicles to maintain their privileged communications with their clients residing at what was then known as the "Marlboro Hilton." The man who appeared in the cubicle in which I was assigned to interview my client was a young, gangly-looking 19-year-old male named Robert Young. I later learned he was charged with misdemeanor breaking and entering—a charge that carries a maximum sentence of three years. He was not charged with first-degree murder, which at the time carried a maximum sentence of the death penalty.

I thought to myself, *"He's 19 and doesn't look like someone who could commit the crimes which our client had been charged with."* However, this was the man whom the jail personnel had brought down to see me. I therefore assumed—incorrectly (as it turns out)—that he was in fact my client.

I sized-up this rather innocent-looking 19-year-old male who did not resemble the description I had been given of my new client. The background I had received was that Robert Willie Young had previously been charged with and acquitted of murder in other cases, and that this was the fourth time he had been charged. I remember thinking to myself, "This kid doesn't look like he could've done all that in the brief time he's been on this earth."

I began our conversation by introducing myself.

"I am Steven Platt, the attorney you have hired, and I am here to interview you and discuss your murder case for however long it takes to do so. I need to explain to you where we're going and how we're getting there, at least for the time being."

The youthful Robert Young immediately grew wide-eyed. He looked terrified and immediately yelled out:

"I broke into a house, but I didn't kill anybody!"

Being a "quick study," I immediately realized this probably was the other Robert Young. I then went back to the deputies and suggested that if in fact another Robert Young was detained there, I probably wanted to see him and not this individual.

All the jail personnel who overheard the inmate loudly proclaiming his innocence and who observed his wide-eyed hysterical reaction to my introduction continued to laugh out loud. They immediately began the task of correcting the situation by taking the 19-year-old Young back and bringing the 33-year-old Young to meet me in the cubicle.

The Company

The "real" Robert Willie Young turned out to be a much more interesting subject to interview. He was "employed" in a capacity I dubbed "Vice President in Charge of Personnel" of a business enterprise run by a gentleman named Linwood Gray. The U.S. attorney for the District of Columbia as well as state and local prosecutors suspected that the business of this company was the wholesale distribution of drugs, specifically heroin, along with racketeering, including violent crimes necessary to carry on the business.

My private investigator and "Pawdner," the ever-present Ben Guiffre, verified that my suspicion was correct and reported much more. The "company" employed as "independent contractors" various individuals who were utilized as couriers, among other duties. These couriers were tasked with contacting suppliers internationally and bringing back inventory—drugs to sell on the streets of Washington, D.C., and the surrounding jurisdictions. "Vice President in Charge of Personnel" Young was responsible for the job performance and morale of the employees and independent contractors who worked for "the company."

The company did not have a retirement plan, nor did it have a 401k program. They did have a strict policy of "non-disclosure" unlike those of mainstream companies. Most mainstream companies with a non-disclosure policy set forth this provision in a written contract that provides a sanction for its violation in the form of an award of "liquidated damages." This company's non-disclosure policy was enforced by the "Vice President in Charge of Personnel" in a way best described as a "liquidated personnel" policy. That is, if you informed on the company, you were subject to being liquidated.

That liquidated personnel policy was in full effect in the early 1980s when a husband and wife acting as couriers journeyed to Amsterdam, Holland, to make contact with a supplier and bring back cartons of Chesterfield cigarettes with packaged heroin to be sold on the streets. For reasons never explained, the Dutch contact was not met; as a result (supposedly through no fault of their own), the couriers returned to the United States empty-handed. Nevertheless, they demanded payment for their "services."

The company's policy when a courier has failed to make contact was to pay the courier's expenses but not to compensate for the unsuccessful connection. The couple, feeling aggrieved that this policy was unfair, particularly as applied to them in this instance, failed to recognize why the company had no employee grievance procedure or suggestion box. They showed up at a nightclub in D.C., which served as a front for the company's real business, and verbally threatened the company CEO, warning:

> *"We'll talk with some people you don't want us to talk to if we don't get paid."*

That ill-advised conversation prompted the CEO to call the "Vice President in Charge of Personnel" to implement the sanction for violating the company's policy of non-disclosure with words to the effect of:

> *"You hired them; you fire them!"*

The "Vice President in Charge of Personnel," now my client, who knew the couple and had initially recommended they be hired, made an appointment to visit socially with them at their apartment. After joining them for coffee and conversation at the kitchen table, he briefly excused himself to use the bathroom. When he emerged, it was with a gun blazing. The female was killed. The male was shot but not fatally. He lay still pretending to be dead and ultimately survived and identified my client as the shooter in open court.

The Evidence

I, of course, knew none of this when I initially interviewed Young. He presented in the jail as calm, cool, and collected—almost routine. This was understandable, even expected, as this was the fourth time he had been charged with murder. The previous times, he was either acquitted based on self-defense or the charges were dropped due to insufficient evidence. Funny how witnesses' memories fail—or they become unavailable as time goes on.

Young denied the bulk of Guiffre's investigation, which matched the actual events. My client also denied any involvement in the company. I have always characterized his and similar behavior as the "I don't know what you are talking about defense." That defense seldom works without a solid verifiable alibi.

My client not only did not have an alibi, he did not even deny visiting the couple on the evening in question. He claimed that nothing out of the ordinary occurred during his visit, and that both the deceased woman and her wounded husband were unharmed when he left. Furthermore, he insisted he had no explanation or even knowledge of the manner in which they were shot or by whom, except to say, "If it had been my purpose to kill them, they would both be dead."

I later advised my client that we could not defend the case on the basis that he was a professional hitman. Young and I discussed the motivations of the surviving victim, the husband, to accuse my client of shooting and killing his wife, as well as shooting him with the intent to kill if someone else actually did it. His "explanation" was that the couple, who had been hired based on his recommendation, "no longer liked him."

With that background, we planned our initial court appearance—the bond hearing in district court. Every accused person has a right in the words of the applicable Maryland Rule of Criminal Procedure "to be considered for release before verdict by a judicial officer which in Maryland is either a District Court Commissioner or a Judge." However, under that same rule, "a defendant charged with an offense for which the maximum penalty is life imprisonment ... may be released before verdict ... only by a judge."

The Presiding Judge

Because Young was charged with first-degree murder and related counts, he could only be released before trial by a judge. Although we had no control over whom that judge would be on the date of his bond hearing, Young got lucky.

The judge presiding that day was the Honorable Sylvania W. Woods, Sr. I had known Judge Woods since I moved into Prince George's County in 1970 when he was an attorney practicing criminal defense law in the Maryland suburbs, Washington, D.C., and Southern Maryland. I met him while helping manage political campaigns in the county in which attorney Woods, Sr. was a candidate for Democratic central committee; and later working for $100 a week while I was a law student for then–State Senator Steny H. Hoyer in the early 1970s.

Sylvania Woods was one of the "go-to criminal defense attorneys" particularly for African Americans accused of both minor and serious crimes. He was also a member of the Prince George's County Democratic Central Committee, having been elected as a result of being on the ticket of the slate of candidates I helped manage in the fall of 1970. In the late 1970s, Woods, Sr. was appointed as a Judge of The District Court for Prince George's County to replace another African American judge, Henry Johnson, who retired.

Judge Woods had a fascinating background. He had at various times in his life run moonshine on the backroads of rural Georgia. He had been a District of Columbia police officer while he attended American University Law School. Upon graduation, he practiced in

D.C. and later in Prince George's County where he lived and worked. His law office was in Landover, Maryland, a majority African American middle-class area in Prince George's County, which, in the 1970s and 1980s, was an area where the demographics were changing dramatically and would, in time, become the wealthiest majority African American county in the United States.

Judge Sylvania Woods, the man, despite his first name now being "Judge," was "street smart"—he was instinctively not judgmental. He believed that everyone was a sinner, and although we should be held accountable for our actions, severity was not always necessary. Bad behavior, even violent behavior, did not surprise him, and he understood "situational ethics."

For a bond hearing, Judge Woods was as good as we could get! Tom Blair, the assistant state's attorney assigned to the case, appeared at the bond hearing, which was unusual at that time. Usually, a fairly new assistant state's attorney handles district court cases including bond hearings; but this case was obviously getting special attention. Tom Blair was one of the state's attorney's most experienced and competent prosecutors. His nickname among the lawyers was "Trooper Blair" because of his reputation for hands-on dealing with the details of every case he handled, including accompanying the police to crime scenes.

The case was called, and Blair argued vehemently for detaining the defendant without bond. He pointed out to Judge Woods that the state believed that Young was an enforcer for an international drug ring, that he was a professional killer, and that this was the fourth time he had been charged with murder. Blair also argued that my client had access to almost unlimited resources and was therefore a flight risk, along with being an extreme danger to the community, in particular, the prosecution witnesses.

When my turn came, I reminded Judge Woods that the purpose of bond is to secure the appearance of the defendant, not to punish him for the crimes he is charged with but not yet convicted of. I then tried to turn Blair's arguments on their head by pointing out that, indeed, this was the fourth time the defendant had been charged with murder. Nevertheless, each time he had been acquitted, and each time he had appeared at every scheduled court hearing and completely complied with all of the court's prescribed conditions of release.

That seemed to turn the tide. Judge Woods surprised both Blair, who was chagrined, and me by setting bond at $25,000 for the murder and $25,000 for the attempted murder. Within hours, Young had been released on bond—posted by someone whom I had never heard of—and was soon off to parts unknown. Among those who did not know where he went was his lawyer—Me!

Oh, Where, Oh, Where Has My Client Gone Now?

When a client fails to appear for court, the ethical obligation of his lawyer, who is an officer of the court, is to counsel him to return to the jurisdiction and turn himself in (if the lawyer has any contact with his client). Young was not in touch with me, so that was easy—no contact, no counsel. The bondsman, meanwhile, was looking for Young to recover his $50,000 bond, which was forfeited when he failed to appear. The court ordered the "bond forfeited absolute" and issued a bench warrant for the defendant's arrest.

I was out of contact with Young for almost three years before I would hear from him again. When I did, he called on the telephone and advised me, his lawyer, that he would be turning himself in. He neither explained the reason he had jumped bond nor the reason he was turning himself in. I suspected that he fled because of my candid assessment of his chances of a successful defense in a case with an eyewitness who knew the defendant and identified him as the murderer.

As to his reasons for returning to face those charges (knowing that he would be locked up until his trial), I suspected that because the leader of the international drug ring for which Young worked, Linwood Gray, had been acquitted of all drug-related charges, including murder and racketeering except for income tax evasion, Young must have been encouraged by that unrelated outcome and thought he could pull off a similar result. That theory was totally misplaced; as it would turn out, the result in Young's case would be completely the opposite.

In the meantime, my client had been indicted for first-degree murder, attempted murder, and related counts. The wheels of justice keep spinning even when you are not around to watch them. The next time I saw Young was when he was back in the county jail.

Court Is Now in Session

The case of *The State of Maryland v. Robert Willie Young* was now in the Circuit Court for Prince George's County. My old boss for whom I clerked, Chief Judge Ernest A. Loveless, Jr., assigned this very high-profile case to the Honorable Audrey Melbourne. Judge Melbourne was the first female judge appointed in Prince George's County. First, she was appointed to the district court and then, shortly thereafter, to the circuit court, both appointments by Governor Marvin Mandel.

Judge Melbourne was a skilled practitioner. Her claim to fame as a lawyer was that she successfully represented the first female jockey to be permitted to participate in horseracing in Maryland. Although Judge Melbourne's reputation was established in that case, she was not considered an ardent feminist. In fact, the "powers that be" who were all male considered her "one of the boys" because she mingled so well with them. That ability brought her political support for both judgeships in rapid order.

Judge Melbourne liked attention. In presiding over this case, she saw opportunities to promote herself through the media and in the courthouse. By sheer coincidence, this was around the time when the Supreme Court of the United States and lower federal and state courts were handing down decisions with limitations and guidance on when judges could "close" courtrooms to the public and to the media.

Naturally, these decisions, and the judges who issued them, drew attention from both print and broadcast media. Judge Melbourne recognized the opportunity that existed in a case that already had received quite a bit of news coverage because it involved a violent international "drug ring's" alleged "enforcer."

Security and safety were grounds under the case law to close courtrooms, so Judge Melbourne closed the courtroom for security reasons. The image of the case as one requiring action to secure the safety of the court, staff, clerks, lawyers, and even the defendant was enhanced by "Trooper Blair's" choice to wear a bullet-proof vest to court allegedly to protect himself from unknown conspirators.

Judge Melbourne then asked me to file a motion to close the courtroom. My client could not have cared less; in fact, he informed me that he was "King of the Jail" and had no reason to be concerned about his safety. I told him:

> *"Unless you object, I'm going to do what the judge asked. It always helps to keep the judge happy, although closing the courtroom has nothing to do with our defense in your case."*

I didn't tell him that we really had no defense, so it was even more important to keep the judge happy.

Although Assistant State's Attorney Blair gave a speech on the rights of "the People" to see and hear the trial, Judge Melbourne predictably granted the motion she had asked me to file.

Two persons remained in the courtroom, apparently in noncompliance with the court's order. Judge Melbourne asked them to identify themselves and to explain their reasons for remaining. One was as an assistant U.S. attorney from Florida who was there to observe the trial to gain information for the prosecutions of gang members in his jurisdiction. Judge Melbourne advised him that he was not exempt from her order and had to leave, at which time he quietly and politely exited the courtroom.

Judge Melbourne, however, knew the second "guest" from her days as a district court judge. That person was my then-wife, who served as the chief administrative clerk for the District Court for Prince George's County. She was 8½ months pregnant with our second child. Judge Melbourne also knew why my wife was there. She turned to Blair and asked, "Mr. Blair, do you have any objection to Mrs. Platt remaining in the courtroom? She has never seen her husband 'perform'?"

At that moment, either my wife or a courtroom clerk pointed to her visibly pregnant stomach prompting Judge Melbourne to clarify the meaning of perform—"NOT THAT WAY!" she exclaimed. Blair voiced no objection, and my wife was allowed to "observe my performance" for the rest of the day.

Within hours, lawyers from the major newspapers and media stations had filed "First Amendment Papers," *i.e.*, motions to reopen the courtroom. Judge Melbourne then inquired, "Mr. Platt, how long do you need to respond?" "Not long, Judge Melbourne," I replied, since I had no intention of spending any time defending an action that was not my idea and did not benefit my client. The next day, Judge Melbourne reopened the courtroom—her search for publicity having been accomplished.

I had no real defense to the serious charges against my client; so, for the next two weeks, I sat with him while we absorbed the hits from one witness after another called by Blair. He was an experienced and competent homicide prosecutor.

I remained quiet without cross-examining most of the witnesses who were called to prove the *corpus delicti*[7] of the crime. No one was denying that the crimes had been committed. The only issue was whether the state could prove that my client was the person who murdered the female courier and attempted to murder her husband. Even when the surviving victim, the husband, testified as the state's star witness and pointed to my client identifying him as the killer, I did not ask him many questions.

I had learned from being mentored as well as watching and listening to some excellent trial lawyers that it takes a really savvy attorney to be able to say, "No questions." That strategy is most recommended for the occasions in which a witness hasn't said anything that hurts your case. However, even when the witness may have hurt your case, a competent and confident lawyer still will not ask questions unless he or she thinks the answers will somehow undo the harm done to the case on direct examination.

---

[7] *Corpus delicti* refers to actions that constitute a crime.

The alternative is what I describe when training or mentoring developing trial lawyers—the "Oh Yeah Cross Examination"—an utterly discredited technique usually involving repeating the testimony that hurt your case; thereby ensuring that the jury heard it, and then asking, "Are you sure?"

During those weeks, I spent a lot of time counseling my client against testifying. My reasons were manifold. First and foremost, every defendant has a right to testify and a right not to testify. If he exercises his right not to testify, the judge instructs the jury about that right telling the jurors that they cannot, in any way, hold it against him for not testifying. In other words, the jurors are told that they cannot infer that the defendant is guilty because he did not testify and deny he committed the crime.

On the other hand, if the defendant does testify, he can be cross-examined on anything in his background and history. In this case, that would include his flight from the jurisdiction while on bond, which the judge would instruct the jury to consider as "evidence of guilt." In addition, Blair, being a very zealous and competent prosecutor, could explore my client's occupation as the "Vice President in Charge of Personnel," how he made a living, his source of funds, etc.

Nevertheless, my client had testified effectively in his other trials and was acquitted on the basis of self-defense. Consequently, he convinced himself that having been an effective witness in his previous cases and successfully convincing those juries that he killed in self-defense, somehow he could be an effective witness for himself in this case.

Only a lethal combination of hubris and hope could have led him to the mindset that he could credibly deny his involvement in the face of eyewitness testimony from the surviving victim, who knew him before identifying him in open court.

I was certain that my client's hunch was wrong. Among other things, I had counseled him that our only chance to win was if the prosecution messed up or a witness didn't show up or surprised them. Otherwise, I advised he had a 95 percent chance of being convicted. However, if he testified and Blair got his teeth into him on cross-examination, his chance of being convicted would increase to 99 percent.

My client chose to gamble on himself and his ability to con this jury. I then dutifully did what was required of me as his lawyer and as an officer of the court. Out of the presence of the jury, I advised Judge Melbourne, on the record, that against my advice, my client had chosen to testify.

Judge Melbourne, again out of the presence of the jury, further advised Young of his right to testify and to not testify; but if he chose not to testify, she would instruct the jury that they could not, in any way, hold his choice against him or infer that he was, therefore, guilty.

My client then testified, against my advice, and predictably got slaughtered by Blair on cross-examination for all the reasons I had warned him about. As it turned out, the only thing incorrect about my prediction was his chance of being convicted. That 99 percent was understated as his fate was sealed upon cross-examination.

Incidentally, he never admitted, even to me, that he killed the woman and attempted to kill the man, which was why I could allow him to testify. If he had told me that he committed the acts in question and was going to lie under oath, I could not have ethically presented his testimony. However, since I did not know whether he committed the crimes, even if I suspected he did, his testimony could be presented.

Sure enough, after a short period of time deliberating, the jury found Robert Willie Young guilty on all charges. He faced a maximum cumulative sentence of life plus 35 years consecutive. We had about 45 days to prepare for sentencing by Judge Melbourne. My preparation would be comparatively simple, particularly when compared to the work necessary to prepare for a 13-day trial with multiple witnesses and expert testimony.

Our evidence to counter the finding was nonexistent. I concluded, by process of elimination, that there was only one possible path to try to save my client from spending the better part of the rest of his life in prison. That path was through a psychiatric prison in Maryland called the Patuxent Institution.

At the time of Young's sentencing, Patuxent Institution was a prison; but unlike other penitentiaries, it operated on the premise that not all, but certain offenders (even violent offenders) could be "rehabilitated" and transformed through intense staged psychiatric treatment while they were confined. If, at any time, the psychiatrists determined the inmate, or as they were called at Patuxent, "the patient," was rehabilitated and no longer sociopathic or dangerous, he or she could be released. This approach was not for the psychotic offender, but rather for the sociopath.

I determined that my allocution at sentencing would be limited to requesting the court, *i.e.*, Judge Melbourne, to "recommend that the defendant be referred for evaluation and commitment to the Patuxent Institution." I decided to avoid emphasizing my client's denial of the charges in the face of the jury's verdict or in any way attempting to minimize the seriousness of the offenses of which he had been convicted.

At the time, under Maryland law, a judge's recommendation of Patuxent was not dispositive of the decision by the Maryland Division of Corrections as to whether a defendant should be referred there, but it was an important factor to consider. Both my client and I knew this, but what I didn't know was that my client, out of vanity, would ultimately refuse to cooperate with my strategy.

At sentencing, Assistant State's Attorney Blair further indicted my client with his entire background. Anticipating my plea for Patuxent, he tried to preempt it by arguing that Young was not mentally ill. He stated:

> *"This man is a cold-blooded killer who needs to be permanently taken off the streets."*

When it was my time to speak, I said:

> *"My client is a single father of a star football player at Northwestern High School and a struggling entrepreneur."*

Then I focused on our request that he be referred to Patuxent. To my surprise, Judge Melbourne responded, "I might do that if he tells me that he needs help." I then whispered to my client, "Tell her you need help." He refused.

I then asked the court for indulgence, which Judge Melbourne graciously granted as she further commented:

> "I'm not asking your client to admit anything; I know he wants to appeal—but he's going to have to say that he needs help if he wants me to consider Patuxent."

I then desperately tried to convince Young to drop his resistance to a totally reasonable condition precedent giving him his only shot at ever seeing society from anywhere besides behind bars. Pleading with him, I said, "Everybody needs help."

He then repeated those exact words to the court.

Judge Melbourne responded, "Not good enough," and refused to make the recommendation. The sentence was life plus 35 years with no recommendation for Patuxent.

Notwithstanding the finality of that sentence, Robert Willie Young was paroled after serving 17 years in the Maryland Division of Corrections. By that time, I was a full-time circuit court judge in the Circuit Court for Prince George's County. Judge Melbourne was a colleague soon to retire.

After his release, I heard from Young once. He shared with me that he had found Jesus in prison, and that Jesus Christ was now a part of his life. Indeed, he was now a minister, bringing the Word of God to people who needed help.

I resisted the temptation to ask him whether he had changed his mind about whether he needed help. In any case, I was pleased to see him utilizing his training in the field of personnel management to help take care of persons needing spiritual guidance and career counseling.

PART FOUR

Donning the Robe:
My Days on the Bench

Chapter 9

The Orphans' Court
A Valuable Lesson, an Emperor, and a Promiscuous Prescription

"Her husband, the Chief, was made aware of the diagnosis, to which he agreed; and he offered to assist in filling the 'prescription.' The 20 men named were friends of Chief Turkey Tayac whom he recruited to facilitate the treatment prescribed."

I DEPARTED THE chambers of Chief Judge Ernest Loveless, Jr. to practice law as a politically involved lawyer in 1976. But by then, I had concluded that I ultimately wanted to be a judge. My experience serving as a law clerk to Chief Judge Loveless (1974–1975) gave me a sense of fulfillment—a feeling I hoped to experience again if I were ever able to attain that goal.

That feeling was defined by the great Judge Learned Hand during his 1927 address to the Bryn Mawr graduating class when he described a judge's life:

> *"There is something else that makes it a delectable calling. For when the case is all in and the turmoil stops and after he is left*

alone, things begin to take form from his pen or in his head, slowly or swiftly as his capacities admit, out of the mirk the pattern emerges, his pattern, the expression of what he has seen and what he has therefore made, the impress of his self upon the not-self, upon the hitherto formless material of which he was once but a part and over which he has now become the master. That is a pleasure, which nobody who has felt it will be likely to underrate."[8]

That feeling, I decided, was preferable to the feeling that would inevitably result if I pursued a political career through elective office. I had learned by observing elected officials and candidates for elective office at every level—federal, state, and local—in three different states (Virginia, New York, and Maryland) that compromises inevitably must be made to have a chance of successfully pursuing public office. In fact, I had participated in the discussions that preceded the decision-making on such compromises in my role as a campaign manager at different levels in multiple jurisdictions.

Although I completely understood that compromises—whether short term or long term and the reasons behind them—were necessary to maximize the chances of success in a political career, I concluded I would not be able to because I ultimately would be unwilling to continually compromise my values and positions sufficiently to sustain a successful political career in the long term.

That realization coupled with my attraction—intellectually and emotionally—to the bench made my choice of careers easier than it might have been. That choice was reinforced by the experience I enjoyed while clerking for Chief Judge Loveless, who remained a mentor and friend long after I left his employment in 1975.

---

[8] C. Landauer, "Scholar, Craftsman, and Priest: Learned Hand's Self-Imaging," *Yale Journal of Law & the Humanities*, vol. 3:2, art. 4 (Jan. 1991), citing L. Hand, The Preservation of Personality (1927).

CHIEF JUDGE ERNEST A. "ERNIE" LOVELESS, JR.

Chief Judge Loveless was, by far, the most beloved and admired circuit court judge in Prince George's County for the 30-plus years he sat and managed that court from 1962 to 1994. He was one of the most influential jurists in Maryland. He pioneered groundbreaking and cutting-edge "treatment" of juveniles and introduced the use of psychological diagnostic tools in family law matters. He cared deeply about children and was a scholar in the field of adoptions, continually supervising and inspiring social workers and agencies in that area.

Prior to being appointed to the circuit court, Chief Judge Loveless served as a state legislator, counsel to the county liquor board, and in numerous other political positions. He was a politician, a diplomat, and a manager of politicians and judges when those skills were still highly valued and esteemed. Chief Judge Loveless was also a humble public servant who cared deeply about his court, his community, his staff, and his family—along with his hobby/obsession of "goose hunting."

I was practically a shoo-in for the law clerk position after having been recommended by State Senator Steny Hoyer, Peter O'Malley, and Chief Judge Loveless's previous law clerk, C. Philip Nichols, Jr.

When I interviewed with Chief Judge Loveless, we spent more time talking about the time he spent as a law clerk serving as "Secretary of the Kingpin Goose Hunting Club" than we did about the duties and expectations for the law clerk position I had come to interview for. Lesson No. 1: "You could be late for court, but not for goose hunting!"

I learned how to judge people and cases from Chief Judge Loveless. Ironically, one of the most valuable lessons I learned was *not* to judge people or cases too quickly, despite the honor of having one's first name changed to "Judge." In addition, as a corollary to Lesson No. 1 was Lesson No. 2: "Most of us human beings are more complicated than either our admirers or detractors would like to believe."

These were lessons in life science, not just judging. I have tried to remember lessons both on and off the bench throughout my life. To the extent that I have experienced "success" and have been able to leave a legacy to document my accomplishments, it has been due in significant part to absorbing and retaining the wisdom of Chief Judge Loveless.

THE BLUE RIBBON TICKET

In 1978, with the support and assistance of County Executive Winfield Kelly, Jr., State Senator Steny Hoyer, and political mentor Peter O'Malley, my name was placed on the Democratic organizations' "BLUE RIBBON DEMOCRATS" ticket as a candidate for judge of the Orphans' Court for Prince George's County—along with incumbents Chief Judge Mary T. O'Hare and my good friend, Associate Judge C. Philip Nichols, Jr.

Being a candidate meant I had to campaign for a position that almost no voter, except the political class, even knew of or cared about. In fact, most voters, understandably if and when they did hear about this position, thought the orphans' court dealt with orphans! In reality, the orphans' court is essentially a probate court. The name "orphans' court" originated in England where the probate court in the 18th century, out of necessity, was concerned with orphans.

Unfortunately, the average voter doesn't know much about probate or care enough to find out. Nevertheless, our opponents in 1978, and again in 1982, labored under that misconception and ignorance, which accounted for the limited appeal our opponents suffered as a result.

In 1978, our only opponent was a genuinely nice lady who was a licensed practical nurse (LPN) by training and occupation. She ran on a platform on which she loudly proclaimed:

> *"As a Practical Nurse, I can do more for orphans than those two lawyers."*

Judge Nichols's and my response was to agree with her while pointing out that the orphans' court did not deal with orphans!

That same year, a true story that recounted a campaign event of mine went as follows: I was door-knocking in Hillcrest Heights with State Senator Peter Bozick at my side at all times, operating on the premise that no one knew what the orphans' courts did or who Steve Platt was.

By sheer coincidence that day, my future colleague (12 years later), Vincent J. Femia, a circuit court judge, was the subject of a front-page article in *The Washington Post* detailing the implementation of his own "Scared Straight" program for juveniles.

Judge Femia summarily "waived" these young people into adult court and briefly put them in an adult lockup cell in the courthouse where he kept them just long enough for them to sample and think about the road they were on and where they would end up if they stayed on that path as adult criminals.

He would then "waive" the juveniles back to juvenile court before the end of the day. These moves were of questionable legality, but not appealable because the decisions began and ended too quickly to appeal. In any case, the tactic arguably worked and, after being publicized, was met with great voter approval.

In 1978, while door-knocking in Hillcrest Heights, a demographically and socio-economically changing neighborhood, I approached the house of a prototype voter. The person who answered was an approximately 250-pound white male with a beer gut protruding out of his dirty t-shirt. In my mind, he resembled the person who would be sent if a producer/director of a production called Hollywood requesting an actor to play a typical redneck voter.

We then had the following polite exchange (*Fake News—1978 Style*):

Platt: "Hi. I'm Steve Platt, and I'm running for judge of the orphans' court."

Voter: "We've already got a good judge."

Platt: "Are you talking about the guy in the newspaper? He's a friend of mine running for a different court. In fact, we are running together as Democrats in this general election as you can see in this brochure (which I handed him)."

Voter: "Oh yeah? What are you going to do?"

Platt: "I'll tell you one thing. Any orphan who steps out of line in my courtroom is going to jail!"

Voter: "Ok then, I'm voting for you and Judge Femia. That'll be two of you who know what you're doing!"

A LAWYER AMONG NON-LAWYER JUDGES

In December 1978, at the age of 31, I was sworn in before the Orphans' Court for Prince George's County and began what would be a 30-year career serving as a judge in Maryland. Nevertheless, I suffered no illusions at this young age. Historically and still in some counties, the judges of the orphans' courts are not even required to be lawyers. Nevertheless, as time went on, at least one lawyer usually sat on an orphans' court. In Maryland's Montgomery and Harford Counties, the circuit courts also function as the orphans' courts.

I felt pretty lucky to be an orphans' court judge at the age of 31, serving with my close friend and fellow lawyer, Judge Nichols. As was pointed out to me, this was a "great part-time job" for young lawyers, which both Nichols and I were. I had my own reserved parking space at the courthouse, which at that time had great value, and modest chambers. In addition, when I was "on duty," I wore a judicial robe and was treated like a "real judge."

The people we worked with and for were ideal. When I was initially elected, the chief judge was the Honorable Mary T. O'Hare. Chief Judge O'Hare was the widow of the Honorable George O'Hare, the former chief judge of the old People's Court of Prince George's County. The old People's Court was a judicial institution that far preceded my time and was ultimately replaced by the district court. Mary T. O'Hare was a wise, smart, and sophisticated lady who knew how to run the court. Yet, she was not a lawyer.

O'Hare also knew what she didn't know and, accordingly, when to defer. She often said when asked to rule on a legal issue with which she was not familiar or knowledgeable, "Let's see what 'The Boys' think about this." Judge Nichols and I were "The Boys." We loved every minute of being "The Boys."

Working with the Honorable Callie Mae Heffron, Register of Wills, was also great fun. She ran a universally recognized, efficient, service-oriented office. We all worked together problem solving. When we needed to, we understood politics, but were not driven by it. We listened to each other and were respectful of our often differing points of view, which, at times, brought exchanges such as:

Register of Wills: "I smell a rat!"

Orphans' Court Judges: "Now, we are not here to create controversy."

After these exchanges, we all could laugh at ourselves and our viewpoints. All of this interaction was facilitated by our administrative aide, Earleen Bowen; our bailiff, Bartley Wood; and our courtroom clerk, J.C. McFadyen.

Such was the setting of the beginning of my judicial career, which began with pride but not pretension. Most of my work, like the work of most orphans' court judges, was administrative (approving inventories, accounts, etc.); but off and on, there would be interesting litigation of issues. This was in spite of the Maryland Court of Appeals's repeated and reported announcements in its cases that the jurisdiction of the Orphans' Courts of Maryland was limited to that which is expressly provided by statute "in light of their historical and present composition."

Presumably, the lawyer judges of the Maryland Court of Appeals were expressing their lack of confidence in the ability of non-lawyer judges to decide complex issues of law.

We didn't necessarily agree with them. We concluded the problem was easily addressed by finding out what "The Boys" thought. But the Maryland Court of Appeals pronounced the law of the land—not "The Boys." So, we declined to challenge that premise.

Four years later, Judge Nichols and I would hit the campaign trail, again operating on the assumption that only a limited number of highly informed voters would know who we are and be aware of the function of the orphans' court. This time, abortion issues unrelated to our jurisdiction were on the minds of certain groups of voters. Of course, the orphans' court would never have subject-matter jurisdiction over any case involving abortion or any related issues.

A woman who identified herself on the telephone as "a concerned citizen" inquired initially of Judge Nichols about his stance on abortion. His response was the most prevalent political response to that question in the 1980s, particularly by candidates for any office who professed to be of the Catholic faith. Essentially, Judge Nichols responded that he was personally opposed to abortion but felt that he should not impose his belief on others. Therefore, the decision should be made by the woman after consultation with her physician, and if she chose, her family and clergy.

The "concerned citizen" was not satisfied with that response. Judge Nichols then called me at my law office to "warn" me about the likely upcoming inquiry. I responded to him by saying, in effect, "Since we don't have a serious opponent, who cares?" This woman probably was not going to like my answer to the abortion question any better than his—but I was ready.

Sure enough, later that week, I received a call from the same "concerned citizen," but she did not ask me the abortion question. Instead, we had the following polite exchange:

Concerned Citizen: "Are you the Steven Platt running for re-election as judge of the orphans' court?"

Platt: "I am!"

Concerned Citizen: "Do you have children?"

Platt: I do. "Two as a matter of fact, ages 5 and 2."

Concerned Citizen: "Do you spank them?"

Platt: "Yes. When they deserve it." (I lied! I never laid a hand on either of my kids.)

Concerned Citizen: "We need more judges like you!"

Later, we discovered that the "concerned citizen" was, in fact, the chair of the Prince George's Chapter of the Moral Majority—the national fundamentalist rightwing organization started by Reverend Jerry Falwell, Sr. out of Lynchburg, Virginia. This realization naturally stirred my memory of my last visit to Lynchburg on behalf of "Robert F. Kennedy for President" some 15 years earlier, when I received the *"Get out of town. You're not welcome here"* greeting at the local Holiday Inn.

In any case, I was the only candidate for judge of the Orphans' Court for Prince George's County in 1982 officially endorsed by the Moral Majority. Friends who knew me then and now often find this fact amusing. I was also one of only three candidates who ran county-wide to receive more than 90,000 votes. The other two were incumbent State's Attorney Arthur (Bud) Marshall and Sheriff Jimmy Aluisi. No one, including myself, professed to understand that large number of votes, but I will always believe in the possibility that my "electoral landslide" resulted from my calculated "focus group tested" position on "spanking."

THE ESTATE OF CHIEF TURKEY TAYAC AND HIS MERRY BAND OF WIDOWS

When I was sworn in as a judge of the Orphans' Court for Prince George's County, I never expected to be confronted with issues that would examine the "Piscataway Indian Way of Life" or to participate in the epic struggle to preserve the "Piscataway Indian Way of Death." These issues were directly presented to the Prince George's County Orphans' Court in *The Estate of Chief Turkey Tayac a/k/a Philip Sheridan Proctor.* When the Prince George's County Orphans' Court responded, the case drew national attention, thereby, once again, illustrating the maxim: "Sometimes historical truth is stranger than fiction."

Until the Prince George's County Orphans' Court spoke, the foremost authorities on the subject of the Piscataway of Southern Maryland were Alice L. Ferguson and Henry G. Ferguson. Their book, *The Piscataway Indians of Southern Maryland,* was published in 1960 and told the history of the Piscataway through the 1950s. By the authors' account, the first person to notice and describe the Piscataway was the famous historical figure, Captain John Smith, in 1608. He described an "empire" that, by 1608, had been reduced to an area encompassing the southern half of Prince George's County and nearly all of Charles County, Maryland, which "could not have exceeded 3,000 people."

In 1608, the Piscataway lived in four towns, the most important of which was Portobak—soon anglicized to what is now known as Port Tobacco. Each of the four individual towns was governed by a chief called a "tayac." The early English settlers called these tayacs "kings." Being sticklers for proper titles, when they found that these tayacs (kings) recognized an overlord, the English naturally had no alternative but to call the overlord "emperor."

The method of succession to the title of Piscataway emperor was that on the death of an emperor, the title passed to his eldest brother; if there was no surviving brother, to the son of a sister. The emperor traditionally kept in his presence "the Great Men of the tribe." These individuals were an informal group of men well-versed in all phases of Piscataway life and politics who acted as advisors to the emperor. Significantly for the case that came before the Prince George's County Orphans' Court, the Fergusons noted that the "Office of Tayac" was kept in one family.

The Fergusons also reported that as time went on, the Piscataway allowed the English governor of Maryland to nominate both the emperor and a few tayacs. This muddied the waters on the rights of succession as described centuries later by the Prince George's County Orphans' Court.

By 1682, the Piscataway, now depleted, had largely departed from Maryland and settled in the "Woods of Virginia." They then migrated again to what is now York County, Pennsylvania. In fact, the Fergusons reported as far back as 1793, the Piscataway made their last appearance (to that point in history) as a tribe at a conference in Detroit, where they used a wild turkey as their signature. Fifty members constituted the tribe.

That was the reality. The legend, which manifested itself in the Prince George's County Orphans' Court, was that the emperor and a few of his "Great Men" and their families did not go to Pennsylvania with the rest of the Piscataway, but actually returned to Southern Maryland. It is from this legend that the decedent, Philip S. Proctor a/k/a Chief Turkey Tayac, emerged two centuries later as the only individual to claim direct descent and, thus, the title "Chief" from the Piscataway "Empire."

On December 8, 1978, Philip S. Proctor a/k/a Chief Turkey Tayac died while domiciled in Prince George's County. On December 29, 1978, a petition for administration of a small estate was filed by the Chief's son, William Augustus Tayac a/k/a Billy Redwing Tayac. A document purporting to be the will of the Chief accompanied the petition having been "removed from safekeeping in the Register of Wills Office." The petition alleged that Billy Redwing Tayac was entitled to be appointed personal representative of the decedent's estate because "he is the son of the decedent and is named in the will as personal representative." It also claimed that Billy Redwing Tayac was entitled to be named "Chief" of the Piscataway.

The only property of Philip S. Proctor listed was a "savings account at American Security Bank in the amount of $5,152.79." The only persons listed as "Interested Persons" or heirs and legatees were six to seven people who were named the full brothers and sisters of Billy Redwing Tayac—the adult children of Chief Turkey Tayac and his first wife. Subsequent petitioners and other parties were not mentioned.

Less than a month later, the cast of this 1980s version of a "reality show" dramatically expanded. Upon discovery of separate bank accounts containing $50,000 and $35,000 in the decedent's name, past "romantic interests" claiming to be the decedent's wives appeared with a cast of lawyers dressed appropriately in seersucker suits and colorful but not coordinated ties.

First, a woman calling herself "Lee Lamar Proctor" filed a document labeled "Election" claiming to have been married to the Chief in Frederick, Maryland, on August 21, 1969, by a "Reverend William Long." She attached a document labeled "Marriage License," but never offered that document into evidence. Her testimony, while illuminating, was not credible.

Under cross-examination, she conceded that she did not know whether she was married to the chief or anyone else. She also enlightened the court by explaining that she made her living traveling the country intervening in the estates of deceased wealthy men, claiming a "statutory share" of each man's estate, and settling for "whatever share I could get." Lee Lamar Proctor's testimony was, in effect, corroborated (albeit certainly not by design) by her only witness who testified that he drove "the parties" to Frederick on August 21, 1969, and was a "witness" to the "marriage." This "witness," upon less-than-penetrating cross-examination, conceded that he had been a "witness" to "at least one other marriage" of "the Claimant" to another individual since August 21, 1969.

Lee Lamar Proctor's "Election" was denied. The law in Maryland (which substantially mirrors the law of every other state) provided the basis and the forum for this claim. Section 3-203(a) of the Estates and Trusts Article of the Maryland Code simply says:

> *"Instead of property left to him by Will, the surviving spouse may elect to take the share which he might take in intestacy under Section 3-102."*

This law enables a spouse to "elect" his or her "statutory share," which in Maryland is one-third.

This statute provided the background for the claims of the women who asserted themselves to be the "surviving spouse" of Philip Sheridan Proctor a/k/a Chief Turkey Tayac. These women included the aforementioned Lee Lamar Proctor as well as her "second coming," under the name of "Frankie Lee Lamar Proctor a/k/a Lee Lamar." Ms. Proctor later returned to court with her new name and her new colorful attorney, "James Hollywood," after being denied a share of the estate as Lee Lamar Proctor. This time, Frankie Lee Lamar Proctor claimed to have been married to the chief in an "Indian Ceremony." Once again, she had neither the law nor the facts to support her claim—which was again denied.

A different fate, however, would await the next "grieving widow," Martha L. Proctor. She claimed her statutory share of the chief's estate as a result of their having lived together and held themselves out as man and wife in the District of Columbia off and on from June 22, 1955, until his death—a period of some 23 years.

Before continuing this episode of the 1980s version of the *Survivor* series, an explanation of the law that enabled Martha L. Proctor to make such a claim is in order. "Common law marriage" is a legal term defined by state law. It either exists or doesn't exist in the state in which the parties reside. Maryland is not a state that recognizes common law marriage if you live in Maryland. However, Maryland will recognize a common law marriage relationship that was entered into in a state in which the validity of common law marriage is recognized. Maryland's neighbor, the District of Columbia, recognizes "common law marriage."

Clearly, if an individual is in a valid common law marriage, that marriage has the same legal force and effect as it would if he or she had been married in a religious or civil ceremony. That means, if a person is common law married, he or she is married unless the couple gets divorced or one spouse dies. And the surviving person is entitled to a statutory share of the deceased spouse's estate.

Martha L. Proctor now had to prove that she was common law married to Philip Sheridan Proctor a/k/a Chief Turkey Tayac. The United States Court of Appeals for the District of Columbia explained in a previous case the steps Ms. Proctor needed to take to accomplish that. That court wrote, "When a man and a woman who are legally capable of entering into the marriage, mutually agree, in words of the present tense to be husband and wife and consummate their agreement by cohabiting as husband and wife, a common law marriage results."

Judge Nichols and I presided over this case together as the law required in 1980. Martha L. Proctor was able, principally through her credible testimony and other evidence, to convince Judge Nichols and me that after the divorce of Philip S. Proctor a/k/a Chief Turkey Tayac from his first wife on June 22, 1955, she and the chief agreed to become husband and wife in the District of Columbia. They consummated their agreement by cohabitating as man and wife in that jurisdiction. However, she was not able to meet this burden without difficulty occasioned by her cross-examination by attorney Donald Danneman, counsel for the "new chief," Billy Redwing Tayac.

Donald Danneman, a skilled trial lawyer based out of Baltimore, whose private practice before this case was largely criminal defense, represented the self-proclaimed new "Chief of the Piscataway Indian Tribe"—at the time numbering somewhere between 10 and 15 members. Danneman's skill as a cross-examiner was apparent to the "triers of the facts"—Judge Nichols and me. That was the good news. The bad news was that the drama Danneman used to accentuate his points was lost on Judge Nichols and me, and the point he was trying to make was beside the point.

If one is common law married, the marriage has the same legal validity as it would if the marriage occurred in a civil or religious ceremony. Logically then, if one is unfaithful to the common law spouse, he or she is still married no matter how many times the infidelity occurred. The effect of the infidelity is the same as if one were unfaithful to a marriage sealed in a religious or civil ceremony. That legal reality is what made Chief Billy Redwing Tayac's lawyer's cross-examination of Martha L. Proctor entertaining but ineffectual. That cross-examination is, however, worth recounting, based on the record:

Danneman: "Mrs. Proctor, isn't it a fact that during the period of time you say you were married to the now-deceased Philip Sheridan Proctor a/k/a Chief Turkey Tayac that you had sexual relations with 20 different men?" [whom Danneman named]

Martha L. Proctor: "Yes, but there is an explanation."

Danneman: "Objection! That's a yes or no answer. We don't need or want an explanation."

Judges Nichols and Platt: "Overruled! We absolutely are very interested in the explanation!"

NOTE: Whether the court's interest in the explanation was prurient, legal, or both is for the reader to determine based on this record.

The "explanation" by Martha L. Proctor was that there came a time when she was increasingly "clinically depressed." Thus, she was referred by her primary physician to a "Georgetown psychiatrist" who diagnosed the cause of her clinical depression to be that she had not being sexually satisfied by her husband. Based on that diagnosis, the "Georgetown psychiatrist" gave her a "prescription" (her word, not mine).

That "prescription" was for her to have sex with as many men other than her husband as soon as possible in the short term. Her husband, the "Chief," was made aware of the diagnosis, to which he agreed; and he offered to assist in filling the "prescription." The 20 men named were friends of Chief Turkey Tayac whom he recruited to facilitate the treatment prescribed.

The court, *i.e.*, Judges Nichols and Platt, found her explanation too strange to be anything but true, ruling that no one could or would make that up. I had the dubious honor of writing the opinion for this case:

> *"We are the judges of the credibility of the witnesses and we believe the Testimony of Martha L. Proctor. Her lifestyle and loyalty to her husband may not have been what some would expect it should have been. Perhaps her marriage to the decedent may well have been the forerunner of the modern day 'open marriage' since most of her extra-marital activity appears to have been with the decedent's knowledge, if not with his approval. In any case, we are not charged with passing judgment on her lifestyle or that of the decedent, and we cannot use what we heard of it to invalidate an otherwise valid common law marriage. We will, therefore, grant her election to take her statutory share of his estate."*

We also admitted to probate the will of the decedent presented to the Prince George's County Register of Wills and to the Prince George's County Orphans' Court by the decedent's son, William Augustus Tayac a/k/a Billy Redwing Tayac, who was named in that document as personal representative. He was therefore appointed personal representative.

These rulings would lay the groundwork for an on again/off again legal fight for the next five years between the deceased chief's family as a result of his common law marriage to Martha Proctor and his original family, *i.e.*, the "newly proclaimed chief" and his brothers and sisters from the deceased's first marriage. During that five-year period, the Prince George's County Orphans' Court ruled it had no jurisdiction to resolve questions of "royalty succession"—the issue of whom, among the 20–35 remnants of those who claimed to be the "Piscataway Indian Tribe" had the right to succeed the decedent as "chief."

We also ruled that the court lacked the jurisdiction to decide the issue of whether the Piscataway had any right, title, and interest to the land claimed by the United States of America known as Fort Washington National Park.

That issue arose when the small ragtag group who identified themselves as the "Piscataway Indian Tribe" showed up one day at around 4:00 pm at the main entrance to Fort Washington National Park in Maryland. In a symbolic but direct confrontation in the face of the security guard on duty, the tribe placed a flag purporting to be the flag of the "Piscataway Tribe Nation State" in the ground next to the security booth while announcing, "We are here to reclaim the park for the Piscataway Indian Nation."

This issue was pled in a "Petition" filed in the Prince George's County Orphans' Court. Testimony at the hearing revealed that the security guard on duty at the time reacted to this intended "provocation" with admirable wisdom and restraint. He immediately looked at his watch and inquired of the group, "Is there any way that you could wait 10 minutes to make your claim? My shift ends in five minutes, and I'll be going home. You can take it from there." The tribe chose to depart, no doubt avoiding what could have escalated to a historic conflagration that might have rivaled the Battle of the Little Bighorn.

As judges of the Prince George's County Orphans' Court, despite our admiration for the demeanor and the restrained action of the security guard, we denied the claim of the "Piscataway Indian Tribe" to the land—perhaps historically misappropriated by the United States from one or more indigenous groups centuries ago. Our ruling was on the basis of the longstanding law that we strictly construed: We had no jurisdiction to determine title to real property or to adjudicate the claims of indigenous persons against the federal government. As far as I know, no serious legal scholar has taken issue with those rulings.

So began my judicial career with a case that not only had a much higher profile than one would expect for an orphans' court case, but it was much more interesting than the mundane cases that typically came before the Prince George's County Orphans' Court.

In 1985, Governor Harry Hughes appointed me chief judge of the Orphans' Court, replacing my friend and colleague Judge Nichols. Less than one year later, Hughes appointed me to the District Court of Maryland. Ironically, eight months prior to my departure from the Prince George's County Orphans' Court, I wrote this opinion closing the case of "The Piscataway Chief and His Merry Band of Widows":

> *"The legend and estate of Chief Turkey Tayac, also known as Philip Sheridan Proctor, the only remaining individual to claim direct descent from the Piscataway Indians, returns to the Orphans' Court for Prince George's County, Maryland, fresh from a legal odyssey along the Indian trail occasioned by the Chief's death. This Native American's journey into the frontiers and settlements of our legal system has so far included stopovers in the Circuit Court, Court of Special Appeals, and the Veterans Administration, as well as the Halls of Congress and the Maryland State Legislature in Annapolis, each on multiple occasions.*
>
> *"In its Opinion and Order of Court dated February 21, 1980, this Court had occasion to examine the Piscataway Indian, "way of life" from the beginning in this State in the 14th century through the discovery and exploitation of their land and heritage by the English in 1608 to the descent and death of their last Chief, the*

decedent herein, on December 8, 1978. In doing so, we started this proud tribe on the legal warpath.

"Now, five years later, this Court is called upon to preside over these proceedings to articulate for posterity the "Piscataway Indian way of death." To this date, those participating in this epic struggle to preserve the "Piscataway Indian way of death" have included no less than 8 lawyers, 14 judges of various courts, 2 alleged wives, numerous state and federal legislators, numerous banking officers, Veterans Administration officials, a freelance "Indian Researcher" named Melvin Mapes, the "spiritual leader of the Sioux Indians" a "Chief Eaglefeather," as well as various Church and civic organizations.

"The Indian death rites of Chief Turkey Tayac in the late 1970s and early 1980s have included two separate funeral ceremonies, one Catholic and the other traditional Indian, the preservation of the decedent's body in a mausoleum for an extended period of time, an Act of Congress, a U.S. Senate resolution, a resolution of the state legislature in Annapolis, and, finally, burial of the Chief in his proper resting place in "Piscataway National Park."

"Casualties in this war have been severe and the physical, emotional, and financial costs of the war have been extensive.

"Martha L. Proctor, whom we determined to be the common law wife of the decedent, has died, failing to outlive both Frankie Lee Lamar Proctor, who rivaled her for the Chief's love and hand in marriage while he lived and for her statutory share after his death, as well as the personal representative, who questioned her fidelity to the Chief. Her heirs have, however, donned their warpaint to protect their mother's name and her statutory share of his estate. In addition, the evidence and the record

shows that the procurement of legal weapons (costs of litigation) and warriors (attorneys) has been at considerable expense to the personal representative and has required, on many occasions, the sacrifice of many of his domestic spending priorities for his tribe.

"Now we have the task to determine who should pay for the horrible costs in wampum and time that this emotional struggle to preserve the traditional "Piscataway Indian way of death" in the fourth quarter of the twentieth century has occasioned."

Completed December 3, 1985, Opinion and Order of Court

The case drew attention in the media again for its novelty if not its historical value. Soon after, I was sworn in as an associate judge of the District Court of Maryland for Prince George's County on August 1, 1986. Planning and campaigning for that position increasingly required my time and political skills for the next eight months.

Becoming a District Court Judge
From "Unknown" to "Most Quali-fied" in Less than 90 Days

*"I have always been able to compartmentalize what
was going on around me and to focus on one thing at a
time when necessary—and in the opinion of some,
even when it wasn't necessary. That skill serves me well
to this day."*

MY LIFE WAS an interesting combination of Ls: litigating, lawyering, and learning. Nevertheless, I decided to act on my ambition to pursue a career as a judge at the age of 36, which meant my tenure as counsel to the Maryland Democratic Party was about to come to an end. I had learned a great deal of value and believed I accumulated knowledge and wisdom (they are not the same) from my years as a political operative and activist. My savvy about politics and the operations of the branches of government would serve me well if I were lucky enough to become a judge.

Among the lessons I had learned was that it is extremely easy for "reformers" to morph into the "machine." I saw it in Virginia, New

York, and Maryland. Another observation was that one person's pressure or coercion is another person's leadership.

A corollary to that lesson learned was that more people want to be led and to follow than want to lead. I find this behavior particularly true when people are uncertain or insecure about their personal or even political future and definitely when they see themselves in a crisis—a reality that cuts across all levels of society.

I also observed that most successful politicians at one level are egotists who believe they have some special talent or skill; but not all egotists are narcissists. In fact, one can be an egotist at one level and still be humble. Persons, such as myself, who get into politics because they believe in themselves usually do not deeply care about many issues—which makes it easier to negotiate compromises when necessary.

I would soon discover whether my lessons learned could be applied to my aspirations of becoming a judge. I was looking forward to the challenge.

WHAT TIME IS IT?

January 1, 1986, besides being my 39th birthday, was the beginning of a year in which my personal and professional life would be transformed forever. My dad, Nathan Platt, had received a diagnosis of terminal pancreatic cancer. This disease would take my father 100 days later in April. It would deprive my father of seeing his son invested as a District Court of Maryland judge only 90 days later—a moment he very much wanted to enjoy.

As I stood in the well of the ceremonial courtroom on August 1, 1986, taking my oath as a District Court Judge, I couldn't help but momentarily flashback to him in his last few days, lying in his bed that he and my mom slept in from the day they moved into our house in Strasburg, Virginia, until the day he died.

My parents' wedding anniversary was April 6. Even while my father's body was racked with pain and filled with increasing doses of morphine to enable him to tolerate it, his mind was focused on the financial security and emotional health of his family—particularly my mom, whom he knew was not handling the situation well. For that reason, I had returned to Strasburg three weeks earlier to help care for him—which really meant just being there for him, my mother, and my grandfather—while we, along with hospice, waited for the inevitable end.

I am convinced my father had decided to exercise whatever will he could summon to keep from dying on my parents' wedding anniversary so that my mother would not have to remember their anniversary and his demise contemporaneously. For that reason, he kept asking me, "Steve, what day is it?" and, "What time is it?"

On April 6, 1986, my father, even more than usual, kept asking those same two questions. I knew why. As the clock struck and then passed midnight, I anticipated the end. Sure enough, at 12:30 am on April 7, 1986, the day *after* their anniversary, my father asked for the last time, "What time is it, Steve?" I replied, "It's the next day, Dad. It's ok."

Within 10 minutes, he was gone. While I confess to being basically an agnostic, my father's passing convinced me that while I cannot articulate the Force's form or substance, there is a God and he or she enabled my father to do what he did for my mom. I will take that further undefined faith to my grave.

My dad had refused to allow my mom to constantly be by his side while he lay in pain waiting to pass because "she cried too much." Telling her was easier than I thought it would be because, on some level, she was relieved that his ordeal was over. Telling my grandfather that his only son had passed ahead of him, even though he expected it, was not.

As the oldest grandson, I had only known my grandfather to be unemotional, tough as nails—a person whose history and demeanor documented that impression. In all my years, I had witnessed him cry just once before. That was when my grandmother, Rose, passed at the age of 84. In the years that followed, any mention of my grandmother's name, or that of my father, could easily draw tears from a man who had never before shed a tear for anyone or anything.

My grandfather lived for over another decade, until the age of 105, in full possession of his mental faculties and in control of his emotions—except when he remembered his wife and only son.

A FOCUS ON THE FUTURE

In the wake of this physical and emotional family-related trauma, I was relieving my tension by feeding my addiction to politics—by plotting and planning to become a district court judge. I have always been able to compartmentalize what was going on around me and to focus on one thing at a time when necessary—and in the opinion of some, even when it wasn't necessary. That skill serves me well to this day.

The flip-side of that "skill" is that if I am concentrating on a particular task or project, there is a serious risk—if not a reality—that I may become oblivious to anything else, even when there is an attempt to bring a different matter to my attention. This character trait has, on occasion, given the impression that I am ignoring someone or something to the point of being downright unfriendly, dismissive, or even rude. My pleas to these charges over the years continue to be:

> *"Not guilty by reason of temporary obliviousness"; "Appearances can be deceiving"; and "We're all more complicated than either our admirers or detractors would like to believe."*

My ability to compartmentalize helped me focus on the tasks I needed to do to become a district court judge in the midst of my responsibilities toward my family during their time of need.

And what I needed to do to be appointed to the district court was clearer to me than to others because of my prior political involvement and experience. Having been appointed to two different courts by two very different governors and having managed several judicial election campaigns, including my own, I was considered uniquely qualified to speak on the subject, "What does it take to be appointed and elected as a Maryland judge?" And I was invited to do so numerous times.

I would always give the classic lawyer's answer to that question: "It depends!" The good news is that the nature of what "It" depends on doesn't change. What "It" depends on is who the current governor is listening to at the time, and what, if any, criteria the governor sets for appointments in order to leave a legacy. For that reason, judges or candidates for judicial appointment must be able to recognize that their chances of accomplishing their goal is based on who they will need for support; and the steps they will need to take to accomplish their goal will change depending on who the current governor is.

A little bit of luck is also helpful!

CHANGE IS IN THE AIR

In 1985–1986, the District Court of Maryland for Prince George's County was changing. The District Court of Maryland was established in 1970 via a constitutional amendment and by statute, thereby replacing a patchwork quilt of courts and quasi-judicial administrative agencies editorially described by *The Baltimore Sun* as "dominated by politics and tainted by petty corruption."

That culture had to be repealed and replaced, and it was not going away easily. As then–Governor Marvin Mandel recognized and noted after he got the new court's creation passed by the Maryland General Assembly—and not without great difficulty:

> *"This was a gargantuan task which required an individual of exceptional ability."*

Fortunately, Mandel found that "exceptional ability" in Robert F. Sweeney, whom he appointed Chief Judge of the new District Court of Maryland. Mandel described Sweeney as possessing "a combination of charm and determination ... an ability to work with people and to organize, to laugh, to joke, but at the same time be strong-willed and controlling."

Years later, Chief Judge Sweeney would become my friend, mentor, and a role model for the rest of my life. Now deceased, I still terribly miss our almost daily conversations and banter.

Upon his retirement a quarter-century later, Chief Judge Sweeney reflected upon what he encountered when he was sworn in on May 5, 1971, as the first chief judge of the District Court of Maryland:

"There were judges who were racists, who had alcohol problems, who were wife beaters and who thought they had found the greatest 10-2 job in the world. I outlived the bastards, the whole collection of them."

Chief Judge Sweeney inherited the original group of judges of the new court as a result of having been "grandfathered in"—a deal that helped obtain the votes to enact the creation of the district court. Among the judges were those whose positions were the result of political deals made to secure the legislation. By 1986, however, those folks had either retired, died in office, or moved on to the circuit courts or one of the appellate courts.

In fact, in the 15 years that had since passed, many of the second generation of "original" judges who were appointed after the court was created had moved on, retired, or were in the process of doing so.

In the winter of 1985–1986, I calculated that as a result of elevations to the circuit court, retirements, and mortality, five vacancies on the District Court for Prince George's County were likely to be filled by Governor Harry Hughes, who had been re-elected to a second term.

Hughes had pledged to "diversify" the judiciary of Maryland and was working at his promise. At the same time, the specialty bar associations and other advocacy groups were responding to the governor's desire to make the judiciary look less white and male by becoming more active in the judicial nomination process. This goal, while generally commendable, was not necessarily good news for a white male applicant for judicial office. A quick look in the mirror confirmed that the task ahead of me would be more formidable than at an earlier time.

GAINING SUPPORT FROM THE BAR

I scheduled interviews and completed applications all in an effort to gain the support of certain bar associations and civic and professional organizations. The criteria for each organization's endorsement differed. Some expressed a single preference while others rated the applicants in a variety of categories. Several organizations were more political than others. Their preferences also depended on the appointments preceding the one upon consideration and the prospects for future appointments.

The Maryland State Bar Association and the Prince George's County Bar Association adopted a rating system that mirrored that of the Seventh Circuit/Fifth District Judicial Selection Commission. That system allowed those voting to rate an applicant "Most Highly and Professionally Qualified"; "Qualified"; "Unqualified"; and "Unknown."

As a practical matter, I defined the ratings as follows:

- *Most Highly and Professionally Qualified* = That's who I'm for.

- *Qualified* = I'm for someone else but he/she is qualified, and I don't have anything against him/her.

- *Unqualified* = He/she really is unqualified, or I don't like this person, so of course, he/she shouldn't be a judge.

- *Unknown* = I really don't know them, or I don't dislike them, so I don't want to hurt them.

The specialty bar associations usually favored their own members or an applicant whose ethnic, racial, and gender identity was the same as theirs—except if a political reason or deal led them to act otherwise.

I always did well in the "bar vote" taken by the Prince George's County Bar Association and was endorsed by the Maryland State Bar Association each time I presented my application. I was also always "approved" by the Women's Bar Association, albeit as a runner-up to their first choice.

My favorite result, however, was the second time (out of five applications) I came before the J. Franklin Bourne Bar Association, the largest African American bar association in the Washington metropolitan area. The first time I applied, I did not even make the list, which set forth in order of preference their first, second, and third choices. Less than 90 days later, I had become their first choice labeled "Most Qualified."

One of my future colleagues commented: "What a remarkable evolution in your qualifications in less than 90 days—from 'not rated' to 'Most Qualified.'" I, too, was amazed but, nevertheless, appreciative that I had been able to become that much smarter in less than 90 days.

Ultimately, I was either endorsed or found qualified by every bar association, specialty bar, and civic and political organization whose approval I solicited. More importantly, the Seventh Circuit/Fifth District Judicial Selection Commission found me to be "Most Highly and Professionally Qualified" the first time and each time I applied. That designation by the commission, which was appointed by Governor Hughes, certified to the governor that I was qualified for the judicial office I was seeking. I was now on "the List" of applicants from which the governor could choose the next judge, a practical pre-requisite for taking the next step.[9]

NOW, ENTERS THE POLITICS

The next step in becoming a district court judge was almost always 100 percent political. Once a judicial applicant was on "the List," which at least in theory, if not reality, certified that the person was "qualified," the process became totally political regardless of

---

[9] Governor Mandel was the first Maryland governor to utilize a judicial selection commission consisting of lawyers and usually community-based lay persons appointed by the governor as a means of limiting the pool from which he could choose for judicial appointments. The system avoided directly confronting political forces, which may be supporting blatantly unqualified judicial applicants. The judicial selection commission largely worked—although sometimes it would consider political factors in its recommendations to the governor.

who the governor was. As a result of my prior experience, I believe I recognized the politics quicker than other applicants.

Moving forward in the context of that reality required calculation, planning, patience, networking, and diplomacy. The most important component of any strategy for attaining judicial office always has been timing. Knowing who to contact, when to contact them, and why is crucial. A potentially important supporter of a different candidate for judicial office could become a supporter of mine if his or her preferred candidate was no longer under consideration.

My political experience provided me with an awareness of relevant political considerations, such as loyalties and relationships to political figures surrounding the governor and his friends. This immeasurably aided me in implementing a workable strategy. My strategy was to lay back and essentially not compete for or contest the first three appointments. It was my "do nothing" strategy, which was easy to implement. I believed I could excel at doing nothing with little effort.

Obviously, I knew that Governor Hughes would take seriously his pledge to diversify the Maryland judiciary. That governed my calculations. Of the five vacancies, I assumed his first appointments would include a woman and an African American. Indeed, they were friends of mine: Theresa A. Nolan and William D. Missouri. It also made sense that my friend, C. Philip Nichols, Jr., would be among the first three appointments.

In addition to being highly qualified in his own right, Nichols's father had served as a Maryland legislator under Governor Hughes. His primary supporters were his and his father's old friends, Secretary of State Fred Wineland and builder/developer Irving Kidwell. The fact that these gentlemen were two of Governor Hughes's most prolific fundraisers did not hurt Nichols's cause. In fact, he and Judge Missouri were appointed the same day.

So far, I was 3-for-3 in the prediction sweepstakes, but I wasn't to become district court judge as a result of my ability to predict the future. The field began to look much clearer; and in April 1986, vacancy number four opened. In addition, number five was coming in August due to the mandatory retirement of Judge Thomas Brooks who was reaching 70. I thought I had a good chance at one of these two seats, and I didn't care which.

Early in the spring of 1986, I received a telephone call from Peter O'Malley. He advised that my friend and, more importantly, his friend, Delegate Gerard "Gerry" Devlin, who represented Bowie and Greenbelt in the Maryland House of Delegates, wanted to be a district court judge. O'Malley and Steny Hoyer felt they should support Devlin as he had backed them for years.

I was aware that Devlin's longstanding and uninterrupted friendship, support, and loyalty to them went back long before I ever thought about moving to Maryland. In that conversation, I was reminded that the next seat would be vacant within weeks and that the situation would be better for everyone if we could "work out" a sequence for filling these vacancies.

I told a number of my supporters, including some senators who called to express "concern" that I had "agreed" to this "arrangement"; that "this strategy wasn't presented to me as a decision I could agree or not agree to." The decision had been made and was therefore a reality.

O'Malley explained that my future was affected, and my support was expected, particularly since I would benefit both in the short and long term. Coincidentally, I was having a very good year—in fact, my best year in my law practice. And Gerry Devlin, whom I truly thought would be a good district court judge, was and remains a friend. All of these factors plus my willingness to support Devlin locked in the support I needed and wanted for the fifth seat, which was less than 90 days away.

Shortly after Devlin's appointment in April 1986, I received two telephone calls, one of which was totally unexpected and the other, although predictable, very gratifying. The first was from Secretary of State Fred Wineland, who advised that the governor asked him to call me to make sure that I "understood why he had appointed Gerry Devlin, that I was not discouraged, and that the news would be good shortly."

As far as I knew, that call was not solicited by anyone else on my behalf; for that reason, I felt good that the governor thought my appointment was important enough to have the secretary of state contact me.

The second call was from O'Malley who, although he certainly didn't need to, called to say:

"Let's go! We're all behind you for the vacancy in August."

He told me what I needed to do and whom I needed to see about the appointment. Besides feeling gratified, I was once again encouraged and happy to conclude that candor, integrity, friendship, and politics could still fuse longstanding, productive, personal relationships.

A DREAM COME TRUE

I got the call in late May 1986 from the governor's office informing me of the governor's decision to appoint me to the District Court of Maryland as an associate judge. However, the call did not come from whom I had expected. The usual protocol for judicial appointments was that the governor would personally call and congratulate the lucky lawyer being appointed. At the same time, the governor would caution the appointee to remain mum for about two hours to allow the appointment secretary, as a courtesy, to notify the unsuccessful applicants before a public announcement.

On this day, however, the call I received was not from Governor Hughes, it was from Appointment Secretary Connie Beims. Although we knew each other, the call still placed me in a state of panic, as it was against the protocol. I thought to myself, *"What did I do wrong?"* since I had been told by my supporters, "It's you in the next couple of days."

Fortunately, Secretary Beims anticipated that I might be alarmed when my paralegal announced that the call was from her and not Hughes. She quickly segued into a bit of "talk therapy," attempting to calm me down. She explained that because the governor was in Europe, he had instructed her to make the call. He did not want me to wait any longer to find out the good news.

The next formal step was my investiture as a district court judge. "Investiture" is a fancy name for the formality of taking the oath of office; in other words, being "sworn-in" to defend the laws and the constitution of the State of Maryland. Investitures usually take on the personality of the judge being sworn in. My investiture was half roast and half toast—serious, but at the same time, fun for my family and friends and a dream come true for me!

The tone of my investiture was both light-hearted and dignified due to my choice of presenters and the response by Chief Judge Robert Sweeney. The local Upper Marlboro, Maryland, paper, *The Enquirer-Gazette*, assigned Estelle Wood, a supporter of mine, as well as a friend of my then-wife's family, to report on the event. Wood began the lead front-page article under the headline, "Judge Platt Sworn to District Court," with the following passage:

> *"Ancient images of civilization preside in the ritual in which judges are robed, and no one in Courtroom 201, The Ceremonial Courtroom, was more aware of those images than The Honorable Steven I. Platt on Monday, August 4, when young Platt was formally invested as the 10th member of The District Court.*

> *"In the jury box sat the family, the beautiful Prince George's bred wife, Patricia, the two picture-book children, Jason the son and Sarah the daughter, the widowed mother, Mrs. Adele Platt and the 92-year-old grandfather, Charles Platt, "a walking fourth of July celebration" and the in-laws, Mr. & Mrs. David Hartlove, (he's the former two-term County Councilman) and their extensive brood. Hovering over the occasion were many memories of "torches passed."*

The article set the stage for the limited pageantry that accompanied the proceedings in what the newspaper described as the "overflowing courtroom." My presenters' remarks, which the *Gazette* reported as "generating laughter throughout the afternoon," were accompanied by sustained applause.

My former boss, Chief Judge Loveless, told the crowd that his former law clerk was "never at a loss for words" but is also "a very down to earth person, practical and energetic ... Steve once told me that he was able to get a lot done by 'avoiding conversations with persons getting a divorce, recovering from an operation or going on a diet—and with joggers.'"

Chief Judge Loveless was followed by my friend and colleague, Judge C. Philip Nichols, Jr., who, with a straight face, informed the crowd that no doubt if Steven Platt had been around in the 18th century, he would have written *the Declaration of Independence* in lieu of his fellow native Virginian, Thomas Jefferson.

Chief Judge Sweeney responded for the district court, noting that he was "happy to preside over this occasion where Patti Platt's husband finally finds gainful employment." Chief Judge Sweeney then solemnly reported a "dilemma," which he explained was the same problem that plagued the Oppenheimer Brothers "who were both geniuses."

The Oppenheimer Brothers, who worked on the creation of the atomic bomb, had cumulative grade-point averages of 96.5 and 97.5, respectively, upon graduating from Princeton. "We, in the District Court, believe we already have the Smart Platt," referring to my then-wife, the chief administrative clerk. The chief judge then proclaimed as he directed his comment to me, "But if you wish to contest for that title—good luck when you get home!"

After catching my breath, I then responded to the court:

> *"I view this position as not just a job. I view it as my profession and my calling for a lifetime, to make this court and our system of justice work, and to always strive to improve it. That means maintaining my sense of humor in and out of the courtroom and taking my job and responsibilities seriously and myself less so. It means being courteous and accessible to the bar and to the*

citizens of our state, who are interested in improving our system of justice."

This was a moment I had hoped for most of my adult life.

Chapter 11

Serving on the District Court Bench

*"The inmates began referring to these court sessions as
'Freedom Court.' Every week, I would receive letters
from several inmates requesting 'to be in Freedom
Court!' Ironically, this approach is now referred to in
the media as 'criminal justice reform.'"*

AS PART OF the orientation process for a new district court judge,
the first order of business was to meet with the Chief Judge of the District Court of Maryland, Robert Sweeney. We had met twice before—
the first time when I was an applicant for the position at a meeting
facilitated by Peter O'Malley, Chief Judge Sweeney's friend and former colleague. O'Malley's theory was that Chief Judge Sweeney
would likely be asked by the governor to comment on my candidacy
among others, and it wouldn't hurt for him to have met me before
responding to the governor's request. Our second meeting was when
Chief Judge Sweeney presided over my investiture.

I traveled to Annapolis, Maryland, to meet with Chief Judge
Sweeney in his chambers. We hit it off better than I ever could have
anticipated. I found it easy to converse with and confide in him. I believe he genuinely felt the same, particularly as our candid conversa-

tions progressed. We found that we both liked to tell stories, which revealed the foundation of an invaluable friendship based on shared values and a practical approach to getting things done. He became my new role model, and the collegiality that accompanied our interactions lasted until his passing in 2010.

During our meeting in his chambers, Chief Judge Sweeney expressed concern that I might aspire someday to be the administrative judge of the District Court for Prince George's County because at that time, my then-wife was the chief administrative clerk of the District Court for Prince George's County and I would be precluded from serving in that capacity for that reason. He aptly reminded me of this in order to avoid any potential conflicts between us. To put the matter to rest, I quickly acknowledged that I was aware of the limitation and had accepted it, and I would not be concerned about it.

However, not long after that conversation, Chief Judge Sweeney changed his mind. He expressed confidence in my administrative and organizational skills and wanted to utilize them to improve the court. Within months, I was given management responsibility for the Civil Division of the District Court for Prince George's County by then–Administrative Judge Graydon S. McKee (Fifth District).

I also was given responsibility for other district court and administration of justice issues besides my normal daily docket of cases. Ultimately, in 1988, I was designated Administrative Judge of the District Court for the Fifth District (Prince George's County) by Chief Judge Sweeney—a complete 180-degree turnaround from his original mindset.

THE CRISIS OF OVERCROWDING

The legal profession and the judiciary often lag behind the culture. This reality can adversely impact its operations, especially if the political and judicial leadership within the jurisdiction is not paying sufficient attention to the events occurring in the world around them.

The District Court of Maryland's original criminal jurisdiction is largely limited to misdemeanor and theft cases. It also has jurisdiction over preliminary hearings, which are held prior to action by a grand jury on felonies to determine if there is probable cause to detain an accused person until the grand jury can consider his or her case. Because the district court has a large volume of cases, the administrators and judges of the court can easily become focused on the daily dockets while failing to address underlying problems.

In the late 1980s, the Prince George's County local jail a/k/a the County Detention Center, which houses defendants who are awaiting trial on both serious and minor crimes, became overcrowded. This situation drew the attention of the U.S. District Court for the District of Maryland, which is the federal trial court in Maryland.

Ultimately, in 1988 (coincidentally, after I was designated by Chief Judge Sweeney as Administrative Judge), the federal court imposed a strict numerical cap on the inmate population that the local jail could house at any given time. This requirement necessitated an immediate short-term solution to limit the inmate population on a daily basis and a plan for a longer-term solution. Until now, this matter had not been on the front burner of the county and state legislative, executive, and judicial branches of government.

This crisis was compounded by an institutionalized lack of consultation and coordination between different agencies of the executive branch of government, *i.e.*, the sheriff, the county police, and the county and state departments of corrections.

THE STING

Sheriff Jimmy Aluisi had a "backlog" of unserved warrants that he wanted to clear out of his system to ensure that those warrants could not be used by anyone running against him. So he set up a "sting." His staff mailed out about 3,000 fake notices to individuals with arrest warrants, telling them that they had won $500 and could pick up their prize money by appearing on a certain date and time at a tent located at an address previously utilized exclusively by cows and horses.

Sheriff Aluisi did not communicate to the Prince George's County Department of Corrections that the jail could potentially add an influx of 3,000 inmates to its already overcrowded facility. How "The Sting" was found out about is unclear; fortunately, Corrections became aware of it in time to "address" the onslaught of incoming residents.

The scene of "The Sting" was of picture-book quality! A large tent was set up in a cow pasture on Lottsford Road in Largo, Maryland. Women dressed in long gowns were stationed along the path to the tent to "welcome" the "prize winners" and escort them to the tent where they would be presented with their $500 check. As they were escorted into the tent, they were arrested and served with the outstanding warrant.

Adding to the color of this Saturday, a smaller tent was situated next to Sheriff Aluisi's more elaborately decorated scenery. There, the district court, with the cooperation of the State's Attorney's office and the Office of the Public Defender, installed a less than majestic facsimile of a courtroom using card tables.

I, starring as the "judge," held "court" on whether these individuals "stung" minutes ago would be incarcerated or allowed to go home with "conditions." My decisions that day would determine whether the jail's population would violate the federal cap. Fortunately, most of the warrants were for failing to appear in court on comparatively minor charges. "The court," operating in this cow pasture, was, therefore, able to provide justice or acceptable conditions of release sufficient to avoid a jail overpopulation crisis.

The Prince George's County government, particularly the executive branch, was grateful. When I was contacted initially about this impending crisis by the Prince George's County Department of Corrections director, I could have taken the position that the problem was not mine to solve. Instead, I immediately dove into "problem-solving mode." I also insisted that the upper levels of the county government itself engage in short-term and long-term problem solving by supporting proposals that I had been presenting (and had fallen on deaf ears) until that time.

Those proposals included:

(1) The creation of a *criminal justice coordinating council* that would institutionalize regular communications between county and state executive agencies and departments of government involved in the administration of the criminal justice system to avoid the kind of crisis management we had just experienced (not for the first time);

(2) The establishment of a *pre-trial release agency* within the Prince George's County Department of Corrections that could supervise inmates outside the Prince George's County Detention Center, including their behavior and drug use as authorized by the courts;

(3) Recognition that *drug use* had a relationship to criminal activity and a substantial enhancement of the county government's ability to test those charged, as well as those on probation, for the purpose of limiting the risk of their continued presence in the community; and

(4) The continued construction of a more modern detention center with *state of the art technology*.

To my delight, all these common-sense measures were approved and funded, thereby proving that leaders should, as Rahm Emanuel once advised, "Never let an opportunity created by a crisis pass."

We acted; Prince George's County was better for it. In return, I took personal responsibility as Administrative Judge of the district court on behalf of the court for monitoring and managing the population of the Prince George's County Detention Center to ensure the inmate population never exceeded the federal court–ordered cap.

THE PROBLEM-SOLVING JUDGE

The management of a jail or prison was never thought to be a responsibility of the judicial branch of government. This arrangement was not in accordance with any precedent or any constitutional separation of powers theory. The facility and its operations, as well as the police powers that when exercised accounted for the detention center's population, were those of the executive branch of federal, state, and local government.

Nevertheless, the judiciary, by its power to commit, could (if so desired) directly and efficiently control that population. Therefore, staying in my problem-solving mode, I agreed to assume that responsibility with the full commitment of county government to provide staff and funding assistance.

It was the county government's job to identify weekly the "100 least dangerous non-violent" inmates in the county detention center. These were folks who were awaiting trial mostly in district court or who were serving a minimal sentence in the jail for a misdemeanor. They were the individuals who could be safely released into our community either in the custody of the pre-trial release agency with drug testing to ensure that our risk calculation remained valid, or via a plea agreement—which included a sentence that put them back on the street either because it was reduced via a reconsideration or the plea agreement.

Many of these individuals already had been incarcerated for longer than the sentence they would have received on a future date had they remained in jail until their scheduled trial date. This was because a judge or commissioner had required a cash or security bond to be posted for them to be released.

Based on the weekly research, the district court would conduct a docket presided over by me with 100 cases on it with the intention of releasing most, if not all, of the systematically identified, "least dangerous defendants." This process served to manage the population of the county detention center and provide justice to the inmates.

The inmates began referring to these court sessions as "Freedom Court." Every week, I would receive letters from several inmates requesting "to be in Freedom Court!" Ironically, this approach is now referred to in the media as "criminal justice reform."

THE BAIL BOND LAWSUIT

Then, as now, not everyone embraced criminal justice reform. The bail bond industry, whose economic viability was decidedly threatened, was not enthralled by the concept or the reality. In 1988–1989, the Bail Bond Association (BBA) sued me, seeking to have the circuit court order me via a writ of mandamus to reconsider my programs and rulings that adversely affected their industry.

While the BBA sued me without initially informing me that it was planning to do so, the leaders and their counsel asked for a meeting. My response upon learning about the lawsuit was to advise them, through my assistant, that when you sue me, you can meet with my lawyer, the attorney general. If you want to meet with me, drop the lawsuit!

When they dropped the lawsuit (after it was dismissed, in large part, on a preliminary motion), I then agreed to meet with representatives of the association and their counsel. I informed them that I held no hostility toward them or their industry, but when I get up in the morning, their welfare is not high on my list of things to worry about.

I candidly expressed the novel view in their world that the profitability of their business was not as important as the efficient and fair functioning of our criminal justice system—which includes the management of the jail population. We parted amicably, at least on the surface. As it turns out, this was a sign of what was to come with criminal justice reform's impact on that industry 20 years later in 2020.

LANDLORDS AND TENANTS

The administration of our criminal justice system was not the only aspect of judicial operations that would be altered by the changing culture and demographics in Prince George's County in the 1980s and 1990s when I was designated administrative judge of the district court.

Prince George's County had voted to become a "Charter County" in 1970 as a result of, among other reasons, an electoral reaction to certain state and local elected and appointed officials and the "commissioner system" of government led by those officials. This government was heavily influenced by developers who contributed to elections. The county commissioners were perceived to be approving uncontrolled real estate development without any planning or concern for the quality of life in the affected communities, in order to repay their contributors for their support.

Development, in many cases, took the form of garden apartments that were more affordable than those in any of the other suburban Maryland and Virginia counties surrounding Washington, D.C. This development incentivized movement into the county by the area's less-affluent citizens, as did the gentrification occurring in Washington, D.C. At the time, more of those less-affluent citizens who took up residence did not resemble those who had lived in this largely rural blue-collar county.

With more garden apartments came more renters, which dramatically increased the volume of cases in landlord-tenant court, a court that fell within the exclusive jurisdiction of the district court. In Prince George's County, however, the conduct of landlord-tenant cases was a carryover from the more rural days of the county.

Furthermore, the judges who presided over landlord-tenant cases in the early days of the district court were themselves landlords or attorneys who had previously represented landlords. These judges were not particularly understanding or interested in the plight of tenants who had difficulty paying their rent or who did not receive the facilities and services they were entitled to pursuant to their leases. In other words, the judicial faces of the district court were not, in any way, moved by the complaints of tenants whose advocacy was increasingly being voiced by organizations at the state and county levels.

The intensified presence in the halls of the Maryland legislature and the county councils resulted in state and county legislation establishing landlord-tenant commissions and rent escrow statutes providing for rent to be escrowed until repairs were made and housing code violations corrected.

Although these laws were on the books, they were not being implemented on a meaningful scale—with a few exceptions. After I was sworn in as a district court judge in August 1986, I conducted my first landlord-tenant docket in this context. That day, I was cautioned by my good friend and colleague Judge Joseph S. Casula:

> *"You will be tested by some of the attorneys who regularly represent the management companies and landlords of some notoriously poorly run apartment complexes. They expect you to automatically do what they want."*

Sure enough, when I entered the courtroom in Hyattsville, Maryland, for the first time, where approximately 150 landlord-tenant cases were scheduled, I was faced with a courtroom brimming from corner to corner. Two lawyers sat in the courtroom holding newspapers in front of them so as to block my view of their faces. I immediately directed my bailiff to instruct those attorneys to put down their newspapers and give their undivided attention to the court.

I then began calling cases. During my training when I sat with another judge in landlord-tenant court, I noticed that the standard practice was to call a case. If the tenant was present, the judge would ask the following:

Court: "The landlord says you owe $_____ rent for the month of _____. Do you owe the money?"

Tenant: "Yes" or "No"

If the tenant answered "Yes," no opportunity was provided for the tenant to explain why the rent had not been paid. Judgment was automatically awarded in favor of the landlord. If the tenant said "No," the attorney for the landlord would always request a continuance, since that attorney likely had no witness present to prove that the rent was owed. That continuance would always be granted to occur about a week later without consulting the tenant who likely would have to take another day off work.

The first day on which I sat in landlord-tenant court alone, I handled matters differently. I advised landlord's counsel that since he had no notice that this practice would not be operational in my courtroom in the future, I would grant his request for a continuance that time. However, going forward, he would be expected to be prepared with his witnesses to present his case on the first day the case was scheduled. I then inquired of both the landlord's counsel and the self-represented tenant as to an acceptable next date. The tenant responded that the next day she was scheduled to be off from her job was in two weeks. I announced that would be the new date. However, my announced decision was greeted with an unceremonious response from landlord's counsel:

Landlord's Counsel: "You can't do that!"

Court: "I think I just did."

Landlord's counsel then "explained" why, in his view, the law prohibited me from continuing the case for more than one week without his consent. I then voiced my disagreement with his interpretation of the applicable statute; but more to the point, I concluded that in that instance, my solution would be to simply deny his request for a continuance completely, which I then implemented. This resulted in the landlord's case being dismissed.

That exchange was witnessed by all the other tenants whose cases were to follow. Based on their observations, they also claimed they did not owe the rent, resulting in their cases also being dismissed.

Following the completion of the docket, I had my bailiff escort the now thoroughly dejected landlord's attorney (who had chosen to take me on in front of a full courtroom) to my chambers. I introduced myself, told him a little about my background, including that my family comprised businesspeople who owned lots of property and were landlord to many tenants. I also told him that if he checked around, he would find that most lawyers would attest that I was easy enough to get along with if not provoked. That said, I advised:

"You made me choose who would run my courtroom—you or me! Whatever faults I may have, I am totally predictable. I

chose me, as I will every time. You will probably have to live
with me in this courtroom and others for the foreseeable future.
You should adjust as necessary to accommodate that reality."

Landlord's counsel then thanked me for my "courtesy." We never had another problem.

That was the beginning of the evolution of landlord-tenant court. After I was designated as Administrative Judge by Chief Judge Sweeney, I intensified my efforts to ensure that the district court judges, who were increasingly diverse and open to a more balanced approach to landlord-tenant cases, were aware of their statutory and administrative tools to ensure fairness in the administration of these cases.

In addition, with the support of Chief Judge Sweeney and the Sheriff of Prince George's County, I implemented a "No Eviction Policy" when the temperature was below freezing (32°F). This took some further adjustments by the property management community and their attorneys, but they survived the changes and remained profitable.

TACKLING DOMESTIC VIOLENCE

The other area in the civil justice system I was especially concerned with while serving as administrative judge of the district court (and even before that as judge-in-charge of the civil division) was the rising incidence and reporting of domestic violence in the county and state—indeed the nation. Once again, the judiciary was operating on its own with virtually no communication with the other branches of government in the county and the state, as well as the organizations concerned with preventing and mitigating domestic violence.

This isolation stemmed from an entrenched traditional view of the function of the judiciary as a branch of government that should not be influenced by the world around it. Furthermore, in that view, cases should be administered and adjudicated based on the evidence presented and the law that applies without regard to impact of the court's decision upon the parties, let alone society.

I rejected that view then and now, although I chose not to argue with colleagues who continued to subscribe to it in the face of trends to the contrary. Instead, I established the Prince George's County Domestic Violence Coordinating Council, one of the first in the state. The wisdom of that innovation was quickly apparent; its continued functioning and utility remains a legacy of which I am most proud.

THE GOOD TIMES

As my 3½ years on the district court bench (including 2½ years as Administrative Judge) progressed, my accomplishments were increasingly recognized. Politicians and lawyers were impressed enough to suggest that I consider applying to become a circuit court judge. My ambition kicked in, especially when being complimented, but that ambition was accompanied by mixed feelings because I was enjoying myself, particularly as administrative judge—an opportunity and experience that Chief Judge Sweeney had predicted would never happen, but which he then made possible by a strategic change of mind.

In addition, the role of administrative judge offered me the opportunity to implement my ideas on the administration of justice and to have fun doing it. I had the opportunity to work with the police department, the corrections department, the clerk's office, all of the courts, as well as lawyers and colleagues.

The largest part of that reward was my professional and personal relationship with Chief Judge Sweeney. He was my mentor and my friend. We talked on the phone almost every morning. I loved the guy!

Below are some of my most enduring accomplishments while serving as a district court judge:

- I collaborated with the Prince George's County police chief and the Maryland State Police superintendent to devise a system to have the courts' computers automatically generate a notice to the chief or superintendent when a police officer or trooper failed to appear in court without a reason or communication. That, in and of itself, reduced police officer "Failures to Appear" by more than 90 percent within 30 days. The county's Fraternal Order of Police (FOP) newsletter described these communications as "Platt's Love Letters," but I was still welcomed at the FOP Lodge for a beer.

- Then there was the lawsuit brought by an attorney who was a friend of mine, Alan Goldstein, against my then-wife as administrative clerk for the District Court for Prince George's County, and me as the administrative judge of the District Court for Prince George's County. I had quashed his subpoenas in 36 DWI cases for the state toxicologist; and because of my order, the clerk refused to send the cases to the circuit court since my ruling was not a final judgment. That case became known in my chambers as the case of *36 Drunks v. Platt & Platt*.

- Finally, there were the 50-plus cases where demonstrators against abortion were charged with trespassing on the property of the clinics where they attempted to block patients' access to facilities. My friend, a pro-life judge and former delegate, Gerry Devlin, served as judge and I was the pre-trial judge trying to work on all these cases. We figured them out with a pre-set menu, which offered the following options:

1. *Plea of Guilty*: Probation before judgment (no resulting criminal record) + pay court costs

2. *Plea of Guilty*: Probation before judgment (no resulting criminal record) + pay court costs + speech for three minutes or less

3. *Plea of Guilty*: Probation before judgment (no resulting criminal record) + pay court costs + acknowledgment by court and defendant that there is a higher authority

My district court days were comparatively short but extraordinarily fulfilling, both personally and professionally. My friends were encouraging me to fulfill my ambition and apply for the vacancy on the circuit court created by the elevation of my friend and eventual mentor, Judge Howard Chasanow, to the Maryland Court of Appeals.[10]

"Your time is now," I was told, "it may not come again." So, I listened.

---

[10] As of January 2023, the Maryland Court of Appeals, the highest appellate court in Maryland, has been renamed the Supreme Court of Maryland.

Chapter 12

The Making of a Circuit Court Judge
One of "Those Guys," a Political Network, and Burgers & Beer

"At that point, I looked over in the jury box of the ceremonial courtroom of the Upper Marlboro Courthouse and saw tears in the eyes of this very strong man like I'd only seen on two previous occasions—when my grandmother and my dad died. To say it was a moment I will never forget is an understatement."

IN THE FALL of 1988, Judge Howard Chasanow was being elevated to the Court of Appeals, the highest court in the State of Maryland. So the admonition that my "time is now" was in response to my inquiries, not a spontaneous outpouring of support. I have never had much patience, nor have I invested a whole lot of credibility in politicians, judges, or other public figures who attribute their seeking office to the insistence of the masses.

Most of us are driven by our own self-generated ambitions, which need very little encouragement to manifest. If we are truthful with ourselves and others, we will readily acknowledge that fact. Nevertheless, the encouragement was coming from a wide variety of sources, including Judge Chasanow, as well as a surprising cross-section of an increasingly diverse political community.

The reasons were self-evident. Prince George's County was changing demographically. The Hoyer-O'Malley political organization's hold on the politics of the county had loosened and was continuing to wane. Steny Hoyer was now a congressman and less interested in county politics; Peter Francis O'Malley was no longer involved in politics on a daily basis, choosing to exercise his still considerable influence only when "one of our guys" sought a political or judicial office.

The good news for me was that I was definitely one of those "guys." When I decided to seek a district court judgeship three years earlier, I had learned that what it takes to be appointed as a Maryland state court judge depends on who the current governor is listening to at the time and what criteria he sets for his appointments and the legacy left behind as a result of those appointments. Fortunately for me, Democrat William Donald Schaefer was now governor of Maryland!

MY SUPPORT SYSTEM

In 1989–1990, Governor William Donald Schaefer was listening to Peter O'Malley and a few others, but more to O'Malley than to others. Why? O'Malley had convinced Schaefer—the same way he had convinced former Governor Marvin Mandel almost 20 years earlier—that his interest was solely in furthering Schaefer's personal and political agenda and that he sought no political or other office, perk, or benefit for himself other than the political, economic, and personal influence that came with their friendship/relationship as it was known to others. That worked for Schaefer and for O'Malley. It also worked for me as I sought a circuit court judgeship.

Schaefer's priority in the appointment of judges was to select the persons whom he believed were most qualified for the particular court. If he valued your judgment, candor, and loyalty, you had a better chance of being appointed. The need for diversity and the politics of each appointment, which Schaefer understood and considered, nevertheless occupied a second tier to his desire that his legacy be that he placed outstanding judges on the bench.

I benefited from O'Malley's relationship with the governor and others whose advice he sought, namely, my friend, Thomas V. "Mike" Miller, Jr., the president of the state Senate; Congressman Hoyer, my former boss; and Thomas Patrick O'Reilly, Prince George's County state senator, whose friendship with me was cemented when we clerked for circuit court judges at the same time.

Other senators supported me, yet some had to be convinced. My favorite exchange on that subject, which I overheard, occurred in the hallway of the State House in Annapolis. It was between state Senator O'Reilly and another state senator who shall remain nameless:

> Senator O'Reilly: "Senator, you're supporting Steve for his appointment to Chasanow's seat on the circuit court, right?"
>
> Other Senator: "I certainly don't have any problem with Steve, but I feel that I should support ... who is from my district. If she doesn't make it, I'll go with Steve."
>
> Senator O'Reilly: "Senator, this is a circuit court judgeship we're talking about, not a crossing guard."
>
> Other Senator: "Ok, but for the time being, let's keep this to ourselves."

Prior to my meeting with the governor, I encountered the other person whom he automatically consulted on all judicial appointments—Edgar Silver, retired Baltimore City circuit court judge, Schaefer's very good and trusted friend since his days as mayor of Baltimore. It was widely believed that Judge Silver could probably get a person appointed to the bench and, for sure, could veto any prospective appointment.

For that reason, to seal my prospective appointment, State Senate President Miller and State Senator O'Reilly arranged for me to meet with Judge Silver in Senator Miller's office the Tuesday before my scheduled Thursday interview with Schaefer. Present were Senate President Miller, Senator O'Reilly, myself, and Judge Silver.

After some brief, friendly small talk about how my supporters had spoken so highly of me, Judge Silver said he wanted to help me. He then gave me his telephone number with instructions to call him the minute I completed my interview with Schaefer. "I intend to make sure that you are the next circuit court judge in Prince George's County," said Judge Silver.

"Why? You don't even know me," I thought to myself. Upon further reflection, the unspoken reason had to be to curry favor with my state senate supporters, including most prominently, State Senate President Mike Miller. In any case, I followed instructions and called Judge Silver after my interview with Schaefer. After a brief exchange of pleasantries, he closed by saying, "I'll take care of this right now." I guess he did because I was appointed not too long after that call.

THE DAY HAD FINALLY COME

On May 7, 1990, I took the oath of office as an associate judge of the Circuit Court for Prince George's County in a ceremony presided over by my former boss, Chief Judge Loveless. My presenters were my friend for over 20 years, attorney William F. Edwards; Circuit Court Judge William D. Missouri, my friend and predecessor as district court administrative judge; and, most importantly, my friend and mentor, District Court of Maryland Chief Judge Robert Sweeney. I had no idea what any of them would say.

Chief Judge Sweeney and I had been talking and even writing back and forth almost on a daily basis. I knew I was going to miss him and our daily conversations. We had reflected on the clear bond we had formed, despite stark differences in our ages, religion (or lack thereof in my case), ethnic background, and, at times, perspective on politics and judicial administration.

We shared a similar outlook on the paramount importance and value of honesty, integrity, intelligence, and practicality in public life. Nevertheless, I was not prepared for the tribute that was forthcoming in his remarks to the circuit court and the family and friends who were in attendance as follows:

"If someone were to ask me to list the ten qualities that I believe—after 19 years as chief judge of this court—the ten qualities that I believe are so important and so valuable and so necessary to the office of judge of the district court, I would list ten qualities that you possess.

"I would list the quality of scholarship, for you have about you the air and the taste and the love of scholarship that has been the hallmark of your career at the bar. I would list, more importantly than that, the quality of decency because, Steve Platt, you are a decent man about whom there is not even the slightest touch of vulgarity or immorality.

"And I would list the quality of goodness because Steve Platt— good lawyer, good judge—he is more important than that. He is a good man, good husband, good father, good son, good friend.

"I would list the quality of courage because courage is an absolute essential of judicial office. Courage is that which you do when you know that the course that you are going to follow is not the popular course, but you follow it because conscience and sense of duty tell you that you can do no other. And you do it regardless of the consequences—a characteristic, I might add, not unseen in your previous life and jurisprudence.

"Also important is the quality of courtesy. I had occasion to listen to tapes of Judge Steven Platt conducting a day's docket in the district court, and those tapes would constitute almost a judge's handbook. Because of the courtesy that you extended to the least, to the lowliest, to those in the audience perhaps who came to the court with less to claim their attention. Courtesy is that quality which, if one really possesses it, does not permit

one to distinguish between the high and the mighty and the lowly of the world, and you are a man of great courtesy.

"And certainly, diligence belongs in the list, and you are a man of diligence—long hours, hard work. And humor—humor has to be there, and you have humor. You not only have the quality of humor that enables you to find enjoyment and mirth and laughter in the world around you, but that even better aspect of humor that enables us to laugh at ourselves. You have that in abundance.

"And you have, too—to put two together—you have, too, the qualities of justice and the qualities of integrity, which I put together because I do not believe they can actually be separated. A sense of justice of knowing, after having heard all of the evidence and applying the law, that what it is that duty calls upon you to do—to put in balance, on the scales, the rights and wrongs of society. And that last, that all important thing of integrity, which is the incapability, perhaps, of consciously doing that which you know to be wrong.

"Those are nine qualities. I left one blank. Because everybody who is in this courtroom and this jury box and on this bench and in this box to my left, everyone who knows Steve Platt could fill in that blank with some tale from your past, some anecdote, and act of kindness, some exercise in compassion that you have rendered over the years. Myself, I filled in the blank by saying you have the quality of friendship that you have extended to me. You have served more than as a judge and administrative judge of this district—you have, in a very personal sense, been for me, a friend and counselor and shoulder and *sounding board. You will be sorely missed. Good luck to you, and God bless you."*[10]

While still feeling the effect of Chief Judge Sweeney's farewell, I delivered my own remarks to the crowd of family and friends, as well as former, present, and future colleagues. I immediately noted that 17 years earlier when I went to work as Chief Judge Loveless's law clerk, "I had not even a dream that I would someday have the privilege of serving on this bench with him as chief judge ... To now be able to serve as his colleague is simply the greatest singular personal and professional honor of my life!"

I went on to recognize my wife, children, my second family (in-laws), and with great focus, "my mother, Mrs. Adele Platt, who, with my father, raised me to believe that there was no goal in this world beyond my horizons and provided me with the pre-legal and legal education to take the oath of office here today."

With great pride, I continued:

> *"My grandfather, Charles Platt, was 92 years old when I was sworn in as a district court judge. At that time, many of you will recall, I mentioned that he was a member of the board of directors of his county's public hospital, a lifetime Rotarian, a former member of his local town council, a Shriner, and active in his community. Today, three and a half years later, at age 96, he continues to serve in all of those capacities. As I said three and a half years ago, he's like a walking Fourth of July celebration having landed at Ellis Island almost 80 years ago without speaking a word of English at the age of 19 with 17 cents in his pocket and a 17-year-old pregnant wife on his arm. He, more than anyone else, by his example, instilled in me that anything is possible in this country and that you have a duty to*

---

[10] Remarks of the first chief judge and architect of the District Court of Maryland, Robert F. Sweeney, a mentor and friend of Judge Steven I. Platt, at Judge Platt's investiture as judge of the Seventh Judicial Circuit, May 7, 1990, Courthouse, Upper Marlboro.

develop your abilities and use them for the benefit of your community."

At that point, I looked over in the jury box of the ceremonial courtroom of the Upper Marlboro Courthouse and saw tears in the eyes of this very strong man like I'd only seen on two previous occasions—when my grandmother and my dad died. To say it was a moment I will never forget is an understatement.

In fact, my grandfather's reaction and pride in my appointment, as well as his expressed admiration of Governor Schaefer's judgment for making it, was something I couldn't resist conveying to the governor himself, particularly after being encouraged to do so by my friend, Peter O'Malley.

I wrote the governor a letter describing my life-long Republican grandfather's "appreciation for your appointing me to the circuit court," and his declaration that he will always be a 'Schaefer Democrat' as a result of your decision."

I certainly did not expect Governor Schaefer to personally read my letter. I was very surprised to receive a response that was personally dictated. In his reply to me, Schaefer stated that he:

> *"enjoyed and appreciated reading about your grandfather and the profound influence that he has had on your desire to excel and to use your extensive talents in service to the people. I am very pleased to have given him further reason to be proud of your achievements and in particular your elevation to the Circuit Court.*
>
> *"You have a special calling for judicial service that has earned you much respect and admiration throughout the community. I shall always recall with fondness our meeting together and the very strong impression that you made on me as one who is committed to using all of your considerable intellectual gifts to make the system work for all of the people."*

The governor then ended his letter with:

> *"I have no doubt that you will do an outstanding job on the Circuit Court and in doing so, make me proud."*

Governor Schaefer then quoted the Honorable Robert C. Murphy, then–Chief Judge of the Court of Appeals, who had sent me a note conveying the same sentiment: "You are known in the gambling industry as a sure thing." The governor must have consulted with the chief judge on my appointment. I'm glad he did.

CRANKING UP THE POLITICAL MACHINE

It was now time to hit the campaign trail. Circuit court judges, then and now, for historical and political reasons and purposes, must run in a county-wide election two years after the vacancy they are appointed to fill. Any lawyer who has been a member of the Maryland bar for five years or more is eligible to run against the judge appointed by the governor. Unlike their opponents, they have not been thoroughly vetted by the bar, community organizations, and ultimately the county judicial selection commission representatives appointed by the governor.

When friends and supporters asked me what my strategy would be for the ensuing election, my answer was, "Do my job well and quietly while anxiously waiting for an African American running-mate to be appointed to fill the next vacant seat." That strategy was wise, and, as it turned out at that time, effective. My friend and former district court judge colleague, Judge Larnzell G. Martin, was appointed by Governor Schaefer, about a year later. I had been cheering for him for my personal and political self-interests, among other reasons.

Judge Martin was supremely qualified and turned out to be a great circuit court judge. He was a great running-mate and became an even better friend while we ran together for the next 18 months. We decided we were the perfect "salt and pepper team" and that we should leverage that fact, so we campaigned together. We visited every elected state and local official as well as any public figure who was even thinking about running for Maryland's 4th congressional district seat that would be on the ballot in 1992. That strategy worked!

We preemptively occupied the field by securing endorsements from politicians, opinion-makers, and leaders at a time when there was no political, racial, or ethnic reason to support any other candidate—partially because none was visible.

We set up a fundraiser, publicized it, and secured the commitments to support it financially. We established an impressive campaign committee chaired by James H. Taylor, a retired circuit court judge and mentor to both Judge Martin and me. Judge Taylor was the first African American to preside as judge in Prince George's County.

Our committee was co-chaired by attorney Diane O. Leasure, who later became a circuit court judge for Howard County. Our treasurer and campaign manager was William "Bill" Connelly, who later in life became the federal chief magistrate judge of the U.S. District Court of Maryland. These steps made it a formidable task to run against us, and we apparently derailed those who otherwise might have thought about it.

The Maryland State Board of Elections in Annapolis is the place to go to file applications to seek a circuit court judgeship. The evening of December 7, 1991, was a cold, wintry, rainy night. Our campaign manager and treasurer, Bill Connelly, volunteered to do the traditional duty of going to the board of elections office and observing who might file, then reporting back to us at the close of business whether we would have any opponents. I decided to go with him. I thought that if someone was going to run against us, he or she would have to walk past me to do it. Connelly and I drove to Annapolis together that evening.

As I searched for anyone who looked familiar, I was tapped on the back by Claire Crawford, a reporter and then-wife of Victor Crawford, state senator for Montgomery County. She said, "Excuse me, sir, you look like you might be considering running for the Circuit Court for Montgomery County." Smiling, she said she was the "Guardian of the Sixth Circuit." In a way she was, since Senator Crawford was a good friend of Jerry Hyatt, a circuit court judge for Montgomery County, who had been diagnosed with cancer and was not expected to survive until the date of the election.

There was some concern that someone would file against Judge Hyatt and that any opponent would win by default if he passed away before November. So the solution to that situation was that if someone filed, Senator Crawford would then file to prevent that cynical play from succeeding.

That plot never unfolded because no one filed against Judge Hyatt. That made my response to Claire Crawford even more poignant when I replied, "Don't worry, I'm the Guardian of the Seventh Circuit."

Thankfully, no one filed against us that night. However, on our way to the board of elections office that night, I had said to my friend, Bill Connelly, "If we don't have an opponent, then drinks and dinner are on me." His response, typical of Connelly, was:

> *"I'm a simple man with simple tastes. All I want is a Fuddruckers hamburger and a beer."*

We had several burgers and beer over the next 15 months. By the time the election was over, we had the next 15 years to do the job we had sought to do. We looked forward to every moment of it.

PART FIVE

The State of
Criminal Justice in Maryland

Chapter 13

Criminal Justice—1990s Style

"The Bail Bond System enabled judges to avoid a more complicated judicial assessment of the level of an individual's threat to public safety and the degree of supervision required to manage that threat."

IN 1990, WHEN I began presiding over cases in the Circuit Court for Prince George's County, the death penalty and life without parole were the sentencing options frequently applied in certain murder cases. The War on Drugs, the rising homicide rate, increased reports of domestic violence, and other violent crimes were in the headlines and being discussed in most courtrooms. Easy answers to the difficult questions were not apparent.

I presided over hundreds of criminal cases, including more than 35 murder cases, during the 16 years I served as a circuit court judge. Those cases and the issues that arose during trial and sentencing were substantively different. However, certain identifiable patterns of criminal behavior were evident. Furthermore, as I would read the newspapers in the morning before going to work and listen to the news upon my return home, I recognized the politicization of the issues I was dealing with as a judge.

CAUSES OF THE CRIMINAL WAVE

The 1990s was a decade that witnessed a sharp rise in violent crime in Maryland and the rest of the country for reasons not easily or quickly understood. That, of course, did not stop talking heads on both sides of the partisan divide from claiming to know the causes of this criminal wave. These talking heads, and the politicians who latched on to their theories for personal and political gain, conjured up a crime spree of epidemic proportions produced by young African American men killing their fellow human beings to steal their Adidas shoes or their Eddie Bauer coats.

The media replayed the visual and audio of "the gym shoe crime spree" over and over, reinforcing policies whose origins were the result of politicians, policymakers, and even some judges ignoring social scientists and expert opinions. Instead, they chose simplistic, politically popular positions designed to pander to their constituents' fears. Those fears emanated from deep-seated racial prejudices and predilections. Most people sought simple solutions to the complex problems of human beings, whose personalities and circumstances were usually far more complicated than their hyper-political and philosophical admirers or detractors wanted to believe.

A SEARCH FOR SIMPLE ANSWERS

Ill-advised policies and strategies adopted in Maryland and other states, as well as on the federal level, in the 1980s and 1990s (and even the first decade of the 21st century) included:

- Mandatory severe sentences for nonviolent drug offenses.
- Pre-trial detention policies based on economic status and discredited punitive rationales.
- Contested elections of circuit court judges based on which candidate could talk the toughest on crime.
- Sentencing guidelines issued to encourage uniformity based solely on averaging sentences of all judges throughout the state, despite the obvious fact that the average sentence isn't

always the best sentence notwithstanding the inefficient, un-fair, and, at times, costly factors surrounding these guide-lines.

Implementation of these and other unjust and unwise policies was justified by a desire for simple answers to complicated questions, including questions generated by the behavior of human beings in certain situations. These questions were not (and still are not) capa-ble of being competently addressed, absent far more rigorous re-search, peer review, and deliberation.

The country and states, under the banner of "criminal justice re-form," have attempted to address these issues as the third decade of the 21st century begins. However, discrediting the policies of the 1990s under the theory that our current understanding is much deeper and superior to our knowledge base in the yesteryears is at best insufficient and, at worst, creates a false hope that we are solving longstanding problems when we are not. Policies that should replace these discredited approaches to criminal justice administration are still unclear and in need of much further research and discussion.

In addition, the unfair, inefficient, and costly bail bond system was, until recently, accepted by many judges without much thought. The bail bond system enabled judges to avoid a more complicated judicial assessment of the level of an individual's threat to public safety and the degree of supervision required to manage that threat.

The acceptance of this unfair system by the judiciary enabled the bail bond industry to ingratiate itself with the legislature through strategically placed campaign contributions and relationships with legislative and executive leadership. That leadership was thereby motivated to conveniently ignore the obvious fact that requiring a person with no history of violence (or other indicia suggesting the risk of flight) to pay for and post a bond would not reduce risk.

I previously had helped set up and supervise a pre-trial release program and agency in the Prince George's County Department of Corrections when I served as the district court administrative judge. The program worked then and is still working today. In fact, it served as a model at the time. Today, this program is labeled "criminal jus-tice reform." I, therefore, can't resist bragging that I was for "criminal justice reform" before anyone had labeled it "criminal justice re-form."

THE RIGHT VERSUS THE LEFT

Some of the dominant theories that drove criminal justice system policymaking for three decades (1970–2000) were as accepted in some quarters in the past as those that are presently labeled "criminal justice reform." These theories emerged from conservative American academics who predicted in the 1990s that "a new breed of superpredators"—youth who had no respect for human life and no sense of the future—would terrorize Americans indefinitely.

This "analysis," in part, drove the legislation establishing mandatory sentences. Fortunately, these theories were proven demonstrably wrong. The "new breed of superpredator" kids turned out to be no more than figments of their imagination and a convenient visual for right-wing media to entertain their viewers.

Other "experts" as well as talking heads predicted crime would keep rising as a result of the decline of the traditional nuclear family and growing ethnic diversity. As the 21st century began, this group on the right held to these beliefs even though crime was clearly on the wane in Maryland, in the United States, and around the world. This way of thinking is undeniably still occurring in parts of certain urban and suburban centers, including Baltimore City.

Many social theorists on the left maintained that crime could never be curbed unless inequality was reduced. More recently, they predicted that the Great Recession of 2008 would interrupt the downward trend of the crime rate. These theories now appear as wrong and as silly as the right wingers' contentions that children growing up in single-parent households and playing computer games would somehow unleash an unstoppable crime wave.

MY MOST CHALLENGING MURDER CASES

In the context of the media hype over "a new breed of superpredators," I presided over 35 murder cases, eight of which are presented in the next chapter to illustrate the dilemmas and the milieu during my tenure as a circuit court judge.

Chapter 14

Murderers' Row
The SODDI Defense, a Death Penalty Debate, Respect for "the Judge," and a Sentence to Last a Century

> *"As it became clearer by the minute that this effort to create serious appellate issues was doomed, Niland ... did not know when to stop. He actually ran out of questions he planned to ask to make his original point and couldn't think of any more."*

STARING DOWN THE FUTURE

State v. William J. Bruce and Arvel Stewart Alston

Two individuals, William J. Bruce and Arvel Stewart Alston, were convicted by juries presided over by me six months after I was sworn in. These two young men were charged with murdering one man, James M. Robertson, execution style, by firing a bullet behind his ear. They tried their best to kill another man by pumping 10 bullets into his body during a March 28, 1990, armed robbery. The motive for these defendants to execute or attempt to execute these two people was neither explained nor discussed during the trial or sentencing proceedings that followed. The "defense" articulated for both of these individuals (and many others accused during these years) was cynically nicknamed by law enforcement criminal justice professionals and lawyers as the SODDI defense.

SODDI was an acronym for "Some Other Dude Did It." It was likely sarcastically coined by lawyers conversing among themselves over coffee or a stronger libation while waiting for a jury to return. My experience as a criminal defense attorney[11] and as a presiding judge helped me reach the conclusion that the SODDI defense seldom worked unless the accused had a convincing alibi that put him or her elsewhere at the time the crime was perpetrated. Neither Bruce nor Alston had an alibi or even suggested one, relying solely on the SODDI defense, without any evidence to support it. Their fate was thereby sealed!

I sentenced Bruce and Alston to life without parole, which in Maryland means what it says. This was the first of seven cases in which I, in effect, sentenced individuals to die in prison. I thought about the impact of the sentence on William Bruce and Arvel Alston before I imposed that sentence because it amounted to a "deferred death penalty" proceeded by a total loss of their rights to ever enjoy liberty and the pursuit of happiness.

I also considered that these two individuals would not be the last persons for whom the state's attorney (who must request such a sentence in writing) would request for me or any judge to impose such a permanent life-changing sentence.

At that time, I decided I would never impose a sentence of life without parole on anyone *unless* I was convinced the person was likely to kill or seriously injure another person if he or she was not incapacitated for life. In setting that criterion, I fully recognized that neither I, nor anyone else, could ever be certain whether a person

---

[11] This includes my representation of the "Vice President in Charge of Personnel" as described earlier in PART THREE: "Private Practice: My Days as an Attorney."

posed that risk. I felt strongly, however, that this aspect of my job as a judge required me to make that assessment based on the available information, evidence, and research.

At the same time, I felt the need to guard against being guided by political pundits, the news of the day, and the stereotypes and implicit biases that had nothing to do with these cases and these defendants. From experience, I have found that human behavior is neither predictable nor capable of instant analysis.

My interest in the relationship between law and psychology helped me conduct a risk analysis of the dangerousness of any defendant, usually based on extremely limited information and data. But it was useful in analyzing whether to allocate the benefit of the doubt to the defendant or to his or her potential future victims—a difficult choice at best, typically hanging on the horns of a dilemma.

If I allocated the benefit of the doubt to the defendant, he or she would not be permanently incapacitated and could violently harm another victim in the future. If I allocated the benefit of the doubt to potential future victims, the defendant would be incarcerated for life and potential future victims would remain safe.

I faced this conundrum many times over the next 15 years as I presided over 35 murder cases and many more cases involving violent crimes. The decision never got easier! I honestly felt that no one could pass judgment more conscientiously than I; that this was a crucial part of my job; and that my decisions always needed to be evidentiary and time-based, which meant a decision could be reconsidered if the facts changed.

Defense attorneys have an ethical duty to zealously represent their clients at sentencing, regardless of the heinous nature of the violent crimes they have been convicted of. I fully understood that responsibility, having served as a criminal defense attorney representing the likes of "The Vice President in Charge of Personnel," who was a clever individual with no regard for human life—at least at the time.

No evidence was brought forth at trial or sentencing that demonstrated that Bruce or Alston valued human life. Both asserted the

SODDI defense throughout the case. I did not have any insight into why either of them executed one victim and attempted to assassinate the other. Their lawyers simply reasserted the SODDI defense, adding that the crime for which they were convicted was "inconsistent with Mr. Bruce's and Mr. Alston's characters."

The criminal records and personal histories of both young men suggested otherwise. I, therefore, found it comparatively straightforward to sentence both of them to life without parole based on the risk of further violence to potential victims. My perception was reinforced by the defendants' behavior and that of their gang-related "support group," namely, four "friends" who sat in the back row of the courtroom.

When I asked both defendants if they had anything they wished to say before the court passed sentence, they responded with silence accompanied by a prolonged glare that appeared to be an ill-advised attempt at intimidation.

After pausing long enough to be sure I was not imagining this incredibly arrogant, stupid attempt to intimidate me, my response was to calmly announce:

> *"It is generally not a good idea to get into a staring match with someone who is going to decide where you reside for the rest of your life."*

Nevertheless, I was aware that this "staring match" and my reaction to it, as well as my sentencing of these two individuals, made good political and courtroom theater for the onlookers and the media covering the trial and sentencing.

LACK OF COMPREHENSION ≠ LENIENCY

State v. Thomas Chapman Weems

On December 28, 1998, Thomas Chapman Weems and Michael Lawrence Pratt invaded the home of Marcus Emilio Simons and his family to steal jewelry and stereo equipment. Mr. Simons was executed by Pratt while Weems raped the wife of Mr. Simons in the presence of their children and his mother.

Weems pled guilty to first-degree felony murder.[12] Weems was hoping for leniency in consideration for his guilty plea. His hopes and pleas were heard but rejected. I sentenced Weems to the following to be served consecutively: life without parole on the first-degree felony murder charge; life for first-degree rape; and life for a first-degree sex offense.

My intention was to incapacitate Weems for the rest of his life, which I announced to him and a full courtroom: "The incomprehensible nature of these acts defies understanding. You won't be released with any piece of paper bearing my name."

PLAN ON DOING THE TIME IF YOU COMMIT THE CRIME

State of Maryland v. Keith Carroll

On December 12, 1998, John Thomas, age 34, was gunned down at a card party at an apartment in Forestville, Maryland. Angela Sipes, age 27, was in that apartment when the homicide took place. She told police that Keith Carroll, age 21, shot Thomas. Three days later, Sipes, herself, was gunned down in that same apartment. Prosecutors believed that Carroll and an accomplice killed Sipes to prevent her from testifying against Carroll.

The issue presented to me as the presiding trial judge, by then–Assistant State's Attorney John Maloney (later to become a circuit court judge), was whether to allow the prosecutors to use a statement given by Sipes to the police two days before she was assassinated, which implicated Carroll in the murder of Thomas.

---

[12] Felony murder is murder even if the actual killing was carried out by another person if committed in the process of perpetrating a felony—in this case, armed robbery and home invasion.

Defense Counsel Joseph Niland argued that the statement should not be admitted into evidence or shown to the jury because it would "cross the line and constitute an infringement on the fundamental constitutional right of the defendant to confront his accuser," guaranteed by the Sixth Amendment. This was the predominant view of the bench and the bar in Maryland at that time.

Assistant State's Attorneys Maloney and Tara Harrison countered Niland's argument stating that although not addressed by either of Maryland's appellate courts, other state appellate courts had addressed the issue and ruled uniformly that a defendant should not profit from killing a witness against him.

I had no trouble relying on those persuasive out-of-state, albeit non-binding, holdings in allowing the use of Sipes's statement, even though defense attorneys would not be able to cross-examine her. I viewed it as likely to be affirmed on appeal, particularly by Maryland's Intermediate Appellate Court with the Honorable Charles Moylan, author of most of Maryland's criminal law and one of my heroes on it. And it was the right thing to do—an irresistible combination in light of how the defendant was viewed as a "cold and ruthless killer."

Ultimately, the jury convicted Keith Carroll of two counts of first-degree murder, witness intimidation, and other related charges. Without any hesitation or regrets, I sentenced him to two terms of life without parole and additional time. The convictions and the sentences were upheld on appeal.

THE EMERGENCE OF VICTIMS' RIGHTS

State of Maryland v. Richard Lawton McLeod

On August 10, 1987, Jacqueline Roberson, age 28, a newly married elementary school teacher, drove to a wooded area off Governor Bridge's Road in Bowie, Maryland, to relax and to wax her new husband's car. There, tragically, she encountered Richard Lawton McLeod, who sexually assaulted her and then stabbed her to death.

Her nude body was found three days later, face down and covered with leaves and branches.

Jacqueline's father, August Bolino, spoke for the victim's family at sentencing after McLeod's trial—five years, two months, and two weeks later on October 27, 1992. He described his daughter as "sublimely happy." He added, "To take that away from her was just the utmost cruelty. I don't think the crying will ever end. We're not vindictive. We don't want revenge; we just want justice."

McLeod, age 24, a landscaper, initially became a suspect in the murder of Roberson after being arrested a few days after her brutal murder for an unrelated sexual assault of a teenage girl. He subsequently pled guilty in 1988 to raping that girl and was sentenced to 25 years in prison for that crime.

Five days after Roberson's murder, investigating police were told by McLeod's mother that while doing her son's laundry, she discovered red gym shorts soiled with car wax residue. Police, shortly thereafter, charged McLeod with first-degree murder of Roberson.

But the Prince George's County State's Attorney's Office declined to prosecute McLeod after having determined that investigators had not accumulated enough evidence to convict him. To their credit, police continued investigating.

Finally, in March 1992, after police found more evidence, the state's attorney charged McLeod with Roberson's murder.

Assistant State's Attorney Laura Gwinn skillfully presented the prosecution's case in a week-long trial, which rested almost totally on circumstantial evidence—traces of blood and car wax on clothes found in McLeod's bedroom and a red bandana and knife found near the crime scene were similar to items witnesses said they'd seen on the defendant. In addition, the bandana was covered with cat hair. Trial testimony demonstrated that McLeod lived with three cats while the victim had none.

The most damaging evidence, however, according to the jury foreman, who agreed to be interviewed by a newspaper reporter after the sentencing, was the testimony of McLeod's mother at the trial regarding a conversation with her son on August 13, 1987. This exchange occurred after Roberson's murder, when McLeod was arrested on the unrelated rape charge of the teenage girl. The defendant's mother said her son told her that he did not know if he had been charged with rape or murder. When asked about the clothes the young rape victim had been wearing, McLeod instead described Roberson's clothing.

"Without that piece of evidence, the verdict might not have been guilty; for us, that was the clincher," said the jury foreman. The jury foreman went on to express both sorrow and admiration for McLeod's mother who had the judgment and courage to contact the police when she found the wax-soiled clothes in her son's room a few days after Roberson's death.

Gary Ward, the Prince George's County Deputy Public Defender, was a competent, experienced criminal defense attorney. He defended McLeod by offering alternative explanations and arguments for much of this circumstantial evidence. He noted that two other men investigated by police in connection with Roberson's death also owned bandanas and knives like those found near her body.

Once again, defense counsel utilized the SODDI defense. SODDI didn't work in this case for the same reasons this approach usually doesn't work. Unless the charged defendant has an airtight alibi and evidence to prove that he was elsewhere when the crime occurred, this defense is generally not credible to juries.

The Roberson case featured other unusual matters. For one, I allowed "other crimes evidence" over the vehement objection of the defense. This meant that I was allowing the other known victim of McLeod, who McLeod was convicted of raping when she was 15 years old, to testify as to how the clothes she was wearing were different from those Roberson was wearing.

Normally, a judge cannot (pursuant to the Rules of Evidence) allow "other crimes evidence" to be presented to avoid the risk that a defendant will be convicted due to his or her unproven propensity to commit similar crimes. However, there are exceptions to this rule.[13]

---

[13] One of these exceptions is that "other crimes evidence" can be admitted proving the identity of the person who committed the crime charged if the "probative value," *i.e.*,

Unfortunately, the young woman, then 20, immediately broke down crying during her testimony when she saw the defendant who had raped her five years earlier. This resulted in a defense motion for a mistrial on the grounds that the witness's outburst "was so prejudicial as to deny my client a fair trial."

My reaction to that motion was to have the jury escorted from the courtroom and to interview each of the 12 jurors and three alternates individually about their reaction to the incident. As a result, I excused one juror who indicated that she would have trouble following my instructions, and I replaced her with an alternate who voiced no such concerns. I then continued the trial with instructions to the remaining jurors to "disregard what just occurred, as you had responded that you could do so."

The other somewhat novel issue that arose in the trial was my granting the state's request to transport the jury to the quiet park on Governor's Bridge Road in Bowie, Maryland—the scene of the crime. On the second day of the trial, the jurors, attorneys, courtroom staff, and police witnesses were guided by Thomas Bruciak, a then–retired county police officer.

Prior to his retirement, Bruciak investigated the case. He led the group about 90 feet through the woods off the road to a small clearing where Roberson's nude body covered with tree branches was found—three days after her August 10, 1987, disappearance.

No testimony, by the police officer or anyone else, other than the physical description of the spot where the evidence was found was permitted. Nevertheless, the jury gained a clearer view and understanding of that physical evidence and the manner in which the crimes against Roberson were committed.

Allowing the testimony of a previous victim, transporting the jury to the scene of the crime, and denying the defendant's motions for a mistrial were all objected to by the defense and were, therefore, issues on appeal. Although I was comfortable with the decisions, I was concerned, as any judge would be, of subjecting the victim's family to

---

importance of the identification is greater than the prejudice to the Defendant." This evidence was admitted under that exception. My decision to do so was affirmed on appeal.

further delay beyond the five years they already had endured, as well as the psychological trauma that would inevitably accompany that additional time.

Considering the mostly circumstantial evidence and legal arguments presented, the jury, after only three days of deliberations, returned its verdict on October 27, 1992: first-degree murder and carrying a weapon illegally. The jury could not find McLeod guilty of any sexual offenses because the condition of the victim's body was too decomposed, which limited the prosecution's ability to produce evidence of sexual assault or other sex crimes. Nevertheless, the assistant state's attorney filed the required motion to request a sentence of life without parole.

I ordered a complete pre-sentence investigation as well as a full-scale psychological evaluation of McLeod. Due to the defendant's demeanor, which stood out because of his total lack of any visible reaction to gut-wrenching testimony implicating him in multiple violent, sadistic acts against different victims, and his criminal and psychological background at the trial, I had become convinced that McLeod might be the most dangerous individual whom I had ever encountered to date.

I was both anxious and interested in learning more about McLeod before sentencing him, particularly since life without parole was an option. As I explained in a previous chapter, I would only consider such a sentence if I believed that a defendant was a danger to maim or kill again unless that individual was permanently, or at least indefinitely, incapacitated.

McLeod was already serving a 25-year sentence at the Patuxent Institution in Jessup, Maryland, for rape. At the time, Patuxent was uniquely a "psychiatric prison." As a practical matter, the facility offered the only hope for any defendant serving a long sentence for a violent crime to ever return to society.[14]

From its inception in the late 1970s into the early 1990s, Patuxent operated on the premise that even the most violent criminals could

---

[14] The reader may recall my unsuccessful effort to get Robert Willie Young the "Vice President in Charge of Personnel of the International Drug Ring," into Patuxent.

be treated and thereby rehabilitated so as to not be dangerous any longer. Every prisoner (referred to at Patuxent as "patients") progressed their way through the tiered treatment plan and process until their treatment was deemed to be completed; and in the opinion of the psychiatrists who designed and supervised the treatment, patients could be and were released.

McLeod had somehow maneuvered his way into Patuxent after his conviction of rape. In addition to my order of a full pre-sentence investigation by the Maryland Division of Parole and Probation and a full psychological evaluation by the circuit court's own mental health consultation and evaluation service, I ordered a full report and evaluation of McLeod's progress by the staff at Patuxent.

I wanted to have as much information as possible before sentencing McLeod because of my initial impression of him during trial. I was, therefore, inclined to sentence him to life without parole unless I gained information that would change my impression. I also believed strongly that there is no such thing as too much due process when contemplating a long-term, life-changing sentence.

Upon receiving the reports, I was not at all surprised that the staff at Patuxent expressed the opinion that McLeod's treatment was progressing "well." My observations and experience over the years is that, generally (with notable exceptions), mental health professionals—including psychiatrists, psychologists, and sociologists—are more optimistic about human nature and the ability of human beings to be "treated," than are judges, lawyers, and law enforcement personnel.

However, I was surprised and further convinced that my impression of this man was correct when I read the report's conclusion. The Patuxent staff had categorically reported that while the patient's progress to the next-to-top tier of treatment was "commendable" and "encouraging," the staff recognized a "substantial risk" that the patient might "re-offend" and commit a further sexual or violent offense if he were to "graduate" and be released to return to society.

On that note, Richard Lawton McLeod was sentenced to life without parole on November 23, 1992.

Multiple appeals of his conviction and, ultimately, his sentence were unsuccessful. The family of the deceased victim, Jacqueline Roberson, fully participated in the sentencing hearing. This participation had not always been routine. In fact, in 1982, only 10 years earlier, the family of Stephanie Roper, a victim of sexual assault and murder, had been denied the opportunity to participate or even observe the proceedings.

The denial of what is now considered basic victims' rights was not because of any malevolence by the judiciary; it was because such participation was not the accepted norm or practice then. Furthermore, no authority or incentive to initiate a more victim-sensitive and compassionate cause of conduct existed back then.

The victims' rights movement was led in Maryland, and indeed the nation, by the Stephanie Roper Foundation, Inc., formed by Stephanie Roper's aggrieved parents—in particular her mother, Roberta R. Roper. That foundation's good work is proof that some positives can come from something really negative.

Below is an exchange of letters after the McLeod sentencing between Roberta R. Roper, director of the Stephanie Roper Foundation, Inc., and me:

Dear Judge Platt:

On behalf of the many crime victims and families we serve, I wish to commend your actions in the recent trial of Richard L. McCleod (CT 920511X). On November 23, 1992, you sentenced Mr. McCleod to life without parole for the first-degree murder of Jacqueline Roberson in 1987.

The Stephanie Roper Foundation provided support to the victim's family throughout the trial and sentencing. For the Bolino family, it was the closing chapter of a very painful period in their lives. And though the Trial itself was a difficult experience for them, they clearly benefited from the victims' rights laws passed during the past decade.

I could not help but compare this family's experience with mine ten years ago. As parents of a murdered daughter and witnesses for the State, the Bolino's were allowed to remain in the courtroom throughout the trial. I was excluded from the courtroom. As victim/survivors, the Bolino's prepared a Victim Impact Statement for the court's consideration at sentencing. The Roper family had no such opportunity. A family member was allowed to speak, and the court listened to some of the crime's consequences for the family. I was denied the right to speak on the grounds that anything I might say would be emotional, irrelevant, and probable cause for mistrial! And finally, your court had the opportunity to impose a sentence of life without parole. No such sentence existed in 1982, and our daughter's killers received two concurrent life sentences plus twenty years, making them eligible for parole in eleven and a half years.

While we are encouraged by the important progress made for victims of violent crime, we recognize that the application of most victim's rights depends entirely upon prosecutors and judges. Your sensitivity and willingness to listen and consider the Victim Impact Statement and Allocution in this case is a good example of balancing everyone's needs and rights --- the State, the Defendant and the victim. Your actions satisfied the need for real justice and won the respect of the victim's family.

Sincerely,

Roberta R. Roper, Director

Dear Mrs. Roper:

Thank you and the Stephanie Roper Foundation, Inc. for your kind letter of November 25, 1992, as well as your "Letter to the Editor" to the Prince George's Journal, which appeared in the November 30, 1992 edition. Needless to say, such letters are not often received in my chambers nor those of my colleagues.

You use the word "progress" in those letters to describe what has occurred in the last ten years with respect to the establishment and application of victims' rights in the criminal justice system. The legal scholar John Berger defined that word as "the action or process of advancing or improving by marked stages or degrees: the gradual betterment of mankind." Even though you generously credit me and my actions in demonstrating that progress in State of Maryland v. Richard L. McLeod in the Circuit Court for Prince George's County, Maryland, in my view my actions were totally routine. I was simply following the laws applicable to that case in 1992—laws that largely you and the other victims of crime and their families who are members of The Stephanie Roper Foundation, Inc. put on the books.

I know your comparison of the treatment accorded you and your family by the criminal justice system in 1982 and the treatment of the Bolino family in 1992 must be both painful while at the same time satisfying to you. Painful because the way you and your family were treated as victims of crime in 1982 was unfortunately routine and in accordance with the law and rules governing criminal procedure at that time.

Satisfying because of the changes in the law, which were certainly not inevitable and in some cases I recognize were quite difficult to bring about, are largely the result of the work of you and other victims of crime working since 1982 to ease the pain of future victims of violent crime such as the Bolino family.

There is still much work to be done to improve the criminal justice system both in the way it treats victims and in the way it utterly fails to come to grips with the function of dealing with the crisis in drugs and alcohol and its relationship to crimes of violence, the inability of our correctional system to rehabilitate criminal Defendants sentenced to its jurisdiction, particularly those who are not necessarily prone to violence when they enter the system, and finally the failure of the leaders of all three branches of government to recognize that they must communicate with each other in order to insure adequate funding for all of the components of the criminal justice system and to use the resources available to the system in the most efficient manner.

The continued efforts of The Stephanie Roper Foundation, Inc. remain therefore both appreciated and essential to the shaping of a properly balanced fair, efficient and compassionate criminal justice system in the future. Good luck to you in all of your future endeavors toward that end.

Very truly yours

Steven I. Platt Judge

BATTERED WOMEN ACCUSED OF HOMICIDE

Who's the Victim Here? A Tale of Two Cases

While serving as a district court and circuit court judge, I presided over more than 250 cases where men with extensive histories of abusive behavior were charged with felonious and/or severe misdemeanor assaults and batteries on their mostly female cohabitants. In contrast, I only presided over three cases in which abused women were accused of killing their abusers. The cases produced very different results.

A 10-Minute Window

The first trial I presided over in which a woman was charged with killing her cohabitant was in the fall of 1990, approximately six months after I was sworn in as a circuit court judge. In 1990, the term "battered spouse syndrome" was an academic term and occasionally a medical term. There was no statutory definition or case law to guide my discretionary decision as to whether to admit into evidence the female defendant's testimony along with that of others who had witnessed the physical and psychological abuse over an extended period of time—abuse inflicted upon her by her now-deceased cohabitant.

Left to my own devices, I allowed the jury to hear the testimony of the defendant and others describing that abuse. I also allowed the jury to hear the testimony of a psychologist about the psychological effects of the abuse inflicted on the defendant who was referred to as both "the victim" and "the defendant."

All of this evidence was admitted over the objection of the prosecutor, whose position was that this evidence was *irrelevant* in the absence of a statute declaring its relevance and mandating its admission. The prosecutor's position was that self-defense, or even what Maryland case law referred to as "imperfect self-defense," was not an available defense in this case because self-defense only applied if the woman was actually under attack or in fear of an *imminent* life-threatening attack. Even "imperfect self-defense," which would apply only if the woman rationally believed that she was or would be under attack even if she really wasn't, was not available as a defense to the second-degree murder charge against her in this case.

There was, depending on whose testimony the jury believed, anywhere from a 10-minute to no-minute interlude between the last act of physical abuse by the deceased abuser and the defendant's homicidal act. Most importantly, there was little dispute of fact, except as to the length of the brief time interval between the last instance of abuse and the stabbing of the abuser by the defendant.

The defendant testified that her actions were in self-defense. In her testimony, she described her abuser as "on the attack." The now-deceased abuser was looking for her in her home for the purpose of inflicting further beatings on her. She perceived these stressful circumstances as making it necessary to stab her abuser to keep him from further beating and killing her. The defense's expert psychologist simply explained that under these circumstances, the defendant's actions were "reasonable," although upon cross-examination, the psychologist concluded that the term "reasonable" was neither intended nor understood as a clinical or legal term.

My ruling was based on my belief, which I arrived at by reading and listening to experts on my own, beginning in the 1980s that courts ought to admit for the purpose of explaining the defendant's motive, state of mind, or both, at the time of the commission of the alleged offense:

1. Evidence of repeated physical and psychological abuse of the defendant perpetrated by an individual who is a victim of a crime for which the defendant has been charged, and

2. Expert testimony on the battered spouse syndrome.

In other words, I believed the truth ought to be admitted into evidence. That seems almost a given today, but it was not the norm in 1990. The prosecutor, even after my ruling, stuck to her original strategy of taking the position that the defendant's explanation for her actions was not legally sufficient and not credible. The jury, for commonsense reasons, thought otherwise. The defendant, an abused woman, was found not guilty of the only charge against her— second-degree murder.

If the state had provided an alternative charge to second-degree murder and an explanation of its position, the outcome might have been different. That said, as a result of the way the prosecutor handled the case, the verdict was a just result. Regarding my decision to allow the facts about the events to be presented and the expert opinion to explain the context to the jury, to paraphrase an old cliché: *"The truth set this defendant free."*

While some trial judges were replicating my rulings, others were inconsistently excluding from evidence the history of abuse that I had admitted. This led to dramatically different verdicts even with similar fact patterns. The Maryland General Assembly reacted two years later. The legislature enacted a statute[15] to provide uniformity and guidance to trial judges from that date forward. That statute provides as follows:

(a)   Definitions – In this section the following words have the meanings indicated... .

(2) Battered Spouse Syndrome" by a spouse, former spouse, cohabitant, or former cohabitant

(3) "Defendant" means an individual charged with:

(i) First-degree murder, second-degree murder, manslaughter, or attempt to commit any of these crimes

A Three-Hour Reprieve

The opposite result occurred in the second case I presided over in which an abused woman was convicted of second-degree murder by a jury composed of 11 women and one man. Like the first case, there had been a long history of physical and sexual abuse of the female defendant. Also, like the first case, the description of this history,

---

[15] Section 10-916 of the Courts and Judicial Proceedings Article of the Maryland Annotated Code.

which was not seriously disputed, was admitted into evidence and presented to the jury along with expert testimony that the defendant was suffering from the effects of the abuse at the time she killed her abuser.

The major difference that accounts for the dramatically contradictory results in these two cases was that in the second case, where the defendant was convicted, the prosecution presented a credible alternative theory to the defendant's version of the pertinent events—unlike in the first case in which the defendant was acquitted.

In the second case, the jury apparently did not believe that the defendant feared, or even had reason to fear, for her life during the three-hour interim that passed after her abuser's last physically abusive contact with her. This may have been because the prosecutor's alternative explanation for the defendant's homicidal actions was more convincing—perhaps for the wrong reasons.

For example, in her presentation, the prosecutor painted the deceased abuser as even more reprehensible than the defense had argued. The prosecutor produced evidence that the abuser was a compulsive womanizer who constantly taunted and angered his then-abused wife, even while he was sexually and physically abusing her. The prosecutor then invoked the age-old stereotype of the "jealous wife." In closing argument to this mostly female jury, she then suggested that the jurors remember, "Hell hath no fury like a woman scorned," while they were considering why the defendant killed her husband as he sat in a chair watching television some three hours after he last abused her.

The jury, by convicting the defendant in the second case of second-degree murder, obviously rejected her version of what occurred, her description of her fear of death or serious bodily harm at the time, and her expert psychologists' explanation of why that fear was both real and rational. Instead, the jury found it easier and more satisfying to accept the prosecution's soap opera–style *"Murder She Wrote/Columbo"*-type theory of the case.

The reasons for that, I believe, were that in the second case there was a three-hour interlude between the last instance of abuse of the defendant by the deceased abuser; while in the first case, the interval was, at most, 10 minutes. The effect and the importance of the timeframe on the degree and intensity of the fear the defendant would experience regarding her abuser was not discussed by the experts in either case.

The defense also did not effectively, through expert testimony, rebut the prosecution's proffered misconceptions battered woman's syndrome and other general stereotypes about women that were put forth as an alternative explanation for her homicidal conduct.

Finally, there was no explanation by the defense's expert in the second case about how the condition of the defendant suffering from battered woman's syndrome came about, the effects of that history of battering, and how the specific circumstances of this case impacted her state of mind *at the time of the killing.* Instead, defense counsel's focus was simply proving that his client suffered from the condition known as battered woman's syndrome and that somehow that fact alone excused her killing of the cause of her condition—her abusive husband.

Defense counsel requested me to instruct the jury as follows:

> *"The state has the burden of proving beyond a reasonable doubt that the defendant was not suffering from the battered woman's syndrome at the time of the killing and that the death was not connected to the battered woman's syndrome."*

I refused to give that instruction to the jury and stated on the record my reasons:

> *"I do not believe, so the record is clear, and I think this is where we disagree, that the legislature by that statute has set up the battered woman's syndrome as an absolute defense, or even partial self-defense.*

> *"They have, rather, said that it can be considered in conjunction with both of those [absolute or partial self-defense] and that is what I have told them."*

My decision in this second case was affirmed by the Maryland Court of Special Appeals, the state's second-highest appellate court. The arguably draconian result was, if not predictable, certainly preventable if the defense had been structured around the specific facts of the case, and a realistic reading of both the text of the battered woman's syndrome statute and its intent.

In a nutshell, because of my refusal to give the jury an instruction that validated the principal tenet of the defense's case, the defendant's attorney was precluded from arguing its main point to the jury. The testimony of the defense expert was, therefore, made to appear to be offered to excuse the defendant's homicidal act rather than explain it. The result was a conviction of the most serious homicide charge available to the jury: second-degree murder.

POSTSCRIPT

As a result of these cases having received substantial media attention, I was invited to participate in a "Roundtable Discussion Conference of Experts" convened by and under the auspices of the Women Judges Fund for Justice, the U.S. Department of Justice, and the State Justice Institute in Washington, D.C., on April 29 and 30, 1995. Thereafter, I presented my perspectives in the University of Baltimore Law Review.[16]

THE CHANGING TIMES

State of Maryland v. Demetrieus Brown

On October 18, 1996, I sentenced Demetrieus Brown, age 24, to 100 years in prison after presiding over his trial. That sentence constituted the maximum sentence permitted under Maryland law for the offenses he had been convicted of. The crimes of which Brown was found guilty by a jury were second-degree murder, use of a handgun in the commission of a crime of violence, attempted second-degree murder, and battery.

---

[16] *University of Baltimore Law Review*, Vol. 25, Fall 1995, No. 1.

The events that led to that sentence were described at Brown's trial:

On September 10, 1995, three armed men forced their way into an apartment occupied by She'kil Gross. The men seemed to be under the impression that there was cocaine in the apartment and went into each room looking for "the stuff." As the men were searching in closets and under furniture, William Miller and Ms. Gross's young daughter returned to the apartment and were immediately accosted by these armed men. Miller was pushed to the ground and questioned about the whereabouts of the cocaine.

Gross attempted to flee the apartment but was shot in the foot by one of the assailants. One of the men then shot Miller multiple times. He died from his wounds.

When the apartment was searched by responding officers, a large amount of cocaine was found. It was established that the apartment had previously been occupied by Lisa Robinson, a cousin of Miller. Gross gave a description of the three men to the police, stating that there was a "tall boy," "a chubby boy," and a "dark-skinned boy." At trial, she testified that the tall boy wielded a knife and a gun and was referred to by the other two men as "Dog." The jury was convinced that Brown was "Dog."

My comments to Brown in imposing the original sentence were as follows:

> "This was one of the worst crimes that I have ever observed, as I said to your co-defendants. As you know from their sentences, I did not attach a whole lot of significance to who was the lead actor. All three, it is clear to this court, were very bad actors. An individual is dead, another one is lucky to be alive, and a third, that child, is probably damaged beyond all comprehension. Following or leading, it does not make a whole lot of difference. The fact of the matter is that the evidence in this case is that the three of you were then, and are now, extreme dangers to this community.

"Why? How you got there is something if I knew the answer to that question, I wouldn't be sitting here. I would be writing a book, and I would change the direction that society is going in. Until we figure that out, the only thing that I can do is attempt to protect future victims from whatever it is that brought you to that location and that caused the death of a human being, the near death of another, and the damage psychologically beyond all comprehension of a child."

Originally, my primary purpose in imposing a cumulative sentence of 100 years was to incapacitate Brown for the reasons stated. Society needed to be protected from him and his criminal cohorts. I found him to be "an extreme danger to the community" because his actions displayed a "total disregard for human life." All other purposes of sentencing were, at best, secondary—deterrence and rehabilitation and even punishment and retribution were incidental.

Twenty-four years later, in 2019, I was asked to "reconsider" that sentence. Brown's lawyer presented the following argument in her pleadings and in open court:

"Demetrieus Brown is a completely different person from whom he was in the 1990s ... He has undergone a phenomenal transition. He is now a great person not just a model inmate."

When that request for sentence reconsideration was made, I was 73 years old and viewing my own mortality and legacy. It had been 13 years since I assumed "senior recalled" status.[17] The times had changed. The governor of Maryland, the General Assembly, and the Maryland judiciary were engaged at this moment in an intense and public debate about ways to reduce the recent dramatic increase in homicides in our state.

As part of that debate, there was the perception that some circuit court judges' sentencing philosophy and practices were causing the

---

[17] "Senior recalled" status describes a judge who has retired from the full-time bench but has been approved by the highest court in the state to be recalled to hear cases.

unacceptable loss of life on the streets of urban communities, particularly Baltimore. Maryland Governor Larry Hogan was among those scrutinizing the judges.

The governor's ascribing of a cause-and-effect relationship to the sentencing philosophy of circuit court judges and the increase in violence was accordingly being examined by all branches of government and the media. In the face of that scrutiny, this senior recalled judge was in the process of dramatically reducing the sentence of a convicted murderer.

The threshold question presented to me was whether the horrifying nature of Brown's crimes 24 years earlier so overshadowed any evidence his lawyer could present to document his "phenomenal transition" to a "great person." If not, then was I convinced that the evidence of his transition was sufficient for me to take the risk of returning him to the community, albeit under strict supervision? Making that decision was my job as a judge, just as much as it was my job to incapacitate Brown by incarceration some 24 years earlier.

As it turned out, Brown's record of institutional adjustment was remarkable, notwithstanding a single minor infraction in the Maryland Division of Corrections over the 23-year period in which he was incarcerated. That sterling record, coupled with the uncontradicted documentation of Brown's rehabilitation by prison officials, including guards, made for a very unusual and credible narrative about a complete personal transformation.

That transformation, which was complemented by Brown's detailed reentry plan with the support and involvement of his family, convinced me that the risk of his recidivating and hurting or killing another victim was remote enough to be acceptable to me and the community I continued to serve.

Coupled with his own demonstrated remorse in thoughtfully addressing this court's comments in imposing the original sentence persuaded me that Brown, indeed, at least at the moment, felt in his written words "forever connected to Your Honor" and "seeking to do great things with the remainder of this life."

That connection Brown spoke of was very real to me because there was much at stake. As I weighed the risks associated with my decision to reduce Brown's original sentence, my concerns were two-fold:

(1)   My decision to provide him a second chance to live in our community and contribute to society as he promised to do by devoting the rest of his life "to catch the children at a very early age before the gangs do" could turn out to be in error, thereby resulting in further injury or death to other innocent victims, and, ultimately, landing Brown behind bars for life; and

(2)   My own competence and judgment would be justifiably questioned—and by some, condemned.

As Demetrieus Brown wrote, his and my futures are, indeed, "forever connected."

THE DEATH PENALTY IN MARYLAND

In Maryland, in 1996, the death penalty was alive and well, although it was constantly being litigated in every case in which the State of Maryland requested that this ultimate sanction be imposed for a first-degree murder conviction. First-degree murder was the only crime in the State of Maryland for which sentencing was up to the jury not the judge.

Therefore, if the jury decided that the sentence of death should be imposed on Heath William Burch, I, as the presiding judge, would be required to impose that sentence. Conversely, a jury or a judge had no authority to impose a sentence of the death penalty unless the State's Attorney's Office requested that ultimate sanction formally in writing within a specified time.

The history of the death penalty in cases tried in the Circuit Court for Prince George's County was dramatically affected by national, state, and even local trends and events. In the early part of the 1970s, the Maryland Death Penalty Statute, along with death penalty statutes in other states, had effectively been declared unconstitutional by a U.S. Supreme Court ruling. The Maryland General Assembly took the necessary steps to reinstate capital punishment in the face of multiple legislative attempts to abolish it. The votes were not close. The State of Maryland reinstated capital punishment in 1978.

From 1978 to 1996, three different Prince George's County state's attorneys, using slightly different criteria, requested the death penalty in what were considered particularly heinous first-degree murder cases. I have no independent knowledge of the number of cases during that period in which the request for the death penalty was made, particularly since over 20 circuit court judges were on the Prince George's County Circuit Court bench during most of those years. I do know that as an individual circuit court judge from May 1990 to January 2007, I was assigned five such cases.

Prior to that, from 1978 to 1996, one Circuit Court for Prince George's County judge was assigned and presided over most capital cases in the county for reasons that were not clear, although everyone willing to gossip had a theory. Although this judge was considered fair and possessed fine judicial temperament, legal scholarship[18] and capital cases were not considered his strong suit.

For that reason, the convictions and sentences of the three men who received death sentences in the Circuit Court for Prince George's County during the period from 1978 to 1996 were reversed on appeal. This judge's poor track record of making clearly erroneous decisions impacting both convictions and sentencing in capital cases motivated prosecutors to consider plea bargaining potential capital cases to pleas of guilty with maximum sentences of life without parole or life with possibility of parole.

This judge, along with some judges in Baltimore County, was partly responsible for the issuance of a 1996 memorandum from then–Court of Appeals Chief Judge Robert C. Murphy, which was directed to all circuit court administrative judges in the State of Maryland. The memo stated that any judge who had not completed the Maryland Judicial College Course on "Handling of the Capital Case"

---

[18] This infers a thorough knowledge of the U.S. Supreme Court and Maryland Court of Appeals holdings. Note that the Maryland Court of Appeals is called the Supreme Court of Maryland as of January 2023.

would not be assigned to preside over cases in which the death penalty was being requested by a state's attorney.

When this memo was issued, I was one of six judges on the Circuit Court of Prince George's County who had completed that course. As a result, the case of *State v. Heath William Burch* was reassigned to me from a judge who had not completed the course. The switch, and the reason for it, drew the attention of the print media as well as the assigned assistant state's attorney and defense counsel.

District Public Defender Joseph Niland always filed motions in capital cases raising constitutional and statutory interpretation issues regarding the death penalty. However, this time, as defense counsel, he immediately added a motion to disqualify the trial judge. His grounds, ironically, were that I had voluntarily enrolled in, and completed, the course, "Handling of the Capital Case." Niland argued that my enrollment in the course evidenced my clear "bias in favor of the death penalty."

Niland also argued that Chief Judge Murphy's memo restricting assignment of capital cases to judges who had completed that course had the effect of depriving his client of his right to have the selection of the presiding judge be from a "cross-section of judges" whose views on the death penalty were not limited by their judicial education and experience nor by Chief Judge Murphy's memo.

Niland expressed in his motion the theory that any judge who chose to enroll in this course probably had a "military background or at least was simpatico with soldiers, trained to kill," and, therefore, "could not fairly and impartially preside over the trial, and if necessary, sentencing of a defendant who faced the death penalty."

The complete absurdity of this theory, and, therefore, this motion, particularly in light of my history of serving in the National Guard, was not lost on me. Niland (now deceased) was a "fighting Irishman" and an experienced capital case litigator. We were not close friends, but we had known and respected each other for nearly 20 years. Our relationship and respect for each other enabled us to battle in the courtroom, then have a beer after the case and laugh about those tense moments. We had socialized before this case and were able to do so again after it ended.

In the meantime, Niland was searching for any legal issues he could find, as the facts of this case could not form the basis for a viable defense to the charges. The state's attorney could prove that Burch killed two people without any doubt—reasonable or otherwise. Therefore, legal issues were the only hope for the defendant to avoid a conviction and possible death sentence. There is an old maxim in the world of lawyers and judges:

> *"If you don't have any facts, use the law. If you don't have any facts or law, attack the police or the prosecutor and pound the table when you are doing it."*

Following that maxim, Niland attempted to create appellate issues whenever and wherever he could. Appellate issues are legal issues that are created by an attorney making motions and/or objecting to evidence or other rulings (*e.g.*, motion denied/objection overruled, etc.). When that occurs, the record and the case reflect the adverse rulings.

If the party loses its case, these rulings are then appealed and a Maryland or federal appeals court is asked to "reverse" the trial court's decision and grant a new trial or a different result based on the erroneous ruling.

During the two days of hearings held on all the motions filed in this capital case, defense counsel demanded he be allowed to *voir dire* (ask questions of) me on the issue of my "pro death penalty" bias, which he had alleged should disqualify me. I am sure he expected me to refuse to let him do so and, thus, create an appellate issue.

Had he thought about it and known me better, he would have known that I would not react as such. Instead, I advised defense counsel on the record that "I would be happy to answer your questions and concerns. What do you want to know?"

Niland's questions were directed to the issues he raised, including inquiring whether I served in the Armed Forces of the United States. I could not avoid thinking about the irony and the humor inherent in this line of inquiry considering my personal history and journey to date. But I also knew enough not to try to be too funny in a death penalty case. Nevertheless, I could not resist. My response to his question was "kind of."

Niland: "What does that mean?"

Judge: "It means that I served in the Maryland National Guard, which, at that time, was kind of like serving in F Troop."

Defense counsel's ultimately fruitless line of questioning continued.

Q. "You enrolled in and completed the Judicial Institute Course on 'Handling the Capital Case,' did you not?"

A. "Yes."

Q. "Why did you enroll in that course?"

A. "It seemed like the most interesting course available. The instructors, Court of Appeals Judge John McAullife, Judge Joseph Murphy, and Judge Dana Levitz, are all knowledgeable, interesting, and entertaining."

Q. "What was the central message of that course?"

A. "That your decisions will receive much more rigorous scrutiny than in any other kind of case, and if you are in doubt, find in favor of the defense. Always be fair."

Q. "What was the most important lesson you learned in that two-day course?"

A. "Again, when in doubt, rule in favor of the defense."

As it became clearer by the minute that this effort to create serious appellate issues was doomed, Niland, like many lawyers in this type of situation, did not know when to stop. He actually ran out of questions he planned to ask to make his original point and couldn't think of any more. Yet, he couldn't resist asking yet another question.

Without thinking it through, Niland asked me a question that he read from the book judges use to ensure that potential jurors understand their roles and responsibilities:

Q. "The Judge will be giving you instructions on the law that applies in this case, and he will tell you that you will be required to apply that law to the facts as you find them to be. If, as the Judge is explaining the law to you, you were thinking 'I don't agree with that,' could you still apply the law as you would be instructed to do?"

My answer reflected (I hope) more humor than hubris, but honestly contained a little bit of both:

"I could. I have the highest degree of confidence and respect for this particular judge."

That ended the hearing. I detected a smile on Niland's face. He realized he had asked one question too many. In doing so, he had enabled me to inject humor into an otherwise humorless situation. I did so, well aware that humor was to be limited in a capital case. Nevertheless, we had both done our jobs and the result was clarifying and fair.

State of Maryland v. Heath W. Burch

On March 19, 1995, Heath William Burch, age 25, broke into the home the Capitol Heights, Maryland, home of his neighbors, 72-year-old Robert Davis and his 78-year-old wife, Cleo Davis. Burch was looking for money to buy drugs and guns. While there, he stabbed Robert Davis more than 30 times. He then attacked Cleo Davis as she tried to call 9-1-1. After killing them, he stole the Davises' pickup truck in which he transported himself, four guns, and $105 from the scene of the crime.

Approximately a year later, a jury voted unanimously to convict Burch of these crimes. Burch and his lawyers (experienced capital case litigators) admitted that he killed both of the Davises but attributed his heinous acts to being high on drugs and to a brutal and abusive upbringing by an alcoholic father. At some level, the cause-effect connection of Burch's abusive childhood to his crime could not be discounted.

However, the perfect fit of the perpetrator's background into the hyped-up media profile of predators likely lessened the degree of sympathy for Burch. He needed all the sympathy he could get from his jury to avoid the death penalty being sought by the State of Maryland.

Burch did not testify until the end of the sentencing hearing stating only:

> *"I'd like to say I'm sorry to the family, knowing that there's really not too much I can do. I ask you all for a fair decision on what my sentence will be."*

At the time of his conviction, Burch's only previous criminal record was for "storehouse breaking." However, he previously had been charged with another murder. That case was pending. The law, therefore, prohibited the jury from even hearing about the earlier matter—only convictions could be considered.

a. State v. Burch: The Trial

Jury selection in this capital case took one and a half days. With a less capable and experienced team, it would have taken twice that long. Earlier in the year, I had convened a meeting with the prosecutor, defense attorney, and my courtroom clerk, Barbara Patterson. She was invaluable in this case and many others. Patterson and I knew each other well before I became a judge and she became a courtroom clerk.

Coincidentally, we began working at the circuit court at roughly the same time and trained together. I will concede that Patterson "trained me well." I was keenly aware of the consequences of not taking my direction from her. That said, my courtroom was considered one of the best run the entire time we worked together, for 11 years, before she became a supervisor and then a manager.

This case typified how well we worked together—the administration of justice and the case benefited from our collaboration. We developed a written questionnaire that contained the *voir dire* inquiries, which effectively allowed us to preliminarily screen out jurors who, because of their background and/or opinions, could not serve on the jury in this case. This procedure and the questionnaire to implement it were agreed to by the attorneys in the case, which took extra effort because the lead prosecutor and defense attorney were not fond of each other. Furthermore, their interests were obviously adverse. That questionnaire was mailed to 250 potential jurors with instructions.

The questionnaire was designed by me to assist in identifying "Death Qualified Jurors," *i.e.*, jurors who were not predisposed to convict the defendant simply because of the specific charges against him or to impose or not impose the death penalty in this or any other case. Most importantly, we required jurors willing to decide whether to impose a sentence of death if it became necessary based on the law explained to them, regardless of their personal and political views.

The Jury Commissioner's Office received back almost 100 percent of the questionnaires. After examining their answers with the assistant state's attorney and defense counsel, we divided the responses into three categories: (1) Death Qualified (2) Death Unqualified (3) Unclear/Arguable.

- "Death Qualified" reflected that both the assistant state's attorney and defense counsel agreed that the juror's response was not disqualifying.

- "Death Unqualified" meant that the prosecutor and defense counsel agreed that the juror's response was disqualifying.

- "Unclear/Arguable" meant the prosecutor and defense counsel did not agree on whether the juror's response was death qualifying or disqualifying and, therefore, it was up to the judge to make that determination.

In the final analysis, we had 85 jurors identified as "Death Qualified." That number yielded enough jurors without further decision-making on those who ranked that I decided not to include the "Unclear/Arguable" category since we didn't need them to get the required 12 jurors and six alternates.

I was pleasantly surprised that neither the assistant state's attorney nor defense counsel chose to exercise the right to object to omitting the "Unclear/Arguable" jurors (which each had a right to do).

Utilized during the jury selection process, peremptory challenges are objections that both the state and the defense are allowed by procedural rule to eliminate a potential juror from being selected. In a murder case, each side is allowed 20 peremptory challenges. They may be exercised for any reason except for race or gender of the potential juror. In this case, all peremptory challenges were exercised by both the state and the defense.

The result, after the completion of jury selection, was a jury of 12 persons comprising by sheer coincidence six men and six women (six Caucasians and six African Americans) plus six alternates. I inquired of both the state's attorney and defense counsel on the record if they were "satisfied with the jury as selected." Both responded, "Yes."

That was important because by responding affirmatively to that inquiry, arguably, they were withdrawing any previous objections they may have lodged.

The "Guilt-Innocence" phase of the trial then proceeded without interruption. The defendant never denied that he killed both Mr. and Mrs. Davis. The jury took less than five hours deliberating before returning a verdict of guilty on all charges. One week later, we would reconvene for the sentencing hearing.

b. State v. Burch: The Sentencing Phase

The only criminal case for which a jury would sentence a defendant in Maryland was a capital case. Therefore, the same jury that had decided to convict Burch of first-degree murder would also decide whether to impose a sentence of "death by lethal injection," "life without the possibility of parole," or "life with the possibility of parole."

In making that decision, the jury considered my instructions on the law when deciding which sentence to impose, as well as further evidence and argument by counsel, victim impact statements by the

Davis family, and a plea for mercy by the defendant, himself. There-after, my role as presiding judge was simply to impose the sentence as directed by the jury.

The jury took less than four hours to direct me to sentence Heath William Burch to death by lethal injection for the first-degree mur-ders of Robert Davis and Cleo Davis. I expected to reflect on my ac-tions while imposing the sentence more than I actually did. But there were extenuating circumstances that kept me from reflecting as long as I might've.

First, my oath as a judicial officer required that I impose the sen-tence the jury directed. Second, I knew that at least five to 10 years would pass before the sentence conceivably would be carried out. Third, I foresaw that my sentence, in fact, might never be carried out in light of the noticeable shift in public opinion on the issues of the death penalty and the strong possibility that this shift might ultimate-ly result in legislative action to abolish the death penalty (which, in fact, occurred a decade later).

c. A Psychological Study

In the interim, I had received a telephone call from a team of pro-fessors from William and Mary Law School and their Graduate Psy-chology Department. The professors and their staff were conducting research on jurors who imposed death sentences. In doing so, they had become aware of the Burch case. They requested permission to interview those jurors, strictly on a voluntary basis, at the courthouse.

The William and Mary team was also offering counseling services to any jurors who agreed to be interviewed, having concluded as a result of their research that these jurors often needed, and wel-comed, counseling as a result of their experience.

I agreed to inform the 12 jurors of this "opportunity" and to invite them back to the courthouse strictly on a voluntary basis, making it clear that they were not being ordered to participate nor was I re-questing that they participate.

I assured them that I would be present at all times during the interviews to ensure that no issues would be created that would complicate matters as the case would, no doubt, be reviewed by both Maryland and federal appellate courts. Admittedly, I was quite curious about the input and reactions that would be revealed in the interviews.

I was pleasantly surprised that eight of the 12 jurors voluntarily appeared and fully participated, including the 56-year-old woman whom I had selected to serve as the foreperson of the jury.

In Maryland, the foreperson is chosen by the presiding judge. I always select someone whose background indicated that his or her work involved supervision or management of personnel, since these are the skills required to effectively manage a jury.

This particular individual listed her occupation as "supervisor and manager"—perfect fit as it turned out. As I listened to her interview, the wisdom of my selection became apparent—not because of her verdict, but because of her obvious management skills.

The principal argument for "mercy" for the defendant was that he was poor and African American and had grown up with an alcoholic father who physically, psychologically, and sexually abused his spouse and children—including the defendant.

As a result of a traumatic childhood, Burch was a drug addict, which accounted for his need to break into the home belonging to the Davises to steal money for drugs and to "defend" himself when confronted by 72-year-old Robert Davis who greeted Burch with a loaded rifle.

Addressing this plea for mercy, the foreperson told her interviewers that she empathized with Burch's childhood experiences and she understood her own history and childhood experience was different from that of the defendant as she had not grown up poor and African American; however, she had been physically and sexually abused as a child. Nevertheless, she was not a drug addict and hadn't ever thought about killing anyone.

Through her interview, the foreperson made it clear to the interviewers, as well as to me as I listened in, that she had extended full respect for the diverse views expressed by each juror during those intense deliberations.

On a considerably less important but amusing note, each of the eight jurors interviewed told the researchers that the lead defense attorney should not have argued with the judge as much as he did since the judge was "more than fair to the defendant and his counsel, and we really liked him."

The lesson to be learned was that if more than one attorney is representing a criminal defendant, particularly in a capital case, whichever attorney will ultimately be asking for mercy should leave the other lawyer to do most of the objecting and arguing that might annoy the jury.

The jurors' feedback also told me (for which I was grateful) that, at least in 1996, a judge was one of a rapidly shrinking number of authority figures still respected by the citizenry.

d. Abolition of the Death Penalty

Finally, at the time I sentenced Burch to "death by lethal injection," I predicted to my staff and "bet" that Burch would outlive me. Years later, when the State of Maryland abolished the death penalty, Burch was one of five defendants on Maryland's "Death Row" to have his sentence commuted to "life without the possibility of parole." In Maryland, this means exactly what it says and is the sentence Burch is currently serving.

As for my "bet," only time will tell who the winner of that wager will be! Like all capital cases, this one was appealed, as well as post-convicted (meaning the conviction was affirmed) in both Maryland's appellate courts and the federal courts at least seven times.

The appeal process included three requests to the U.S. Supreme Court to consider the issues decided in state and federal trial courts and appellate courts. All these requests, which are called "requests for writ of certiorari," were denied.

I have written on the subject of the utility of the death penalty, which was subsequently abolished in Maryland. In 1996, when Burch was tried, convicted, and sentenced in the Circuit Court for Prince George's County, Maryland, the conventional wisdom was that because of the emerging demographic changes in Prince George's County's population, juries, which had become primarily African American, would not impose death penalty sentences. The jury in the Burch case contradicted that conventional wisdom—at least in 1996.

In spite of respected research that arguably creates a question about the death penalty's deterrent effect, I never believed that the death penalty significantly deterred violent crime based on the events before and after it was abolished.

Although Burch's homicides were heinous, he was not the most evil person I had tried while serving as a judge, nor were the homicides he perpetrated the most shocking or even reprehensible.

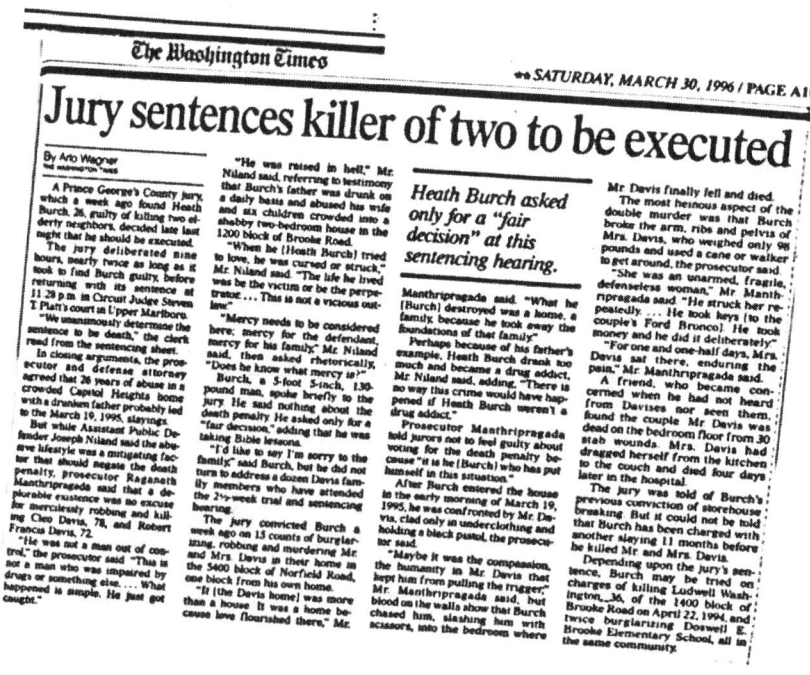

PART SIX

The Civil Docket

Multiple Personalities, a Half-Million-Dollar Penalty, the Making of the Drug Court, a Model for the Nation, and Judicial Job Performance

Chapter 15

Civil Justice Served in Prince George's County, Maryland: Family Law Division and Reform

> *"The resistance from the bar came mostly from that portion of the domestic relations practitioners who made their living serving middle- and lower-class clients. Contrary to the stereotype that lawyers make a lot of money, these lawyers do not get rich practicing law."*

WHEN I WAS sworn in as a circuit court judge, and before that as a district court judge, I stated:

> *"I view this position as not just a job. I view it as my profession and my calling for a lifetime, to make this court and our system of justice work, and to always strive to improve it."*

For the first four years of my tenure as a circuit court judge, I was tasked with the management of the soon-to-be legislatively mandated family division of the Circuit Court for Prince George's County. Involving myself in the administration of justice was not difficult for me to do.

I viewed the work as both personally and professionally fulfilling based on my experience as a politically active practicing attorney, orphans' court judge, district court judge, and as Administrative Judge of the District Court for Prince George's County, Maryland.

At the time, civil justice was changing. At the same time, criminal justice was grabbing headlines of a different sort.

Beginning in the late 1980s and into the 1990s, the dissatisfaction of litigants and lawyers, as well as some court administrators and academics, with the traditional adversarial methods of handling family law disputes became more visible and vocal. The law schools started experimenting with, and law professors started writing about, "alternative dispute resolution" as a more efficient, economical, and fairer way of resolving family law disputes.

There was also increased attention on research documenting the negative mental and physical impact of the litigation process, particularly of custody and visitation issues, on the children whose future was being decided.

Changing this paradigm required a change in the legal and judicial structure and culture of the courts as well as the mindset of the judges and the professional, paraprofessional, and clerical personnel of the court.

The structure of trial courts and their processes were set up in a rigid hierarchy—from case intake to trial—to prepare the case for trial before a judge or a jury. All personnel—including clerks, staff attorneys, paralegals, and masters (now called magistrates)—had very specific duties and job descriptions to match. Litigation was the default dispute resolution process.

The court's structure and the business model it served as well as the work processes that accompanied it had to be changed from one that served the interests of the judges and lawyers to one that encouraged the families to resolve their own disputes with the assistance of counsel and court personnel.

That meant increased flexibility and training of non-judicial personnel to work with the families to resolve their disputes and figure out how to relate to each other—if for no other reason than the mental and physical health of their children. It also meant earlier and in-creased transparency—particularly of the court's education and evaluation of the parties' parenting suitability and skills.

This dramatic change required substantial additional resources. Those additional resources included changes in the physical struc-ture of the court, improved and enhanced technology, additional conference rooms, education tools, projectors, and so on, to expo-nentially increase parent education and to provide for training of custody mediators, evaluators, and clerical staff.

In fact, I chose to revive a management tool from yesteryear, "total quality management," as it seemed to fit perfectly with the retraining needed by the paraprofessional and clerical personnel of the court. This previously discarded and forgotten management tool and phi-losophy encouraged initiative and the exercise of judgment at all lev-els of an organization. It had never previously been utilized in a court setting.

The first mandatory custody and visitation mediation program in the state was established with mediators who were independent con-tractors, despite legal challenges to the court's authority to order mediation in its cases. The result was an over–70 percent case set-tlement rate, well above our initial expectation. In addition, a man-datory parenting education program was established.

Finally, the court's magistrates' talents were redirected. Their du-ties were shifted and expanded from strictly preparing recommenda-tions on cases for judges to conducting pre-trial settlement confer-ences in domestic relations cases with a focus on settling these cases in lieu of preparing them for trial.

These changes were implemented despite some resistance both from the bar and the bench. The resistance from the bar came mostly from that portion of the domestic relations practitioners who made their living serving middle– and lower-class clients.

Contrary to the stereotype that lawyers make a lot of money, these lawyers do not get rich practicing law. In fact, some barely eke out a living. They felt economically threatened by the changes. Their con-cerns were at least partially addressed when we pointed out to them that they could now expect to be paid in full for doing less work in less time, whereas previously they would get only partially paid for more work in a longer period of time.

The resistance from the bench came from some of the older generation of judges who were accustomed to having the court's clerical and professional personnel focused on their needs, not those of the families. Their concerns were assuaged when we pointed out that a much higher rate of settlement would reduce their overall workload and make it less difficult to reach decisions.

The result was the evolution of the modern family division, which is still developing, but has provided access to justice and a much clearer path for families.

In the meantime, these model programs were being cited by proponents of legislation that would mandate the creation of family divisions in the circuit courts across the State. The judiciary's position was that the legislative creation of formal family divisions had to be accompanied by the resources necessary to implement the concept. After three years, the family divisions were legislatively established with rules to implement that legislation.

While this was going on, a recession hit the nation accompanied by a "foreclosure crisis." With that crisis came some malevolent characters who sought to take advantage of vulnerable, usually older, adults. I had one case that arguably involved the "worst of the worst" of those malevolent characters. That story follows.

Chapter 16

Foreclosure Fraud

"On a scale of one to ten as to its reprehensibility ... this court rates this an eleven. If the defendant sleeps at night, this court can't help but wonder how."

TOMMIE MAE SMITH V. VINCENT ABELL

ON APRIL 26, 2004, Vincent Abell's agents/employees arrived on Tommie Mae Smith's doorstep. At the time, Smith was 83 years old, financially distressed, emotionally vulnerable, and physically infirm. Praying on Smith's desire to remain in her home, Abell, through his agents/employees, fraudulently induced Smith to sign away her home for minimal, if any, consideration in order to "save her home from foreclosure."

On May 5, 2005, Smith filed a complaint for declaratory relief and other related relief alleging intentional misrepresentation (fraud) in preparing and recording a deed and breach of contract. Smith requested the court (1) declare the contract and the deed null and void and (2) award Smith $50,000 in actual damages[19] and $500,000 in punitive damages.[20]

Defendant Abell did not file an answer to the complaint. A hearing was held during which Melanie Sims, Esq., the aging, frail, and vulnerable victim's granddaughter and a South Carolina attorney, testified. Michael Greg Morin, an attorney in private practice, testified as to the conduct of Abell, which can only be described as reprehensible.

Abell's attempt to defraud Smith out of her home had succeeded until this court nullified his actions. As presiding judge, I explained my decision to award $500,000 in punitive damages in addition to compensatory damages in this case as follows:

> "Mr. Abell's tortious conduct evidenced an indifference to, or a reckless disregard for Ms. Smith's health. Ms. Smith, an elderly lady, was at the time of this tortious and reprehensible conduct, generally in poor physical health. She suffered then and continues to suffer from diabetes and hearing loss. It is certainly foreseeable that losing her home because of Mr. Abell's fraud could have easily aggravated her health problems. In fact, she recently suffered a minor stroke as a result of a thrombosis.

> "Ms. Smith was also financially vulnerable at the time of Mr. Abell's tortious conduct. Roughly one month before Mr. Abell committed the fraud, foreclosure proceedings on Ms. Smith's home had been initiated. Ms. Smith later filed Chapter 13 bankruptcy. She is currently fulfilling her obligations under the Chapter 13 plan approved for her.

---

[19] Compensation of "actual" monetary damages is an amount of money that the tortious conduct actually costs the plaintiff.

[20] Punitive damages are an amount of money in addition to actual damages where the conduct is so evil or malicious that it should be deterred by requiring the bad actor to pay a cash penalty.

"The harm caused by Mr. Abell's tortious conduct was the result of intentional malice, trickery, and deceit. Because Mr. Abell exhibited actual malice as described supra. The defendant, Mr. Abell's tortious conduct in this case constitutes the most reprehensible actions this court has ever observed in his 28 years on the Orphans' Court, the District Court, and the Circuit Court, save only the physical violence and death routinely visited on the court's conscience in criminal cases. On a scale of one to ten as to its reprehensibility, one being slightly reprehensible and ten being super reprehensibility, as often described in the popular talk show, The McLaughlin Group, this court rates this an eleven. If the defendant sleeps at night, this court can't help but wonder how."

This case, in particular, my decision, and the award of punitive damages drew national attention. It was covered in major legal newspapers and periodicals. I received many requests for copies of the opinion and order in the case and was advised by attorneys from all over the country that even though it was a trial court decision, it was being cited as a template and as a model deterrent remedy for foreclosure fraud. I was pleased to have made a difference.

Chapter **17**

The Little Girl with 25 Personalities

"I decided that I would not contribute to the further abuse and neglect of Jennifer Marlette Chapman, nor would I further traumatize this little 8-year-old girl by deferring to that previous jurisprudence. Instead, I chose to directly confront the Victorian ideals ..."

THE MATTER OF JENNIFER MARLETTE CHAPMAN

EXACTLY ONE YEAR after my investiture, I was assigned the case of *In the Matter of Jennifer Marlette Chapman*, or as it was known in my chambers, "The Case of the Little Girl with 25 Personalities." It was assigned to me by Chief Administrative Judge Ernest A. Loveless, Jr., my former boss. When I was appointed to the circuit court bench, Chief Judge Loveless was approaching his mandatory retirement at age 70.

Recognizing his approaching judicial mortality, he made it clear to me in a series of informal and personal conversations that he, in effect, was willing me his responsibility for adoption cases. Judge Loveless believed that I would carry on the care and attention he had given the children who were the subjects of such proceedings.

Chief Judge Loveless had literally adopted two of his own children right out of his courtroom during the period in which he presided over and administered adoption and termination of parental rights cases. He cared deeply about these cases and the kids involved. Perhaps because he trained me as his law clerk and then as his protégé, the judge felt that I should handle the administration of these matters, particularly once he was required to leave as a full-time judge. I gladly accepted. I firmly believe this was why and how I was assigned the case of Jennifer Marlette Chapman.

Jennifer Chapman was born on August 15, 1982, at Prince George's County Hospital Center in Cheverly, Maryland, as a result of the unfortunate and ill-fated union of Norman Douglas Chapman and Bonnie Chapman. On February 12, 1987, this child, who was then 4 years old, came to the attention of the Prince George's County Department of Social Services (DSS) as a possible "child in need of assistance."

For the next four years, Jennifer was in foster care as a result of court orders by other judges of the circuit court before I was appointed. Finally, on January 4, 1990, prior to my appointment to the circuit court bench, DSS petitioned the circuit court for guardianship with the right to consent to adoption and/or long-term care of Jennifer. This meant that the department was seeking to terminate the parental rights of Jennifer's biological parents. They both, for different reasons and on different grounds, vehemently opposed that petition. Both were represented by counsel separately.

The trial began on May 6, 1991.The proceedings lasted 21 working days. The first exhibit introduced in this lengthy trial was a photograph of Jennifer taken in February 1987. She was 4 years old at the time and appeared to be her age in the photograph. The child was smiling. By all accounts, she should not have been!

Jennifer suffered from a mental condition known as multiple personality disorder." Before this case, if I had been asked whether I believed in such a condition, I would have expressed disbelief. After seeing and hearing the evidence, I had *no* doubts. This 8-year-old girl also suffered from attention deficit disorder (ADD). The causes of these conditions were apparent from the testimony and records of multiple mental health professionals, as well as the physical appearances and testimony of Jennifer's parents.

Bonnie Chapman, the natural mother of Jennifer, was diagnosed by her own treating psychologist, Dr. Roger Pasternak, as having severe borderline personality disorder, the symptoms of which are anger and depression as well as drug and alcohol abuse. All of these symptoms manifested themselves in Mrs. Chapman during Jennifer's infancy and thereafter. Psychotic episodes are symptomatic of this disorder. She was of "low average/borderline intelligence" and suffered from a severe learning disability.

Mrs. Chapman, herself, suffered from a history of sexual abuse and assault as a child, with recurring hospitalizations since 1987 for psychiatric and/or drug and alcohol problems:

- September 15, 1987, when she was diagnosed as suicidal;

- A May 1988 outpatient hospitalization;

- An emergency on June 22, 1988, at which time she was suicidal;

- October 4, 1989, and October 31, 1989, for the same reason—suicidal;

- On February 20, 1990; March 7, 1990; and again, on May 12, 1990; for mental health reasons;

- And her latest hospitalization occurred during the trial of this case.

Dr. Pasternak had not been involved in all of Mrs. Chapman's hospitalizations. He was not able to keep her in treatment without interruption. She followed neither her hospital physicians' nor Dr. Pasternak's instructions per follow-up and out-patient treatment with any consistency.

Apparently, Mrs. Chapman, while under the influence of drugs, chased after Jennifer when the child was between 2 and 4 years old with a kitchen knife until she was restrained by her husband, Norman Chapman. She also threw a glass Christmas ball ornament at Jennifer before Jennifer's fifth birthday while her daughter was in her care and control. In addition, Mrs. Chapman had sexual relations with at least one non-marital partner in her 4-year-old daughter's presence. Considering the circumstances, I was convinced that Jennifer observed this act, perhaps without Mrs. Chapman's knowledge.

Dr. Pasternak testified during the trial that Mrs. Chapman could tend to her own basic needs "since she was married." He stated if she were not married and did not otherwise have a caregiver, she would need vocational rehabilitation to be able to tend to her personal needs. It was made clear that she could not take care of herself or Jennifer.

Norman Chapman, the natural father of Jennifer, was 33 years old when this case was tried. He was born on December 15, 1957, in Maryland, the oldest of seven children. Employed as a master printer, he graduated from Bladensburg High School and received eight credits from Montgomery College. In his words, his childhood was "no different than anyone else's." Mr. Chapman testified that the last time he used drugs was in 1978.

After the incident in which he rescued Jennifer from the threat of her knife-wielding mother, Mr. Chapman testified that he became concerned about his daughter's physical safety. He explained that he had become the primary parent in Jennifer's life; and thus, toilet trained the child, taught her reading, counting, and colors. In describing the situation, Mr. Chapman testified without any sign of emotion despite the allegations against him. He was a glib, articulate, and matter-of-fact witness, characterizing his relationship with his daughter as more "father-son than father-daughter—we were buddies."

Mr. Chapman was tested psychologically when he was seen initially by Dr. Pasternak in 1987. He was administered the Minnesota Multiphasic Personality Inventory test and also took the Rorschach (ink blot) test. Based on the results of these tests and his personal history, Dr. Pasternak testified that Mr. Chapman "functioned within normal limits and did not present any anti-social personality disorders."

However, Dr. Pasternak pointed out that this testing does not tell whether a person is capable of committing a sexual offense, since "thought disorder is not a prerequisite to committing such an act."

Dr. Pasternak testified that he had seen persons who tested normal but were sex offenders. Jennifer's father was treated actively until December 1987; thereafter, his psycho-social treatment history became sporadic.

Mr. Chapman engaged in the following exchanges on the stand with his counsel:

Q. "Did you abuse your daughter?"

A. "No".

Q. "Did you ever come close to abusing your daughter?"

A. "I don't know what you mean."

Q. "Did you ever come close to abusing your daughter?"

A. "Not that I know of."

Then later in his testimony:

Q. "Did you ever abuse your daughter?"

A. "No, sir, I do not ever remember abusing my daughter."

Mrs. Bobbi Lyn Dozier, the special foster mother of Jennifer at the time of the trial, met the little girl on October 12, 1986. Subsequently at Jennifer's parents' request, Mrs. Dozier arranged daycare for Jennifer at St. Matthews Church, as well as babysitting at her home on many occasions, during the time between October 12, 1986, and February 1987. During that period, Mrs. Dozier befriended Mrs. Chapman and, in doing so, assisted her in getting to and from doctors' offices on many occasions. On one occasion, at the request of one of Mrs. Chapman's physicians, Dr. Singer, she transported Mrs. Chapman to the hospital.

When Mrs. Dozier first met Jennifer in October 1986, the little girl made sexually explicit comments and requests such as "lick her," "play the married game," and "make love." When Jennifer told Mrs. Dozier she wanted to "make love," the child made reference to movies she had seen, apparently at her parents' home. From October 15,

1986, to October 31, 1986, this 4-year-old child constantly talked about "taking care of her father" while her mother was in the hospital.

Also in October 1986, when she first began babysitting Jennifer, Mrs. Dozier observed that Jennifer's clitoral area was enlarged and reddened with obvious abrasions. From October 1986 until the child left her parents' home, these conditions appeared and disappeared intermittently as did Jennifer's complaints of itching in her vagina.

In the fall of 1986, an incident occurred that heightened Mrs. Dozier's concern. While babysitting Jennifer, Mrs. Dozier witnessed Jennifer reach inside her panties and say, "My pussy stinks." As a result of this unprompted action and comment, Mrs. Dozier inspected the child's genital area and panties wherein she observed red spots that appeared to be blood, plus the familiar swelling and redness she had observed intermittently since caring for the child.

That evening, when Mr. Chapman picked up Jennifer, Mrs. Dozier advised the child's father of the events of the day and that she had seen what she believed to be blood. His reaction, as characterized by Mrs. Dozier, was to "brush it off." In doing so, he suggested that the red spots "must be juice." This incident, coupled with other actions and comments by Jennifer, caused Mrs. Dozier to consult with her pastor, Reverend Tom Rogerson.

Another incident took place in November 1986, when Jennifer told Mrs. Dozier about bugs climbing in her window and into her private area. Jennifer then explained how to swipe the bugs with a hand motion. Another such incident occurred in early February 1987, when Jennifer explained to Mrs. Dozier that "Dad had to scratch and kill the bugs."

On February 12, 1987, Jennifer was the subject of a referral to the Prince George's County Department of Social Services by Reverend Tom Rogerson. He reported that the child's caretaker, Mrs. Dozier, and certain persons (whose names were not reported) at the St. Matthews Episcopal Church on Nicholson Street in Hyattsville, Maryland, where the child attended a daycare facility, had reported "strange behaviors." They suspected sexual abuse.

That behavior was described on the DSS intake form as follows:

Touch her here because it feels better (child told Mrs. Dozier this).

Asked babysitter to lick her pussy.

Blood spotting in her underwear.

In the fall of 1988, Jennifer began talking about her "make believe friends." She was also observed talking as if someone else was present when, in fact, she was alone. Mrs. Dozier then observed Jennifer blinking and then rolling her eyes in the back of her head followed by looking up in a manner that made her appear different physically, as well as speaking with a different tone of voice. This caused Mrs. Dozier to report her observations to both social workers and Dr. James Lewis.

Dr. James Lewis, a renowned neuropsychologist, was accepted without objection by any party as an "expert witness in psychology and in the diagnosis and treatment of sexually and physically abused children and their families." For three and a half days, his opinions in this case were heard and considered; however, not without controversy.

Dr. Lewis first evaluated Jennifer in July 1987 after she was referred by the sexual assault center. That evaluation involved two to three hours of psychometric tests with his staff, plus 10 hours with Dr. Lewis personally. That initial evaluation was followed by 90 to 100 hours of treatment beginning in September 1987 following Dr. Lewis's diagnosis.

In the fall of 1988, Dr. Lewis began to suspect that Jennifer had symptoms of a dissociative disorder. Dr. Lewis explained this term by analogizing it to a continuum—with a dissociative state such as amnesia and less severe lack of memory at the beginning of the continuum, and the most serious dissociative disorders such as multiple personality disorder at the end.

Dr. Lewis personally observed further evidence that Jennifer suffered from one of the most severe forms of dissociative disorder, multiple personality disorder. He witnessed and conversed with the "host personality" Jennifer. He then witnessed multiple alter egos: "Bad Jennifer," a male personality named "Glany," a personality named "Melissa," and an older girl personality named "Amy." The doctor personally observed the transition of the host into the alters, "Bad Jennifer," "Glany," and perhaps "Amy" in his office. He saw Jennifer's eyes roll in the back of her head and then she went behind the couch. On one occasion, she came out as "Glany" and started talking to Dr. Lewis.

Dr. Lewis testified that perhaps other alter egos existed in various stages of development, whom Dr. Lewis had not personally observed, but whom he had heard about from Jennifer. They had names such as "Zem Zimbawe," another "Melissa," "Zaney," "Gonzilla" (one male and one female), "Princess Elana," "Michelle," and "Katey."

Dr. Lewis distinguished these alter egos, whom Jennifer referred to in therapy as her "inner friends," as different from a typical child's imaginary playmates. A typical child's imaginary friends are positive—Jennifer's "inside friends" were violent. They wanted to kill. They wanted to kidnap. They had sex. A typical child's imaginary friends are separate personalities, while these alter egos had taken over the child; Jennifer became these people!

Dr. Lewis informed the court that the most developed of these alter egos was the one known as "Bad Jennifer" whom he testified was known to the "Host Jennifer" as Mr. Chapman's wife. "Bad Jennifer" made Jennifer scratch her genital area and sexually act out in public.

Based on his evaluation and treatment, including tests and numerous interviews with the child, Dr. Lewis had asked her non-leading questions in an attempt to have her verify her self-report of abuse and asked her leading questions "in the nature of cross-examination." The doctor was trying to shake the child's faith in her own story. Dr. Lewis formed an opinion, to a reasonable degree of psychological certainty, that Jennifer had been physically abused by her mother and chronically sexually abused primarily by her father. He further opined that Jennifer's dissociative disorder resulted from the cycle of abuse inflicted on her by both of her biological parents at least while she was between the ages of 2 and 4 while in their care, control, and home.

Dr. Lewis's observations were not contradicted on cross-examination or by other expert witnesses. His opinions were questioned by Dr. Pasternak because he considered the self-reports by Jennifer on which Dr. Lewis partially relied as "contaminated." Dr. Pasternak, however, offered no contrary opinions; nor was he willing to state that Jennifer's self-reports were untrue or that Dr. Lewis's opinions were incorrect. Dr. Pasternak would only say that based on his review of the relevant reports and depositions in this case, he would not be prepared to render an opinion on the issue of whether Jennifer was sexually abused by her father because of the unacceptably high risk that the information available on which to base such an opinion was "contaminated."

This court did not then, nor do I now (some 30 years later), share Dr. Pasternak's reservations about Dr. Lewis's opinion or his methodology. I was aware of the factors mentioned by Dr. Pasternak, many of which Dr. Lewis acknowledged, which can cause a child's self-reporting of incidents—particularly of physical and sexual abuse—to be "contaminated." Nevertheless, I was convinced (based on his testimony as well as his training and experience) that Dr. Lewis had taken sufficient steps to verify the child's self-reports. In doing so, he had identified and effectively neutralized those factors that would otherwise render those reports unreliable.

For that reason, I found Dr. Lewis's unequivocal and uncontradicted opinions clear and convincing. Based thereon, along with medical findings that were not inconsistent with those opinions and the other factors (particularly the report of the Sexual Assault Center), I found clear and convincing evidence that Jennifer Marlette Chapman was chronically sexually abused between the ages of 2 and 4 while living with her natural parents. I also found the evidence to be clear and convincing that her primary abuser was her natural father, Norman Douglas Chapman; and that on multiple occasions, she was physically and emotionally abused by her natural mother, Bonnie Chapman, during that same period.

Notwithstanding those findings, I held no delusion that the termination of the rights of Jennifer's biological parents would be affirmed by Maryland's appellate courts. In Maryland, the biological parents' rights to the custody and care of their children were deemed fundamental. In 1991, this was deeply embedded in the jurisprudence of Maryland and other states. Furthermore, regardless of the circumstances, a DSS was required to take steps to reunify a child with his or her biological parents before considering other custodial arrangements, even with a history of documented physical and sexual abuse and neglect.

My prior experience as Chief Judge Loveless's law clerk and later as a lawyer representing biological parents, couples seeking to adopt children, and the children themselves, convinced me that in cases such as this, an attempt by DSS and/or the court to reunify a child with his or her abusive and neglectful biological parents(s) would itself constitute further abuse and would violate one of my life's lessons lived and learned—"Do no harm!"

Unfortunately, the jurisprudence of our state did not reflect the same ideology. At the time, I had seen countless reversals of circuit court judgments terminating parental rights and criticism of DSS for failing to make sufficient efforts to reunify children with their historically abusive and neglectful parents. These actions often cited biblical authorities and other theories rooted in religious dogma—not reality!

Nevertheless, in this case, I decided that I would not contribute to the further abuse and neglect of Jennifer, nor would I further traumatize this little 8-year-old girl by deferring to that previous jurisprudence. Instead, I chose to directly confront the Victorian ideals:

> *"We have also considered all the services offered by DSS, as well as the other agencies and professionals who have provided services to both Jennifer and her natural parents in making these findings.*

> *"Based on this Court's consideration of that evidence, which is clear and convincing that the natural mother in this case has*

disabilities that render her unable to care for the immediate and ongoing physical or psychological need of Jennifer Chapman for long periods of time, and our further finding that there is clear and convincing evidence that the natural father in this case has committed acts of sexual abuse and the natural mother has committed acts of physical abuse toward the child in the family, and after evaluating the efforts made and services rendered by DSS to the natural parents as set forth earlier herein, we find by clear and convincing evidence that the waiver of the Prince George's County Department of Social Services obligations under §5-313 (c) is in fact in the best interest of the child in this case. Alternatively, we find that even if not waived, that the Prince George's County Department of Social Services has offered those services designed to facilitate reunion of Jennifer Chapman with her natural parents at the times and to the extent that they were consistent with what was and is in the best interest of the child during the tortured history of this case.

"Norman Douglas Chapman has said he "is entitled to notice and an opportunity to defend against the allegations of the County." He had that opportunity in this case for 21 days.

"Norman Douglas Chapman says "the Court, and not the County, is the proper agency to determine a factual finding of abuse." We agree. We have made that finding.

"The issue is not whether Prince George's County is justified in seeking termination of Mr. and Mrs. Chapman's parental rights. Rather, the issue is whether pursuant to §5-313 of the Family Law Article of the Code whereas in this case the child has, in a prior juvenile proceeding, been adjudicated a child in need of assistance, this Court finds by clear and convincing evidence that it is in the best interest of the child to terminate the natu-

ral parents' rights as to the child. We find by clear and convincing evidence, that it is in the best interest of Jennifer Marlette Chapman, to terminate her natural parents, Bonnie Gail Chapman's and Norman Douglas Chapman's rights to this child.

""Due process is a word about which we have heard spoken and written a great deal in this case.

"For all its consequence, 'due process' has never been, and perhaps can never be precisely defined." Lassiter v Department of Social Services of Durham Cty., 101 S. Ct. 2153, 2158 (1981). "Unlike some legal rules, this Court has said due process is not a technical conception with a fixed content related to time, place and circumstances." Cafeteria Workers v McElroy, 81 S. Ct. 1743, 1748. Simply put, "the phrase expresses the requirement of fundamental fairness." Lassiter, supra.

"Norman Douglas Chapman and Bonnie Gail Chapman have received due process of law, much of it at a high cost to the formative years of their eight-year-old daughter's life.

"Jennifer Chapman is a little girl, who between the ages of two and four years of age, was rejected and physically abused by her natural mother, randomly and without warning, and when she turned to her natural father for protection, got a sexual relationship with him instead. Jennifer Chapman is a little girl who developed multiple-personality-disorder to cope with the trauma of these events. Jennifer Chapman is a little girl, who instead of having the kind of real as well as imaginary friends that other children her age have, has "inside friends" who want to kill and have sex with her as well as have sex with her father. Jennifer Chapman is a little girl, who instead of having dreams like other children, has nightmares about being kidnapped and *other violent acts. Jennifer Chapman is a little girl whose world, for the last four years, has been made up of lawyers, judges, psychologists and social workers whom she worries will disrupt her life again. This little girl deserves a chance for a safer and more secure future. She is entitled to fundamental fairness. She is entitled to substantive due process without further delay. Today, she receives it."*

Early in my tenure on the circuit court, and for a variety of personal and professional reasons, this case literally and figuratively reinforced my reasons for serving as a judge. To me, the opportunities to employ my analytical skills and to experience good work was what judging was all about. The headlines in the print media, as well as the lead-ins on local television stations for the month I presided over the trial, reinforced my sense of justice as they proclaimed:

- "TRAUMATIZED CHILD AT CENTER OF CUSTODY BATTLE"
- "DISTURBED CHILD'S FATE IN HANDS OF COURT"
- "MULTI-EGO CUSTODY CASE GOES TO JUDGE"
- "HAVEN FOR ABUSED GIRL WITH 25 PERSONALITIES CREATED BY JUDGE"

The findings and decision in this case were set forth in a 76-page opinion. The decision was not appealed by either of the biological parents. The "requirement" that reunification of a child with his or her biological parents be sought regardless of the circumstances, including abuse and neglect, withered away in cases that followed.

Shortly after the decision was published and the last part of it read on various Washington-area television stations, my former boss, Chief Judge Loveless, left word for me to come see him one afternoon. I was then 43 years old. I walked into his chambers and he summoned me into his office. Holding the 76-page opinion in his hand, my former boss uttered these simple words I'll never forget:

"Steve, I am very proud of you. No one could have written this but you."

That was, and remains, the most gratifying "Attaboy" I have ever received!

Dr. James Lewis and I became friends. We talked about the Chapman case often. We even presented two programs in which we discussed the case—his role and mine—in front of professional organizations exploring the developing relationship between the law and psychology. Later, Dr. Lewis became a neutral and consultant with the alternative dispute resolution group, The Platt Group, Inc., a company I formed after I "retired" as a full-time judge.

Approximately one year after the case ended, I had the honor and pleasure of presiding over the uncontested adoption by the Dozier family of Jennifer Marlette Chapman, who became Jennifer Marlette Dozier. She was 10 years old. Jennifer attended, and this time her smile was natural and warranted. I am, to this day, happy that I helped make that smile possible.

Chapter 18

The Drug Court Experiment

*"We trained all the stakeholders including the counse-
lors, many of whom were 'recovering addicts.'"*

FROM THE FAMILY division, I moved on to manage the criminal
docket and operations of the Circuit Court for Prince George's County. In addition to presiding over drug cases and, at least in part, trying
to expurgate the 1990s version of the War on Drugs, Administrative
Judge William D. Missouri tasked me with designing and implementing a "drug court."

Drug court was, and still is, a concept that operates on the premise that treatment, not incarceration, is the ultimate solution to address drug addiction; and the criminal justice system should "make
love not war" on people who are addicted to drugs. That means that
the court selectively offers the drug court option to defendants who
either on their own are motivated to seek treatment or choose it in
lieu of incarceration for their criminal behavior.

The drug court treatment program is designed and implemented
by a team: the judge, the prosecutor, the defendant's attorney, the
probation agent, the drug program counselor, and other persons or
agencies necessary to address the defendant's addiction and the

criminal behavior emanating from it. The members of this team when participating in drug court cases depart from their traditional adversarial roles to work collaboratively to advance the agenda of the drug court—to rehabilitate criminal offenders whose conduct is at least partially driven by their addiction.

Rehabilitation is accomplished via a multidisciplinary combination of drug education and counseling, intense drug and alcohol testing, vocational counseling, and psychological counseling. Any noncompliance with the program's requirements by the offender is addressed immediately with coercive sanctions ranging from a brief period of incarceration to increased testing and essay writing, among other things, and further counseling.

Working with Administrative Judge William D. Missouri, we selected the initial "team," which included the first drug court presiding judge, the Honorable Maureen Lemasney.[21] We trained all the stakeholders including the counselors, many of whom were recovering addicts. During their training, they had to be persuaded that their continued employment by the program required them to report their clients to the court if they violated the program's protocols.

This was a difficult but essential requirement to accept for some of these recovering addicts, which we understood; but in order to make the program work, it was absolutely necessary. These recovering addict counselors ultimately bought into their new job description or were told to seek alternative employment.

The drug court program worked and still does. In fact, most drug courts around the country, if they are structured and staffed properly and given the necessary and appropriate resources, "work" far more efficiently and compassionately than the traditional criminal justice adversarial system. The challenge is to persuade the taxpayers and their elected representatives to fund these courts on a scale that enables them to make the difference they can make in the long run.[22]

---

[21] I designed the program but declined the honor of being its first presiding judge because I wanted to move on to other assignments.

[22] I have written on this topic in one of my other books, *The Winding Road*—"Part One: Criminal Justice in the 21st Century," which I recommend to you, my readers, for further analysis.

I hope the government will continue supporting this program because even though it's a cliché, *"An ounce of prevention ultimately costs less than a pound of correction."*

New plan for drug offenders

DRUGS from A1

What drug court supporters want to do is simplify and shorten that process by offering treatment at the early stages, if the accused is willing.

However, the court system cannot move forward without state funding and a commitment from the governor to expand drug treatment services in the state, Platt and Missouri said.

"Legislative support is an absolute precondition of doing this," Platt said. "It could be a fad, but it appears to be working."

Sen. Gloria Lawlah, D-26th-Hillcrest Heights, who could not be reached for comment yesterday, has been behind an effort to create a drug court statewide, Missouri said. Lawlah sent a letter last month to Maryland Gov. Parris N. Glendening in support of creating drug treatment oversight panels similar to Delaware's.

U.S. Rep. Albert R. Wynn, D-4th, who will host a discussion with county officials Monday, has asked the House of Representatives to consider a $15 million increase in funding for drug court programs nationwide. That program was underfunded by $10 million last year, according to a spokesman for Wynn's office.

Officials from the county State's Attorney's Office, circuit court bench and state senate delegation have made public statements supporting the creation of a Treatment Access Committee (TAC), which would monitor treatment centers, and a Treatment Access Center (TASC), which would expand drug treatment centers in Maryland. TAC and TASC are the backbone of Delaware's drug court system, officials said.

Platt said judges sentencing drug offenders to treatment programs rely on the Departments of Parole and Probation or Juvenile Justice to select an appropriate program, but do not have enough time to monitor the quality of the program.

One of the most promising features of Delaware's drug court program, they say, is a committee that monitors the quality of private drug treatment programs where drug offenders are sent.

Platt said the problem with many current drug treatment programs is similar to the much publicized lack of regulations in private home detention firms.

"There are a lot of private programs that have spring up overnight with no quality assurance," Missouri said. "There is no one to hold the line."

"Salvation Army and Second Genesis are excellent programs, but there are others who don't do a good job and slots are limited," Missouri said. Salvation Army and Second Genesis offer in-patient treatment.

Close to 100,000 drug offenders nationwide have entered drug court programs since their inception nearly five years ago. More than 70 percent are still enrolled or have graduated from the program, Wynn's office reports. That rate is more than double that of traditional treatment programs, according to Wynn's office.

Chapter 19

A New Case Management Program, Class-Action Fees, and the Management of Other Judges

"[A] movement that was national in scope but growing in intensity in Maryland became more visible and audible as the 21st century dawned. Business lawyers and their clients in the business community expressed widespread dissatisfaction with the way the courts handled 'business litigation.'"

A MODEL FOR THE NATION

FROM MANAGING THE criminal docket and operations, I then moved to jointly manage the civil (non-family) docket and operations of the Circuit Court for Prince George's County alongside my longtime friend and then-colleague, the Honorable Thomas P. Smith.

We jointly decided the civil (non-family) division of the court needed a whole new look, structure, and protocols to go with it. Our ideas on how to accomplish that collaboratively were developed in a weekend at Judge Smith's house in Bethany Beach, Delaware, in between glasses of good wine.

In doing so, we recognized that our collaboration was unconventional, but the system we developed worked well enough that Judge Smith and I believed it might well have been the best-case management system ever developed while under the influence. More importantly, the bench and the bar were content, and it served the court well for a number of years.

In the meantime, a movement that was national in scope but growing in intensity in Maryland became more visible and audible as the 21st century dawned. Business lawyers and their clients in the business community expressed widespread dissatisfaction with the way the courts handled "business litigation." These complaints were noticed by all three branches of state government, although the response was not embraced uniformly.

The Honorable Casper Taylor, then–Speaker of the Maryland House of Delegates, initially captured the mood of the business community and introduced legislation to require the judicial branch of Maryland's government to create a new "business court." This bill stirred the judiciary, through its Chief Judge Robert M. Bell, to formally acknowledge "the problem." At the same time, the judiciary reiterated its longstanding resistance to the executive or legislative branches of government attempting—through legislation or administrative fiat—to dictate the structure and/or management of the operations of the separate, independent, judicial branch of government.

Ultimately, a compromise was negotiated by Chief Judge Bell with Speaker Taylor to amend the original legislation (HB-1). Instead of creating a new business court, the bill established The Maryland Business and Technology Case Management Project Task Force. This task force included a diverse membership chosen by the governor, the speaker of the house, the president of the senate, the chief Judge of the Court of Appeals, and the Maryland State Bar Association. An icon of the legal profession, Woody Preston, Esquire, was designated chair, and I was named vice chair.

The task force, which included representatives of the business community as well as the legal profession, met regularly for about nine months. Finally, in a surprisingly unanimous vote, it recommended the establishment of the Maryland Business and Technology Case Management Program. I was appointed chair of the judiciary's implementation committee by Chief Judge Bell.

In about eight months, the program had become operational. Specially trained and experienced judges were recruited and educated to preside over cases involving complex business and technology issues. A strong alternative dispute resolution requirement was made an integral part of the administration of those cases. A premium was placed on quick, predictable, and accurate decision making in these cases.

Headlines followed in major business and legal newspapers and magazines, including *Case in Point*, the periodical of the National Judicial College, and *The Business Lawyer*, a publication of the American Bar Association—both of which cited the program as a "model for the nation."

A MARYLAND JUDICIAL CREATION

With the birth of the Maryland Business and Technology Case Management Program came its first operational challenge. In the 1999 Maryland Court of Appeals decision in *United Cable Television of Baltimore Limited Partnership v. Louis Burch, et al.*, the court declared that virtually any and all commercial enterprises in Maryland that financed the payment for whatever product or service they sold by charging a late fee, likely violated the 6 percent per annum cap that the court determined was proscribed under Article III Section 57 of the Maryland Constitution.

This precipitated a flood of lawsuits filed by lawyers from law firms across the state and the country who specialized in the litigation of class action suits. These lawsuits were filed on behalf of late fee–paying customers. Of necessity, they were for comparatively small amounts varying from $5 to $50 per customer. The suits were against not only cable companies, but also equipment rental companies, automobile financing companies, car dealerships, telephone companies, utilities, tire centers, healthcare companies, and health insurance companies.

Most of these suits filed in almost all the circuit courts in Maryland were assigned to me and, if necessary, transferred and/or consolidated in my court by the chief judge of the Court of Appeals. This was done out of concern that if these suits were decided by different courts, inconsistent rulings could disrupt not only the courts but the economy of the state. Certainly, my role as the acknowledged principal architect of the Maryland Business and Technology Case Management Program played a role in that administrative decision.

The cases were settled quickly and efficiently upon applying the lessons learned while the Maryland Business and Technology Case Management Program was being designed and developed by the task force and then executed by the judiciary's implementation committee, which I chaired. Those lessons were that the court should be predictable, which was and is as important as being correct, and it should act in a timely manner so affected businesses and industries can survive the litigation-induced disruption and plan their future operations.

In addition, these cases raised an important question, which the national and state media covered extensively: Did the Maryland judiciary and other courts across the country wish to encourage lawyers who specialize in class action litigation to continue to file class action suits to recover small but fair amounts of compensation for every late fee–paying customer in their state by awarding substantial attorney's fees for filing and litigating these claims?

While I was considering this question in the context of whether to approve the settlements of these circuit court cases and the requests for attorney's fees contained in the terms of those proposed settlements, the Maryland General Assembly made its own independent determination by enacting legislation that retroactively overrode the original decision of the Court of Appeals. Maryland's highest court then summarily declared that legislation unconstitutional. At that point, it was "back to the future" for me and the attorneys whose fees had been legislated against and were again being litigated.

That "future" turned out not to be what counsel had in mind. For a variety of legal and economic policy reasons, I denied the class plaintiff's motion for final approval of class action settlement, award of attorney's fees and expenses to class counsel. In summing up the reasons for my decision, I pointed out that the U.S. Supreme Court in the Microsoft Corporation antitrust litigation case stated that the primary purpose of a class action lawsuit is to "provide a mechanism for litigation of small claims that no individual plaintiff would have the incentive to bring," and that, in my opinion, this purpose is undermined by what economist Ronald Coase refers to as "transaction costs" or "social costs" if these costs are disproportionate to the benefit received by society.

With that in mind, I explained that the transaction costs of the proposed recovery, particularly the attorney's fees of $13 million, for restoring moneys illegally charged and collected as late fees ranging from $5 to $50 from customers was not justified by the small benefit received by those customers.

These consolidated cases triggered a thorough examination in the media and academia of class actions in Maryland and the nature and role of the plaintiff's class action bar. Ultimately, I approved a revised settlement and recalculation of attorney's fees based on the commonsense proposition that attorney's fees awarded "shall not exceed a reasonable percentage of the amount of any damages and prejudgment interest paid to the class," as per the U.S. Supreme Court.

MANAGING JUDGES

As I became more and more involved in court administration, that activity ultimately led to my appointment as co-chair of the Maryland State Bar Association Special Committee on the Management of Judicial Personnel.

This was clearly a "Blue Ribbon" committee, as I was serving alongside Nell B. Strachan, Esq., Venable partner, who was my predecessor as chair of the Maryland State Bar Association Judicial Administration Section Council.

The special committee later included Chief Judge Robert M. Bell, future court of appeals judge Sally Adkins, and a diverse cross-section of the bench and bar.

The special committee spent two years comprehensively reviewing every aspect of the recruitment, selection, education, training, compensation, and discipline of trial and appellate court judges. Our time resulted in a substantive report on the entire spectrum of "managing judicial personnel," which included a controversial recommendation that Maryland establish a system of "judicial evaluations."

The very concept generated intense resistance, particularly from the judiciary itself. The report was issued in 2000 and its adoption in Maryland, to say the least, is not forthcoming. Nevertheless, the media focused solely on the most controversial aspect despite the headline in *The Daily Record* and other print media:

ADMINISTRATION OF JUSTICE

Panel Recommends Major Overhaul Of Court System in Maryland

Committee Urges First-Ever Performance Review for State's Judges Says Judiciary Would Have Chance To Recognize Weaknesses

Chapter 20

Time Marches on (Transitioning Off the Bench ... and Then Some)

"I always enjoyed the intellectual challenge inherent in presiding over complex litigation with experienced, at times, elite lawyers—the best at their craft."

IN AUGUST 2002, at the age of 54, I began thinking about life after the bench where I had spent the last 16 years. This tour made me eligible to "retire" or assume "senior status" when I would turn 60, some six years into the future. I was aware that Maryland judges were constitutionally mandated to retire at the age of 70, which, in judicial circles, was referred to as "constitutional senility."

The difference between a judge retiring and being approved for senior status is that if senior status is requested and approved by the highest court in the state, the senior judge can be recalled to sit and be compensated on a per diem basis for each day the judge works, based on the salary the judge earned in his or her last full-time position. This per diem compensation is paid in addition to the judge's pension. Both the pension and the per diem increase proportionately whenever the judiciary receives a pay raise.

Whether the judge is retired or on senior status, the judge's pension is two-thirds of whatever salary the judge received in his or her last full-time judicial position. Although a senior judge cannot engage in the practice of law and concurrently be recalled, he or she, by rule, can engage in private alternative dispute resolution (ADR) activities for pay and concurrently be recalled to sit as a judge, subject to strict ethical standards and disclosures. Significantly, this distinction does not exist without some controversy.

I decided that I certainly would not wait until I turned 70 to transition from the bench. My reasons were both personal and professional. During my judicial career, along with presiding over many, many cases, I accumulated significant administrative and management experience. I had been assigned total management responsibility for two of the trial courts that I served on. I had been Chief Judge of the orphans' court for two years and Administrative Judge of the district court for two of the three years I served on that court.

In addition, I was assigned management responsibility at one time or another during my 16 years on the circuit court for every division of that court except juvenile. I enjoyed judging, and I enjoyed the management of judicial personnel, staff, and clerks, as well as operations and systems.

As time marched on, however, I had become increasingly frustrated with what I perceived to be bureaucratic inertia and reluctance by the judiciary to recognize what I viewed as the changing legal culture and to adapt its institutions and operations to address the altered expectations of the citizens that we served. In addition, on a personal level, I found that the job of a circuit court judge was changing in a way that made it less fulfilling than it had been previously.

I always enjoyed the intellectual challenge inherent in presiding over complex litigation with experienced, at times, elite lawyers—the best at their craft. As the years passed, I found myself doing far less of that and more refereeing of disputes between self-represented litigants. That took a toll. While I recognized that my personal fulfillment was required to take a back seat to the need for increased access to justice, I was nevertheless driven to look elsewhere to keep my life interesting.

The various leadership positions I held while serving as a full-time circuit court judge allowed me to look at the judicial system more broadly and holistically. By January 2007, I had served as vice chair of the Maryland Business and Technology Case Management Program Task Force; chair of the judiciary's Statewide Business-Technology Case Management Committee; chair of the Circuit Court for Prince George's County Strategic Planning Committee; and co-chair of the Maryland State Bar Association Special Committee on the Management of Judicial Personnel.

Finally, I had been recognized as the architect of the Prince George's County Circuit Court drug court and the total restructuring of the operations and staff of the Prince George's County Circuit Court family division.

This "feeling" or mindset that I had accomplished all that I could as a full-time judge led to my decision to "*retire*" from the full-time bench.

PART SEVEN

Thriving as a Professional Mediator and Arbitrator

An Incarcerated Politician, a Thankful Mayor, and a Record-Setting Settlement

Chapter 21

The Rise of ADR

"I was able to grasp the intersection of the economic,
political, and legal dimensions of the disputes I was
hired to resolve perhaps quicker and easier than some
other neutrals. Lucky for me, my skillset was recog-
nized by market forces sooner than I expected."

THE PROFESSION OF private alternative dispute resolution, or ADR, began to emerge alongside the development of "problem-solving courts." These new institutions and occupations were the result of a subtle cultural change that began in the 1990s but became more evident toward the beginning of the 21st century.

This shift was precipitated by the recognition that the underlying causes of most disputes usually are more economic and psychological than legal or factual. Perhaps not surprisingly, this thought was met reluctantly and, in some cases, with resistance and controversy in the law offices of certain lawyers and the chambers of some judges.

Was this change a result of economics, including a severe recession (2007–2010), a generational shift in the litigant population, or was it a byproduct of all three branches of government's focus on providing increased access to justice? This shall remain a question to be explored some other time. What we know is that this change in society's expectations for its judicial institutions was not accompanied by a sophisticated understanding of the constitutional, statutory, and, most importantly, practical limitations of the judicial branch of government's ability to delve into disputes to the extent expected.

Nevertheless, the change was clearly the result of the hue and cry from all segments of society at the beginning of this century to reduce the costs of dispute resolution for litigation in both the short and the long term. That realization was accompanied by the further recognition that in order to reduce the costs, these disputes needed to be resolved in a manner that economically and efficiently addressed the cause so the dispute would not be repeated.

Public and private institutions, including law firms and courts, were compelled to dramatically change their business models and work processes to accommodate these enhanced expectations. This trend was no doubt accelerated by the Great Recession, which caused even the wealthier corporations, LLCs, and individual clients to conclude that they either could not or would not pay the skyrocketing cost of full-blown litigation.

As a result, corporate in-house counsel, law firms, and individuals began looking for cost-effective alternatives to full-blown "all the way through trial and appeal" litigation in order to remain economically viable. Courts began to incorporate ADR into the dispute resolution services they offered in order to remain relevant, lest they be replaced by private alternatives or, as feared by some, devolve into the lower level of an economically tiered civil justice system.

The evolution of private ADR and its increased utilization—including arbitration, neutral case evaluation, mediation, and conflict coaching—resulted from this cultural shift. The development of the ADR profession was accompanied by a proliferation of education and training programs of varying quality, along with discussion and debate within the State of Maryland.

As I transitioned off the full-time bench, consulting opportunities came my way—courtesy of my friend, retired North Carolina Chief Judge Ben Tennille, and the U.S. Departments of State and Commerce. They included missions to the beautiful city of Dubai to "consult" and instruct Iraqi and United Arab Emirates judges on how to preside over business litigation.

This was a very interesting and fulfilling experience that would not have been possible if I had remained on the bench full-time. I wrote about my Dubai experiences in Chapter 10 of my book *The Winding Road*. In addition to that adventure, I had the opportunity to consult on business courts, jury trials, and arbitrazh court administration in Russia through the Russian American Rule of Law Consortium (RA-ROLC). I traveled to Russia three times after being invited to join in this "labor of learning" by Maryland Court of Appeals Senior Judge Alan Wilner.

Finally, I accepted an invitation to accompany a small group of judges to travel and witness the work for peace, security, and justice at The Hague, which is described in *The Winding Road* in Chapter 11.

By the time I had decided to leave the full-time bench, one of my mentors, Judge Howard Chasanow, had established himself as a premier mediator. Among many others, John McCammon was establishing a formidable group of retired judges and senior practitioners in Virginia to be known as the McCammon Group; while JAMS had begun to establish a national and international presence and reputation.

THE MARYLAND BUSINESS AND TECHNOLOGY CASE MANAGEMENT PROGRAM

As ADR started to take off, the judiciary was belatedly recognizing a primarily economic and cultural, but also legal and political, reality. The courts' reaction was to form panels of potential mediators, particularly for family law cases. The courts also began to establish problem-solving courts and specialized case management dockets to meet the special needs of the parties, which, when distilled, usually could be defined as addressing not only the case but the underlying causes of the parties' disputes.

These problem-solving courts would then resolve these disputes or problems in a more holistic and timelier fashion designed to secure more rational, legally correct, and predictable dispositions.

The courts began to recognize that when handling business cases, an arbitrarily or unduly delayed resolution of a case or dispute could economically devastate one or both parties' ability to continue to operate. Similarly, a legally incorrect, impractical, or illogical ruling, particularly on a request for temporary restraining order or a preliminary injunction, could unfairly and irreparably leverage a business party's position so that it could not recover legally and—more importantly—financially and operationally.

For those reasons, among others, the Maryland Business and Technology Case Management Program was developed, and ADR was integrated into it as a means of timely meeting those special needs. This program became the most prominent among the problem-solving courts and the specialized case management dockets in Maryland.

MY ADR PRACTICE TAKES SHAPE

Because of my background and experience, I was able to grasp the intersection of the economic, political, and legal dimensions of the disputes I was hired to resolve perhaps quicker and easier than some other neutrals. Lucky for me, my skillset was recognized by market forces sooner than I expected.

My multifaceted experience and advanced training in ADR techniques have shaped the ADR services that I provide in a market concentrated on professional liability cases, business litigation, and disputes arising from political and governance issues—particularly police and corruption cases and construction litigation.

Since my retirement, and assumption of Senior Status, I have been hired to investigate and report on allegations of employment discrimination for various municipal and private corporations, including charges of nepotism.

I have mediated and arbitrated hundreds of cases over the last decade, the details of which cannot be disclosed because of confidentiality and ethical requirements that preclude their disclosure. These cases include the breakup of medical LLCs, law firms, and other professional entities. They also include cases of sexual harassment, wrongful termination of executives, and cases bordering on blackmail.

Among the personal injury and business divorce cases that came my way, there was an "emergency arbitration" of a dispute between a same-day lender and a retired NFL player who was a party in the class action suit resulting from head injuries he suffered during his playing days.

I have previously written about the "lessons learned" from these days, which began in January 2007 and continue today. Those "lessons learned" are described in Part Three of my book, *The Winding Road*, titled, "Dispute Resolution and Access to Justice."

Rather than "cases," a better word to describe the narratives of the mediations and arbitrations from which these lessons were learned would be "stories." And since I love to tell "stories," prepare to read some of my favorites over the next couple of chapters.[23]

---

[23] The confidentiality in many cases requires that even the names of the parties and their lawyers remain shielded.

Chapter 22

Corruption: Make It Go Away!

"My job as a mediator was apparent. The Baker administration did not want the 'corruption of Prince George's County' to be a topic of discussion in the media or in the community any longer than it already had been."

JACK JOHNSON, ALMOST from the time he was elected to his first term as a county executive for Prince George's County, had set up a corrupt county government where almost all services, particularly those associated with commercial development and construction, were illegally surcharged and had to be paid for through him, his campaign, or persons whom he appointed to run agencies of county government.

Prince George's County's reputation as a place where you had to "pay to play" was thereby reinforced, solidified, and, in fact, taken to a whole new level by Johnson.

Four years earlier, Rushern Baker had run to replace Johnson as a reformer who would restore honor and integrity to the operation of Prince George's County government. He ran again on the same platform, this time with Johnson precluded from running for re-election by term limits and by a criminal conviction that would ultimately land him in federal prison for eight years. This time Baker won.

The lawsuit I was privately hired to mediate was brought by a developer/builder and some of his financial backers who were rehabilitating a long-standing hotel to convert into a mixed commercial and residential building. In doing so, they were finding that every license, permit, and inspection required a payment to someone over and above the cost for the government service, and the project was held up until the fees were paid.

The defendants were The Prince George's County government, Jack Johnson individually (as a private citizen by this time, incarcerated in federal prison), and an assortment of past county officials and other prominent citizens who were accused of being part of a corrupt network that controlled the county. All of these allegations were set forth in a complaint filed in the Circuit Court for Prince George's County.

By the time I was hired as a private mediator, a number of the individual defendants had been dismissed from the case, including one who was accused of activities his attorney facetiously referred to as "lobbying malpractice," which he defined as paying a bribe to an official to take a certain action, but the official doesn't do what you bribed him to do. The trial judge ruled that "lobbying malpractice" was not a viable cause of action in the State of Maryland; therefore, the court would not enforce the "contract" or sanction as a tort[24] the defendant's failure to keep his promise.

My job as a mediator was apparent. The Baker administration did not want the "corruption of Prince George's County" to be a topic of discussion in the media or in the community any longer than it already had been. Thus, a global settlement (not only with the county, but with all the defendants, including Johnson) was necessary in this case. The case and the image of Prince George's County associated with it needed to be dismissed—never to grab attention again.

---

[24] Tort is defined as a wrongful act or an infringement of a right leading to civil legal liability.

Understanding that political reality, I pressed the attorney representing the county to involve the administration at its highest levels in order to determine and communicate the financial consideration they would be willing to pay to arrive at a global settlement. The plaintiff had heavily contributed to Baker's campaign and had held a press conference with him at the site of the construction project to emphasize the candidate's pledge to eliminate the corruption once and for all.

The plaintiff was not going to accept any amount of compensation less than everything the county could offer; he would also need to be convinced that the number the county would offer was coming from the elected county executive after conversation with his financial administrative and political people. This was not a case to be worked on by "risk management" personnel.

When my advice and counsel were finally accepted on the third day of mediation, the case was globally settled against all defendants for an amount I am not at liberty to disclose. Even the case against Johnson, individually, was dismissed. This accounts for why Baker, Johnson's political opponent, paid for Johnson's lawyer in this civil case. The entire case needed to disappear, including Johnson's part in it, for the political "new day" that the Baker administration wanted to project in the county.

Chapter 23

The Police Brutality Cases

"In this case, Prince George's County had much at stake as this case would cost it millions of dollars while further damaging its reputation. The chief of police had already lost his job."

I WAS HIRED as a private mediator to try to resolve law enforcement excessive force cases including wrongful death. The names of the victims in these cases were and are familiar in law enforcement, legal, and community circles—Calvo, Green, Espina, to name a few. Most preceded the spotlight on the Black Lives Matter movement. In addition, some did not directly involve Black lives.

LOCAL MAYOR TARGETED:
THE CHEYE M. CALVO CASE

The first of these cases, the Calvo case, involved Cheye Calvo, then–mayor of Berwyn Heights, Maryland, his family, and his beloved dogs who were killed as a result of the "mistake" of the Prince

George's County Police and Sheriff's Department. That mistake resulted from Prince George's law enforcement executing a no-knock search warrant" on the mayor's home, looking for drugs based on incorrect information, and needlessly killing the family pets in front of the family who were present to witness the raid. Law enforcement then refused to be held accountable administratively, even internally or civilly, in the Circuit Court for Prince George's County.

These events occurred while Jack Johnson was still county executive. In the immediate aftermath, the Johnson administration legally defended or, alternatively, minimized the action of his police department and the sheriff's department as simple "mistakes"; therefore, they were immune from liability.

However, by the time the actual mediation of the case occurred, an election had taken place and County Executive Rushern Baker was occupying that office on the fifth floor of the County Administration Building.

When I mediate a dispute with an emotional component, I have learned that I must listen to all members of the complaining family carefully, particularly the first time I talk to them in private caucus to fully understand their issues and the mindset that conditions their positions. The emotional issues may be more nuanced and complicated and may also vary among family members—even though they are together as plaintiffs. I could, and often did, end up mediating among family members.

I also realized the importance of who is in the room. In this case, I immediately knew that the wrong people were in the room representing Prince George's County and the sheriff's department. The assistant county attorney with limited authority and the county's "risk manager" clearly did not possess the negotiating skills, authority, or the awareness of the factors that would need to be weighed to settle this case.

I quickly concluded that they also were unsure of their job security and roles in this and other cases as they were both temporary holdovers from the previous Johnson administration.

For that reason, when they persisted in defending the actions of law enforcement in the Calvo case, I requested that the actual county attorney join us. When she did, she persisted in defending the indefensible, which led me to point out:

> *"Are you aware that there was an election and that the position you are taking is contrary to the position the current county executive took in his campaign?"*

I was not surprised by the hold-over county attorney's response that she had not spoken to Baker or Michael Erico, his acting chief administrative officer whom I knew. Once I reached out to open a conversation with Mayor Calvo and his family, their counsel, and Erico, we were able to work out an agreeable financial and nonmonetary settlement agreement.

The outcome satisfied Mayor Calvo's desire to have a voice in the effort to "reform" the practices that led to the county law enforcement actions (*otherwise known as mistakes*). Furthermore, the financial settlement reflected the seriousness and emotional trauma inflicted on Mayor Calvo's family, including the loss of two pets.

This was my first police case as a private mediator, which would establish my reputation as a professional who understood the complexity of the interrelated political, financial, and psychological issues that must be addressed to resolve cases involving law enforcement's interaction with the individuals and communities they serve and protect.

That reputation was confirmed by the gracious unsolicited note I received from Mayor Calvo after the case was over:

> *"I write to thank you for your efforts to bring about a settlement with the County ... There were times during our mediation, which I was prepared to walk out the door; and it was only through your patience and thoughtful facilitation that we remained on track. Please know how much we appreciate your assistance and service to us and the County."*

AN UNEXPLAINED HOMICIDE:
THE WILLIAM GREEN CASE

Years later, in the wake of the rise of the Black Lives Matter movement including, but not limited to, the deaths of George Floyd, Ronald Greene, Eric Garner, Breanna Taylor, Daunte Wright, and Jonathan Price, events unfolded that would lead to the mediation of the case of the *Estate of William Green v. Prince George's County, Maryland.*

On January 27, 2020, just after 7:00 pm, William Green was driving his car and accidentally struck three parked cars, a mailbox, and a tree. Michael Owen, Jr., a Prince George's County police corporal, and another Prince George's police officer, Corporal Ricci Villaflor, were dispatched to the scene. When they arrived, they found Green asleep behind the wheel of his car. The officers then woke Green and got him out of his car. Green was frisked for weapons and/or contraband. Following that, he was handcuffed behind his back.

Owen then walked Green to his police cruiser, placing him into the front seat of the vehicle with his hands still cuffed behind his back. Several minutes later, the sound of gunshots was heard by the other officers on the scene, as well as bystanders who witnessed the events unfolding.

Villaflor, not knowing where the shots were coming from, ran to Owen's police cruiser where Green had been placed. There, he discovered that Owen had discharged his police-issued Smith & Wesson 9mm Luger handgun at Green at point-blank range seven times, striking him six times in the torso.

Green was taken to United Medical Center where he was pronounced dead at 8:35 pm that evening. No weapons were found anywhere on the scene. Subsequent investigation revealed no evidence of any altercation between Owen and Green.

Within 24 hours, then–Chief of Police Hank Stawinski issued felony criminal charges against Corporal Owen for second-degree murder, manslaughter, involuntary manslaughter, first-degree assault, and use of a firearm in the commission of a crime of violence. After requesting bail three separate times and being denied by three different judges, Owen remained in jail in St. Mary's County, Maryland, for his own protection while he awaited his trial.

Accompanying his request for bail, Owen provided a written "use of force" statement authored at 10:40 pm, the same date as the shooting:

> *"While on duty, a suspect attempted to obtain my firearm. In fear of my life, I discharged my departmental handgun at the suspect."*

That "explanation" was viewed by three different judges and even by Chief Stawinski as factually impossible. Green was handcuffed behind his back. He physically could not have reached for, let alone accessed, a weapon while locked inside the police cruiser. Furthermore, Owen's handgun was tested for DNA after the shooting by the special investigation response team at least in part to provide any conceivable cover for Owen's version of the facts. Owen's DNA was recovered, yet no DNA of Green was found.

Apparently, Owen had yet another, very different, explanation for his actions, which he related to an acquaintance after the shooting. That acquaintance was interviewed by the Prince George's County Police Department. His version of events, which I will not dignify with a description here, was equally implausible for the same reason: Green was handcuffed behind his back and restrained in a police vehicle.

Neither Chief Stawinski nor Prince George's County Executive Angela Alsobrooks found Owen's "explanation" for his actions credible; they then issued this statement: "There is absolutely nothing that is acceptable about this incident." The Green family's lawyers contacted the county regarding the family's claim stemming from the actions of Owen and the Prince George's County Police Department.

Enter the law firm of Murphy, Falcon & Murphy. The firm was totally committed to the Green family and this case.

I was well aware of the firm, its history, and reputation, particularly that of William H. "Billy" Murphy, Jr., the founding partner, who was well known to me as a result of his multiple appearances before me when I served as a circuit court judge.

In addition, I had earlier become acquainted with his father, William H. Murphy, Sr., who had served as a Maryland District Court judge when I was Administrative Judge of the District Court for Prince George's County. Judge Murphy, Sr., and I shared an affinity for storytelling that I think carried over to his offspring. We also shared a similar sense of humor and an appreciation for superlative trial skills.

For that reason, I admired the trial advocacy skills of his son, who was as quick on his feet and prepared as any lawyer I'd witnessed in my 27 years on the bench. That said, I also noticed that Billy Murphy didn't then, and doesn't now, suffer fools very well. Neither do I, but I have always been able to hide it better than most, including Billy Murphy.

Although we had never met before this case, the firm's managing partner, Hassan Murphy's, excellent reputation preceded him. I could not help but admire and respect anyone who could "manage" his father and their law firm.

Attorney Malcolm Ruff did the work and did it well. I noticed that the Murphys made an effort to recognize Ruff's abilities and gave him credit where due.

I also had worked with the capable lawyers who would be representing Prince George's County in this case. Rhonda Weaver had worked with me in my capacity as mediator while serving in her previous positions as an assistant Prince George's County attorney and as the county attorney for Charles County. In fact, I had worked with her on a complex case involving multi-years of taxes on Charles County utilities and a power plant, which settled after months of intense mediation.

I had also worked and tried cases with Deputy Prince George's County Attorney Andrew Murray while in his previous positions as Prince George's County assistant state's attorney and assistant Anne Arundel County attorney. He was and is an experienced, competent litigator whom I greatly respect.

The plaintiffs, Brenda Foye Green (William's mother); Shelly Green (William's daughter); William Little (William's son), all suffered in a manner that can only be characterized as profound and traumatic. The plaintiffs' expert described Brenda Green as "severely depressed, unable to control her emotions and socially isolated." Shelly Green was diagnosed as suffering from "increased anxiety and panic attacks." Finally, William Little was diagnosed as suffering from "serious anger issues."

The cumulative cost of what could amount to a decade of treatment was estimated to be close to $1 million!

In this case, Prince George's County had much at stake as this case would cost it millions of dollars while further damaging its reputation.

The chief of police already had lost his job. Alsobrooks, the county executive, whose reputation was excellent, had to handle this case in a way that recognized the financial costs to the county, the legal reality, and the political ramifications of either a trial or settlement resulting in a multi-million-dollar payout on her short-term and long-term ambitions for the county and herself in this era of racial reconciliation.

In this atmosphere, we began the mediation in person at the Law Offices of Murphy, Falcon & Murphy on July 14, 2020, in the middle of the COVID-19 pandemic—properly masked and socially distanced. Present were the Murphys, Ruff, lawyers and staff of their firm, and the Green family. County Attorney Murray was present representing the county. His experience in such cases was extensive and known.

I suffered no illusion that this case could be resolved in this first session. My goal was to gain the trust of the parties, specifically the Green family, to lay the groundwork for subsequent discussions, and to determine clearly who the decision-makers were.

This was nobody's first rodeo. The Murphys's successful track record in cases involving police use of excessive force, including wrongful death, was well known.

The firm had most recently been in the news by representing the family of Freddie Gray, which resulted in a $6.4 million settlement. For that reason, I suspected that Prince George's County would initially view the Freddie Gray case as a template for this one. My experience told me that it would not be. The facts in this case were uniformly bad—worse than the Freddie Gray case and arguably as bad as or worse than the George Floyd case.

Predictably, the first day of mediation confirmed that my instincts were correct. We informally reached the $6.4 million settlement level, but we also clarified that it wouldn't resolve this case. After we adjourned, I knew that all the "lessons learned" in previous cases, some of which are described herein, would have to be applied in this case to get it resolved. That meant a series of Zoom conferences, telephone calls, and communications with counsel and with Alsobrooks, her attorneys, and administrative staff on the subject of the amount of the monetary settlement and the terms of the nonmonetary settlement.

I had known Alsobrooks since she was an assistant state's attorney and had served on her transition team when she was initially elected state's attorney for Prince George's County. In addition, I had predicted to numerous friends and colleagues that she and her friend, Tara Harrison, now–chief administrative officer of Prince George's County, would be "stars" in the Maryland firmament. The only question being in which universe would they "shine?" Alsobrooks's universe turned out to be the executive branch of government and politics.

My meeting with Alsobrooks and her attorneys and staff via Zoom was on July 29, 2020. At that meeting, I made it clear that the Murphys, as the family's representatives, would not give serious consideration to an offer unless they were satisfied that the offer was fair and reasonable and emanating from the highest level of county government. I was pretty sure such an offer would require eight figures—somewhere between $15 million and $25 million.

I also made it clear that in my view, the opinion of the Murphys was that there were substantial differences between the Freddie Gray case and this one, both in facts and value. Finally, I advised that the

Green family trusted me but only because the Murphys trusted me. I knew that the Murphys would only go to their clients once with what they believed was the county's final offer, and then only if it was clear that was all there was to offer. That decision had to be made by Alsobrooks. As a result of that meeting, she promised to make a decision.

Following that meeting, there was a communication to me from the Murphys that provided very damaging documentary evidence of the county's awareness of Owen's prior history of the use of excessive force through their own records. This evidence had the potential to dramatically expand the risk of a very large jury verdict if this case was tried before a jury in federal court.

Apparently, the police department knew about (or at least should have known about) Owen's history, but the county administration and the office of law did not. Alsobrooks was prompted to settle the case for $20 million. Upon my recommendation and the persuasive skills of Murphy, Falcon & Murphy, the Green family accepted the offer.

I was surprised to be requested by both parties and their counsel to participate in the press conference to jointly announce the settlement. It was hosted by Alsobrooks, the Green family, the Murphys, and Malcolm Ruff.

I agreed to participate after making sure the waiver of their rights to confidentiality was comprehensive and that they understood it was irrevocable. While answering questions from the press, I found myself accepting more than my fair share of the kudos.

The stark reality that a verdict by a predominately African American jury, who would have been keenly aware of the Prince George's Police Department's history and Owen's personal history, could have been considerably more than the $20 million.

Billy Murphy credited Alsobrooks for being a visionary by recognizing that the county and the country are in the middle of a racial reckoning and that this case truly gave meaning to the Black Lives Matter movement. I also believe that this case laid the groundwork nationally for the $27 million settlement of the George Floyd case.

Needless to say (but I will anyway), the settlement of this case was the most gratifying to me of all the cases I have mediated and arbitrated since I "retired" from the full-time bench.

I have received a few "thank you" messages as a judge, but I have received many more as a mediator. I have also received, in addition to my compensation, gifts including my most cherished remembrance for settling a dispute between two lobbying firms—a Trump-style, red baseball cap with the words "Make Lobbying Great Again."

It's what keeps me going, along with the kinds of cases described in the next section entitled "Comic Relief."

PART EIGHT

Comic Relief

Chapter 24

Jury Duty for the Judge, PTSD for the Defendant

"And then ... do you know what they did?"

THE CIRCUIT COURT for Prince George's County prided itself on having everyone, including its judges, report for jury duty. In each county of Maryland, citizens at least 18 years old who are registered voters and/or licensed drivers are randomly summoned to serve as jurors. I was summoned more than once while I was a judge, although I was never selected to serve on a jury.

I did, however, serendipitously expedite the administration of justice in at least one case for which I had been called to serve as a juror. The defendant had decided to rob a 7-Eleven store several months earlier. No doubt, he lacked the capacity for strategic thinking and picked the wrong store located on Route 301 in Bowie, Maryland.

As the robber displayed his gun while facing the clerk behind the counter and demanding the contents of the cash register, three customers witnessed it and even videoed the encounter. The cashier then pressed a button that set off an alert in the Prince George's

County Police Headquarters on Route 301, which summoned five officers to the location.

Within five minutes, those officers entered the store just in time to witness the defendant committing the crime. Subsequently, the defendant confessed, thus enhancing an already "slam dunk" case against him.

The assistant state's attorney assigned to prosecute the case recognized that the defendant, who had a substantial criminal record, had no defense. She therefore refused to plea bargain but offered to accept a plea to the most serious count of the indictment—robbery with a deadly weapon—and a sentencing recommendation based on the Maryland Sentencing Guidelines.

The defendant, seeing no reason to plead guilty if he wasn't guaranteed a break for doing so, insisted on exercising his right to a jury trial; that is, until it dawned on him that there was a judge on his jury panel.

After three requests by his attorney to have me disqualified as a juror "because he is a judge," the presiding judge refused, stating:

> *"I'm not going to do that—he took an oath to be fair."*

Jury questioning and selection continued until the process suddenly halted, a recess was announced, and the presiding judge, the court staff, the prosecutor, the defense attorney, and the defendant adjourned to another courtroom. My fellow jurors and I wondered what was going on.

Apparently, the stressed-out defendant, in an excited but resigned state of mind, recognized that his case was not looking good and his future bleak. He had whispered to his lawyer, Public Defender Dent Lynch:

> *"Jesus Christ, Mr. Lynch—three eyewitnesses, five cops, a video of me committing the crime, my dumbass confession, and now they put a motherfucking judge on my jury. I give up. They got me!"*

Dent Lynch, who is a friend of mine, later filled me in on what transpired. He and I then speculated that his client, while incarcerated for the crime he had committed, might've described his dilemma to his fellow inmates in this manner:

"And then ... do you know what they did?"

Chapter 25

Everyone Needs a Hero

*"Unfortunately, I could not save her from herself.
The plaintiff did not settle and the Circuit Court
for Prince George's County dismissed all her claims
as I had predicted."*

AS A MEDIATOR, I have to be able to recognize what's going on not only between the opposing parties and their lawyers, but also each party and their own lawyer. In one of my cases, my attention was directed to a lawyer who was representing an attractive woman who had unwisely and tragically listened to her then-husband. At her husband's request, she signed papers that pledged her personal share of their joint multi-million-dollar life savings and investments as collateral for one of her spouse's far too risky investments. The husband's investment predictably failed; all was lost.

The client then compounded her problems by doing the following:

- Hiring the wrong lawyer to rescue her from the results of her ill-advised decisions. The lawyer gave her bad advice by recommending futile, expensive, and foolish legal actions that were now drawing my criticism;

- Instructing her lawyer to sue two different lawyers and law firms for malpractice when neither had done anything that bordered on malpractice;

- Hiring me to mediate between her and these law firms that were represented by very competent counsel who knew, as did I, that their clients were not the cause of her problems.

I explained to the woman and her lawyer that a court was likely to dismiss both of her separate cases against these law firms summarily, but that if we moved quickly, I could probably get these two much-respected law firms to resolve her claims by paying her a combined low six figure "nuisance-value" settlement.

These firms, in my opinion, could have been persuaded to settle her claims for considerably more than what her claims were worth simply to avoid the publicity associated with being sued. I then pointed out to her and her lawyer once more that the alternative was probably outright dismissal of all claims and the further expense of paying for her own lawyer.

The plaintiff then told me that she had not read the documents she signed and that she was dyslexic. My response, which demonstrated my basic grasp of both law and logic, was to point out that it is well-settled law that signing something without reading it is not a defense to a claim stemming from the contract that is signed. Furthermore, I added, "Being dyslexic doesn't affect the case if you didn't read the document to begin with."

At that point, the woman's counsel looked me in the eye, pointed to his very attractive client, and said:

Counsel: *"Judge, do you see her?"*

Judge Platt: *"I do."*

Counsel: *"I may have to litigate this case to prove there are still heroes in this world. Some women still need to know that there are heroes who can save them."*

Judge Platt: *"Any chance that I could be her hero and save her?"*

Unfortunately, I could not save her from herself. The plaintiff did not settle, and the Circuit Court for Montgomery County dismissed all her claims as I had predicted. Furthermore, in a touch of irony, the woman's attorney who wanted to be her "hero" ended up suing her to collect his fee.

Chapter 26

Contempt—An Elusive Concept

Assistant State's Attorney: "Your Honor, I hereby request you hold Mr. Murphy (attorney William H. Murphy, Jr.) in contempt."

Judge Platt: "For what?"

Assistant State's Attorney: "He called me a motherfucker!"

Judge Platt: "Where did this take place?"

Assistant State's Attorney: "In the hall during your last recess."

Judge Platt: "Denied—no jurisdiction."

Chapter 27

The Wizard of Oz Effect in Mediation

"Sure, but I don't want you to go back to Texas without knowing why we're okay."

I MEDIATED A high-profile civil case in which an off-duty police officer moonlighting as a security guard for a property management company in one of the "projects" the company managed allegedly murdered one of the tenants for the "crime" of trash-talking him. The liability insurance company for the property management company hired one of its most competent outside attorneys and assigned the claim to one of its senior claims representatives whose base of operations was in the "Great State of Texas."

The first day of mediation did not go well; we made very little progress because the Texas-based claims representative was rejecting my description (based on substantial experience) of how the case would proceed and be managed by the judge in the Circuit Court for Prince George's County, and how a jury would react to the competing narratives about the events leading up to the death of the tenant.

In rejecting my evaluation of the case, the claims representative repeatedly lectured me and his counsel about the manner in which this case would be handled in Texas. At the end of the first day of mediation, the claims representative announced to us that he be-lieved:

> *"This case will not settle. If it doesn't, it will be because of Judge Platt and the opinions about the case he has expressed."*

I agreed with him on his first point and acknowledged that he was entitled to his opinion about the second point. I also assumed that we were done.

About two weeks later, the scheduled three-week trial of the case began. On the fourth day of the trial, I received a call from the property management company's legal counsel inquiring if I could "come back." I pointed out that it would be an "understatement" to say that the claims representative was "unhappy with me."

Counsel responded that the claims representative had changed his mind about me and reevaluated his position on the case, as everything I had predicted had either occurred or was now occurring. I then mentioned that the presiding judge would certainly not recess the trial so that we could further mediate. Counsel then requested that we reconvene on the upcoming weekend. I agreed to meet if all parties and counsel agreed, which they did.

We reconvened on the following Sunday. After 4½ hours of further mediation, the part of the case that involved the claim against the property management company settled. The settlement was approximately $1 million more than it could have been three weeks earlier on account of what I had previously described to the claims representative as a "risk" had now become the reality.

After our work was finished, the Texas-based claims representative attempted to use his Texas charm (Ted Cruz-style) to explain, without being asked, his earlier behavior and comments. After a brief attempt, he looked at me and inquired, "Are we okay?"

My response was, "Sure, but I don't want you to go back to Texas without knowing why we're okay." I added:

> *"When you were incessantly lecturing me on how this case would be handled in Texas, 'because I'm a smart guy,' I imme-*

diately grasped that the information you were providing had nothing to do with anything that mattered. That said, I'll show my advancing age by admitting that the only thing that I was thinking while you were talking about how this case would be handled in Texas was that scene from The Wizard of Oz in which Dorothy and her dog, Toto, are whisked out of Kansas and land in Oz. Dorothy then turns to her pet and says, 'Toto, I don't think we're in Kansas anymore.'

"I gather you now agree with me that Prince George's County, Maryland, is not like Texas; just like Kansas was not like Oz. I'm sorry it cost you and your company an extra $1 million to find that out."

Chapter 28

Strippers versus Strip Club
In the Mood?

*"I would anticipate possible enforcement and interpre-
tation issues if a violation of the resolution of the 'hostile workplace' complaint is ever necessary."*

PERHAPS THE EASIEST and yet the most difficult "settlement" I
ever mediated was when an "attendant" at a "spa" (actually a mas-
sage parlor licensed as a "health club") brought suit in the Circuit
Court for Prince George's County. The "attendant" complained that
the "spa" and its owners, a female and her male significant other, had
violated federal and Maryland wage and hour statutes by paying her
less than those laws required.

At issue, among other things, were the records and the calculations of "tips" for "extra services" introduced into the mediation of
the case and the settlement.

The principal issues of the case surprisingly settled quickly. Then I
inquired of the plaintiff and her attorney what amount of money they
thought the "spa" owed her. The plaintiff responded that she be-

lieved her employer owed her around $200,000, but that she could only prove $20,000. It didn't take a rocket scientist to figure out why.

I then made the mistake of inquiring into "any other issues" to look at since we had time left to do so.

Plaintiff: "I believe the owner and management of the health club were running a hostile workplace."

Judge Platt: "And where did you hear that phrase?"

Plaintiff: "My lawyer explained the term to me."

Judge Platt: "What convinced you and your lawyer that the owner and manager were operating a hostile workplace?"

Plaintiff: "The owner required me to participate in a ménage à trois with her and her significant other as a condition of employment."

Judge Platt: "Do you still want to work there?"

Plaintiff: "Oh, yeah—I don't mind doing that if I am in the mood."

Being a highly trained, experienced, and skilled mediator, I immediately recognized the potential for a resolution of this "quality of life issue" and suggested that this "further agreement" be set forth in the final settlement agreement and final releases.

That said, I would anticipate possible enforcement and interpretation issues if a violation of the resolution of the "hostile workplace" complaint is ever necessary. Until then, I will be left wondering how the Supreme Court of Maryland[25] would define "in the mood" as anything other than an old song.

---

[25] The Maryland Court of Appeals, the highest appellate court in Maryland, was renamed the Supreme Court of Maryland effective January 2023.

Chapter 29

The Tiki Bar Grand Opening
Be Careful What You Ask For – You Might Get It – Then What?

"I asked you what you wanted me to do. You told me and I did it. You won! Congratulations!"

EVERY YEAR IN the spring, "Grand Opening Weekend" occurs in Solomon's Island, Maryland, a resort community on the water in Southern Maryland (Calvert County). The upside of the Grand Opening is that spirits, usually in paper cups, flow freely, and the seafood is tasty and plentiful.

The downside is that for residents who live on the streets adjacent to the main drag, this celebration is noisy and spreads rapidly beyond the bars and restaurants that derive huge profits from it.

In turn, those neighbors complain to the Calvert County government and to the businesses whose opening weekend events and commercial activities are disturbing their peaceful neighborhoods. When the response or lack thereof is inadequate, the perception in Solomon's Island and Calvert County (where everybody knows everyone) is that the authorities are "looking away" at the behest of the

Tiki Bar and other similarly situated bars and restaurants that greatly profit from the weekend activities.

This perception has lingered from year to year, long enough to become a full-fledged, locally-based conspiracy theory. In turn, the conspiracy theory stimulated a level of frustration that motivated the neighboring homeowners to hire an out-of-county lawyer. The lawyer filed and financed a lawsuit against almost every institution and official of Calvert County government, as well as the Tiki Bar.

In Calvert County, as a practical matter, everyone knows everyone. That includes the Calvert County judges who, in those days, regularly recused themselves in these cases because of their relationships with many of the parties and their attorneys. For that reason, an "out-of-county judge" had to be assigned to the case. That judge was me.

Calvert County's Southern Maryland charm and civility remained intact each of the three years I traveled to Prince Frederick to hear the same case. That case, in a nutshell, alleged the conspiracy described above. The defense was the testimony of each elected and appointed official that no conspiracy existed and they were doing their jobs.

No direct evidence supported the articulated suspicions of the plaintiffs that the elected and appointed officials were "looking away" and conspiring to allow prohibited activities such as possession of open alcoholic beverage containers, loud and disorderly conduct, and public drunkenness, as well as the use of drugs.

While anecdotal circumstantial evidence surfaced every year indicating that some of these legally prohibited activities and behavior were occurring, it was not on a massive scale.

At the end of the case's first year, upon hearing the closing arguments of plaintiff's counsel and the County officials' attorney, I commented on the evidence or lack thereof. My comments were followed by this exchange:

Judge Platt: "It's not clear to me what it is you want me to do."

Plaintiff's Counsel: "Your Honor, we want you to order the Governmental Defendants to do their jobs and enforce the law and to order the Tiki Bar and the other commercial defendants to comply with the law."

Judge Platt: "No problem! So ordered!"

Plaintiff's Counsel: "I'm afraid it's not that simple, Judge."

Judge Platt: "Sure it is ... I asked you what you wanted me to do. You told me and I did it. You won! Congratulations!"

I then made further general remarks to the effect that the plaintiffs have a right to live quietly and peaceably in their homes and neighborhoods.

Apparently, all the defendants took my remarks seriously enough to quiet down for the rest of the Grand Opening Weekend. The local press noted the compliance with headlines:

"OUT-OF-COUNTY JUDGE'S WARNINGS HEEDED"

Proof that words matter. Here they did, and they were enough!

Chapter 30

ATTENTION, Shoppers!

"I just reviewed the applicable Maryland Rules and do not see any exception to their application for individuals who, when they speak, markets move."

AS FAR AS I know, I am the only judge to ever be sued in an original action in the highest court in Maryland, the Court of Appeals, now renamed the Supreme Court of Maryland. The case arose as a result of an order I issued in a case assigned to me.

CRYSTAL DENEEN BLAND V. SEARS ROEBUCK AND COMPANY

Crystal Daneen Bland had alleged that she had been sexually assaulted while visiting her parents' residence. She accused an employee of Flagship Cleaning Services who was hired to perform carpet cleaning services as an "independent" subcontractor of Sears. Sears admitted Flagship was the company's licensee, but every corporate representative and employee deposed disclaimed any knowledge of the circumstances that led Sears to hire Flagship and its employee, who, by this time, was in prison for this offense.

Arthur C. Martinez, chief executive officer and chairman of the board of Sears Roebuck and Company, was required to submit to a deposition in connection with the Bland case. The purpose of plaintiff's counsel seeking to depose Martinez was not to find out what he knew or what involvement he had, but rather to show that Martinez and Sears were stonewalling about any knowledge its corporate management had about related issues, such as negligent hiring and negligent supervision.

Absent the existence and availability of a more informed corporate representative, I, therefore, had no trouble ordering Martinez to submit to a three-question deposition in his Chicago corporate office with plaintiff's counsel's consent.

The Chicago lawyers representing both Martinez and Sears, along with local Maryland counsel, argued against the deposition stating, among other things, that this 10-minute, three-question deposition would be "unduly burdensome" because of Martinez's stature and busy schedule. To emphasize Martinez's great annoyance with my ruling, his counsel chose to point out at a hearing: "When Arthur Martinez speaks, markets move!"

Upon hearing that statement, I pulled out my red *Maryland Rules of Procedure* and remarked, "I just reviewed the applicable Maryland Rules and do not see any exception to their application for individuals who, when they speak, markets move."

SEARS ROEBUCK AND COMPANY V. STEVEN I. PLATT, ASSOCIATE JUDGE, CIRCUIT COURT FOR PRINCE GEORGE'S COUNTY

I was informed about the complaint filed against me by plaintiff's counsel and by Assistant Attorney General Julia Freit, who accepted service of process on my behalf. I then wagered as to how long it would take for the case to be dismissed for, among other reasons, lack of jurisdiction. It took less than 15 days!

By sheer coincidence, however, my friend for 40 years and then-neighbor, Glenn T. Harrell, Jr., a Maryland Court of Appeals judge, called me the day I found out about the lawsuit to ask for a ride home since his car was in the shop. I could not resist "informing" him of the pendency of the "case of first impression" in his court in which I was a party.

I expressed faux caution and concern about being accused of attempting to ex-parte[27] him about my case if I were to give him a ride home. His only response was, "Steve, you will be absolutely amazed at what will happen in your case if you *don't* give me a ride home!"

My work certainly has had moments of mirth and merriment even when involving serious cases.

---

[27] *Merriam Webster Dictionary* defines ex parte as something done with respect to or in the interests of one side only or of an interested outside party.

Conclusion

Older & Wiser

"These positions are taken by people who either never had or have lost their sense of humor and any semblance of humanity."

THIS BOOK IS titled *Lessons Lived and Learned: My Life On and Off the Bench* for a very specific reason. It describes the thoughts, opinions, and, dare I say, personal, cultural, and political analytics derived from my life's journey through the worlds of law, economics, and politics.

These "Lessons Learned" are presented in the context of a deep sense of humility developed over a period of time—from my ascendant teenage years, self-centered twenties, and even thirties and forties when I was focused on climbing the perceived mountain of outward success and professional achievement that ultimately led to a successful law practice and three judgeships.

That road briefly descended in my fifties to a disquieting personal valley of midlife divorce and doubt for a period of time. That time was comparatively brief, although it resulted in an intense learning experience and a much greater appreciation for the true meaning of life and the value of the love of my children, grandchildren, friends, and family—even my ex-wife.

Later, in my sixties and now in my seventies, I am convinced that I am both older and wiser, very aware of the research by, among others, Marc Freedman, chief executive at Encore.org and author of *How to Live Forever: The Enduring Power of Connecting the Generations.* Marc Freedman's work documents that "there is a U-bend of happiness in life—on average, we're upbeat early on; then hit the skids in midlife before growing happier later."

That midlife skid is further explained by Jonathan Rauch's writing, which adds that in our fifties, we can see the deficiencies of the first half of life, but haven't figured out the second half's imperatives, even though as Stanford psychologist Laura Carstensen explains:

> *"We realize that there are fewer years ahead than behind. This realization drives us to seek the deeper connections than we had previously with those we care about."*

In this book and in others I have authored, I hope the older and wiser Steven Platt has been able to relate the lessons of his life's journey with the two big "Hs": humility and humor.

Australian-born writer Clive James wrote:

> *"A sense of humor is just common-sense dancing—Those who lack humor are without judgement and should be trusted with nothing."*

I agree!

Finally, and if there is an ultimate message that I hope those who read all my books will take from them, most of the narratives in this book are about the people, institutions, relationships, commitments, and trust that I and others have relied on during our lifetimes. Particularly now, many of them sometimes appear to be failing and under attack.

They should be cherished, defended, and reinforced with all their complexity intact. Arthur Brooks, former president of the American

Enterprise Institute and author of *Love Your Enemies: How Decent People Can Save America from the Culture of Contempt*, wrote that our problem in America is *not* as widely believed to be incivility or intolerance.

Rather, it is described as "motive attribution asymmetry," which, according to a 2014 article in *The Proceedings of the National Academy of Sciences*, is the "assumption that your ideology is based on love and your opponent's is based on hate."

The researchers found that the average Republican and the average Democrat suffer from a level of motive attribution asymmetry comparable to that which exists between Palestinians and Israelis. That is, each side thinks it is driven by benevolence while the other is evil and motivated by hatred and, therefore, an enemy with whom one cannot negotiate or compromise.

These positions are taken by people who either never had or have lost their sense of humor and any semblance of humanity. They need to either get them back or be replaced by people whose personal transformation has evolved to the extent that they can lead the necessary social transformation.

That evolution, to a certain extent, as columnist David Brooks pointed out, is a product of age—the stage of life when one has reached his or her sixties and is mature enough to recognize that contempt is, in the words of philosopher Arthur Schopenhauer, "the unsullied conviction of worthlessness of another" and is "a noxious brew of anger and disgust."

I believe this book reflects that I am both older and wiser. If that means my words can help rescue our relationships and institutions, my purpose will have been served.

A Letter to My Grandchildren

"As our circumstances are new, we must think anew,
and act anew."

DEAR DYLAN, BENJAMIN, AND CHARLIE,

I am writing this final and most important chapter in this book for you, and since you are reading it, it must be in your hands. It's Monday, June 28, 2021. The July 4 holiday is approaching. I am 74 years old and counting, although not out loud.

Until about two years ago, I had no thought of writing a book about my life or anything else. But as you guys came into my life—Dylan on December 28, 2016, Ben and Charlie on May 17, 2019—and I watched you grow and develop your own personalities, I couldn't help but recall how little time my dad, Nathan (who passed away when he was 70—younger than I am now), had to spend with his grandchildren—my son, Jason, only nine years (Ben and Charlie's dad) and my daughter, Sarah, only six years (Dylan's mom); and how little they would ultimately be able to know and remember about him.

I then began to think about writing to you, like I am today, hopefully to help you remember me when I am long gone.

That's kind of selfish, I know! But I started thinking I've had an interesting life, and I believe I've, at times, done important work; I want my grandsons to know about it and remember me, the life I have led, and the work I have done.

That's when the idea of a book, a memoir, first occurred to me. I followed up those thoughts with conversations with my family: your parents, Jason and Sarah, and their spouses, Anne and Kevin; my Significant Other, Francie Glendening; your grandmother; and now my good and special friend, Patti. All of them encouraged me beyond my expectations.

I would have asked you guys what you thought, but I figured you'd probably want to wait a few years and read the reviews first.

After that, I had further conversations with my well-regarded publisher and editor, Tatia Gordon-Troy (Ramses House Publishing LLC) and my writing coach, Dr. Marilyn Smith, as well as my friend and Administrative Assistant, Penny Simpson. They encouraged me even further to the point that as I pen this final chapter, I am beginning to believe that my story to my grandsons may be of interest to others as well. We'll see.

Nevertheless, this book, the stories in it, and this letter are directed to you, Dylan, Ben, and Charlie. If anyone else is interested, that's great; but here's what I want to tell you.

I've received lots of awards and recognition over my adult life. Much of it was unexpected and probably undeserved. As Isaiah Berlin, the British historian and philosopher, said when receiving similar recognition:

> *"I have been overestimated all my life. I will not pretend that this has been a source of grave distress. As someone once said to me—'It is much nicer to receive more than one's due than one's due and I will not deceive myself by denying it.'"*

With that said, the thing I treasure the most was given to me by my former courtroom clerk and friend of more than 25 years, Barbara Patterson, on the occasion of my "retirement" from the full-time bench.

It was not an award or even a gesture of recognition for something I had done. That engraved plaque defined our "True Friendship" by saying:

> *"True friendship only needs a few key ingredients: undying loyalty, unmatched understanding, an unsurpassed trust, deep and soulful secrets and endless sharing. These ingredients, mixed with personality and a sense of humor can make a friendship last a lifetime.*
>
> *"This is just a thank you, my friend, for all the wonderful and colorful special ingredients you've brought to my life!*
>
> *"If I had one gift that I could give you, my friend, it would be the ability to see yourself as others see you, because only then would you know how extremely special you are."*
>
> *Barbara Patterson, March 2007*

Dylan, Ben, and Charlie, I have had great friends. Some are acknowledged in the front of this book and in the stories that I have told. I chose them, but more importantly, for which I am both humbled and proud, they chose me. That's really important!

This book tells the important parts of the story of my life and some of the lessons learned from it. Other books I have written are:

- *Black Robe Fever: The Role of the Judge in American Society;*

- *Of Politics and Economics: The School of Hard Knocks and Gentle Persuasion;* and

- *The Winding Road: Criminal Courts, Civil Matters, and the Ongoing Quest for Access to Justice.*

All of which set forth the "lessons learned" during my life in much greater detail.

Together, these books are my attempt to tell you, my grandsons, and anyone else who may be interested, how I saw myself; and to the extent possible, shape how you remember me when I am gone to wherever I will go when I am no longer with you. I hope you will find that I led a worthwhile life and that I enjoyed living it.

Finally, I am going to use this last chance to leave you with advice, even though you didn't ask for it. Hopefully, these thoughts will stay with you longer than our last conversation. These "lessons," which I have learned from mentors and experience, have served me well in my life. "Give them the weight you think they deserve." The most important is:

- ☐ **Love and support your family and close friends unconditionally.** Don't try to control or even limit how they live their lives and what they try to do with those lives. Their lives belong to them, not to you.

- ☐ **Don't compare them to you and your way of life or to each other.** What may be right for you might not be right for them. What might be right for one friend may not be right for another.

- ☐ **If they want your advice, they will ask for it.** However, when they do ask for your advice and help, provide it freely, honestly, and unconditionally.

- ☐ The one exception to the second piece of advice, which is not to provide unsolicited advice unless requested, is when you believe deeply that your family member or close friend is making a very serious quality-of-life decision that is a grave mistake and will adversely affect not only them but their loved ones and offspring. At that point, you owe it to your family member or close friend to attempt to intercede for their own good.

I will now immediately and for posterity disregard my own advice to you and provide further unsolicited advice in the form of the most impressive "pearls of wisdom" that I have received from my mentors and others:

1. As per John Casteen, III, former president of my alma mater, the University of Virginia:

   ☐ **"Don't sweat the small stuff"**—seek the company of those with vision, ambition, and worth.

   ☐ **Choose mentors and friends** on the basis of genuine human worth, not title, birth-wealth, or appearance.

2. As per Oliver Goldsmith:

   ☐ "People seldom improve when they have no other model but themselves to copy after." **Accept help and support in your life.** You are lucky to have it.

3. There is nothing wrong or nothing to feel guilty about for weighing how a decision you make will affect you personally, and if you are in politics, politically (particularly in a democracy). If you are a public official in any branch of government or a public figure, you are in politics.

4. There is nothing wrong with manipulation if it's for a good purpose and doesn't hurt anyone or any institution that you care about.

5. Doing a good job is generally good politics.

6. Keep the events and people in your life positive whenever possible.

7. Don't tilt at windmills. Meaning—don't work on or worry about things you can't control. There are too many things in this world that you can do to waste time on things you can't do.

8. Stories are fun to hear, and storytellers are fun to be around. You can learn a lot from both if you listen closely and can laugh at the story, the storyteller, and yourself.

9. Carefully select your conflicts, both personal and political, as well as the battles that you fight.

10. Before voicing an opinion about a person or an idea, ask yourself:

☐ Will it matter? If so, to whom and in what way?

☐ Does voicing an opinion risk adversely affecting a valuable relationship?

☐ How important is the relationship(s) *versus* how important is it to voice the opinion?

☐ Personal criticism should have a purpose other than making a point, particularly if the point has previously been made and nothing positive will result from repeating it.

☐ As per *Washington Post* op-ed columnist Kathleen Parker's father: "Opinions are fine, but it is good to hold those opinions with less than total certainty, it is much healthier." In other words, "Be slow to know."

11. Don't judge people or situations too quickly!

☐ Recognize that all of us human beings and most situations are a lot more complicated than either our admirers or detractors would like to believe.

☐ Don't demonize people that you disagree with or that you simply don't like. There is a little good in even the worst of us and the best of us have at least a little selfish streak.

12. Don't habitually try to escape from reality or be intimidated by complexity. It is all around us and is a challenge, not a burden. Address it directly. It is necessary if you are to enjoy life and accomplish your goals.

As per the late business executive and civil rights activist, Vernon Jordan:

> *"Each of us has to decide in our everyday lives how much verbal nonsense we will tolerate and from whom."*

From retiring UMBC President Freeman Hrabowski, quoting Chinese philosopher Lao Tzu:

> *"Watch your thoughts, they become your words. Watch your words, they become your actions. Watch your actions, they become your habits. Watch your habits, they become your character, and it becomes your destiny."*

From Charlie Platt, my grandfather, responding to a question from his great granddaughter, Sarah, who interviewed him when he was 102 years old:

Sarah: "What is the secret of your success and longevity?"

Charlie: "No secret. Life changes. When it does, you have to change with it. No choice. If you don't, you will fail at whatever you are trying to do. Always help the people who helped you."

Finally, Dylan, Benjamin, and Charlie, as I write this, I can't help but note that for the first time in my 75 years, I have actually heard and listened to some friends, whom I respect, talk about whether it is wise to bring children into the world today.

The country is divided, and, at times, politics seem to drive us in a direction and manner that it shouldn't, but not everyone is so afflicted. We should not, *you* should not, give up hope.

I didn't, and, boy, am I glad I didn't because you guys came into my world while I was still able to give you hugs and watch you grow.

I am also comforted by my faith and confidence that my grandsons, even in a changing world, will continually, individually strive to make not only themselves, but the world, a better place than it was when they came into it.

Love,
Gramps

Appendices

Resolution of the Maryland Judicial Conference Honoring Steven I. Platt

MARYLAND JUDICIAL CONFERENCE

Administrative Office of the Courts
Maryland Judicial Center
580 Taylor Avenue
Annapolis, Maryland 21401

August 6, 2008

Hon. Steven I. Platt

Dear Judge Platt:

It is a privilege to forward to you the Resolution in your honor adopted by the Maryland Judicial Conference on June 13, 2007. With it comes warm regards and good wishes from all members of the Conference.

With warm regards, I am

Sincerely,

Roxanne P. McKagan
Manager, Administrative Services

RPM/peg
Enclosure

(410) 260-1400
TTY Users: 1-800-735-2258

Maryland
Judiciary

MARYLAND JUDICIAL CONFERENCE

Administrative Office of the Courts
Maryland Judicial Center
580 Taylor Avenue
Annapolis, Maryland 21401

RESOLUTION OF THE

MARYLAND JUDICIAL CONFERENCE

HONORING

THE HONORABLE STEVEN I. PLATT

In January, 2007, an event occurred that affected all who work and practice in the Prince George's County Courthouse: The Honorable Steven I. Platt retired from the Circuit Court.

A daily fixture in the courthouse for over 20 years, his retirement was deeply regretted by all who worked with him.

Known equally for his wonderful demeanor and legal acumen, an assignment to his courtroom was relished by lawyers and litigants alike.

Judge Platt was prominently mentioned in the September, 1996, edition of the Washingtonian. He was listed No. 6 in an article called "Best of the Bench."

Judge Platt's lists of accomplishments are too many to include in this Resolution.

(410) 260-1400
TTY Users: 1-800-735-2258

MARYLAND
JUDICIARY

Born in Woodstock, Virginia on January 1, 1947, Judge Platt received his B.A. in Government and Public Administration from the University of Virginia in 1969 and his Juris Doctorate from American University Washington College of Law in 1973.

His earliest achievements include working as law clerk to the Chief Judge of the 7th Circuit, Ernest A. Loveless, Jr., as an administrative assistant to Steny Hoyer and as Chair of the Prince George's County Human Relations Commission.

His judicial career began as an Associate Judge of the Orphan's Court for Prince George's County in 1978. In 1985 he was named Chief Judge of that Court and remained in that position until he was appointed as an Associate Judge of the District Court. In 1988 he was named Administrative Judge for that Court.

In 1990 he became an Associate Judge of the Circuit Court, a position he held until his retirement in 2007. Judge Platt was a leader in the court. He was named by the Administrative Judge as Coordinating Judge for Criminal and Family Courts and Chair of the Strategic Planning Committee.

Among the many awards and recognitions he received are Distinguished Service to the Judiciary Award presented by the Philippine Lawyer's Association of Metropolitan Washington, DC; Conflict Resolution Award from the National Conference of Christians and Jews; the Distinguished Alumnus Award Washington College of Law, the American University; and the Maryland Leadership in Law Award and Innovator of the year award from the Daily Record.

Judge Platt was actively involved in many legal organizations, including President of the Prince George's County Bar Association, and made each organization better because of his participation.

WHEREAS, it is the desire of the Conference to express its appreciation and gratitude, and to recognize Judge Platt's years of service on the bench; and

BE IT HEREBY RESOLVED, that the Maryland Judicial Conference acknowledges its respect for Judge Platt's many years of faithful service to the public and in particular, his contribution as a jurist in the finest Maryland tradition; and.

BE IT FURTHER RESOLVED, that the resolution be made a permanent part of the record of the Maryland Judicial Conference and a copy hereof be delivered to Judge Platt.

ADOPTED unanimously by the Maryland Judicial Conference this 13th day of June, 2007.

Frank Broccolina
Executive Secretary

Remarks of Judge Steven I. Platt
Retirement Celebration
(March 7, 2007)

RETIREMENT CELEBRATION
MARCH 7, 2007
UMD ALUMNI CENTER

First of all, let me thank each of you for simply being here. Each one of you, as well as some people who wanted to be here but couldn't, have been a part of my professional and personal life and for that I am so very grateful. I tried to greet each of you individually thought the evening but I didn't completely succeed. But I can't help but look out and think of how I have drawn strength from the confidence and faith each of you have shown in me.

I have been very lucky in my life. Not too many people can look back and say, as I can tonight, that I have no regrets about the course I took personally or professionally. Indeed I am reminded of what Winston Churchill wrote to his mother, Jennie Jerome, from India "...I have had faith in my star- that I am intended to do something in the world. If I am mistaken, what does it matter? My life has been a pleasant one..."

Let me briefly acknowledge those that have been and are a major presence in my life. My two adult children, Jason and Sarah. Their love has sustained me and will continue to do so. And I am still learning from them about the world as it unfolds before my eyes. The woman who came into my life almost five years ago, Francie Glendening. She has made my life more interesting and continues to teach me to smell the roses- except when I'm driving when she insists "Focus on the Road". An unknown philosopher who I am sure Francie would say was a woman, said "Romance is the appreciation of two people who are celebrating the fact that they love each other". We're still romancing.

I was lucky I have Patti Platt with me for over 25 years and we were both lucky to have been blessed with our two children. In addition, we worked together professionally when I was Administrative Judge and she was the Administrative Clerk under the late Chief Judge Robert F. Sweeney whose friendship and mentorship of me, will forever be treasured. I also want to introduce my brother, Howard, who traveled all the way from his home in North Carolina to be here with me tonight on this occasion. He is a Sports Director for a radio station and prognosticator. There are also rumors about his administration of football pools. Those attorneys, who have experience defending gambling cases, please leave you card with him before you leave.

Finally, I want to thank my Boss in the Courtroom for 15 years, Barbara Patterson, and my support, my Bailiffs, Bill Wiggs and Bill Watson. We had fun! And our days were interesting. My secretary for seven years is here, Sara Baldwin. She enabled me to do much of what you're heard about tonight. Before her was Martha Folea whose quiet dignity helped me in the first 9 years of my stay on the Circuit Court.

My Clerks, who hosted this event, all of whom made me look good and wrote much of what I got credit for. I particularly want to thank Mike Winkelman who not only broke iron ceiling in my chambers but also chaired this event, Tara Lehner who helped manage it and Connie Lynch who helped out with the arrangements and the evening.

Kathy Le Marck took care of my last year in courtroom and Terri Burton is taking care of me in my new professional life as a Mediator, Arbitrator, Consultant and Adjunct Professor. Jennifer Gallagher is doing a great job staffing my Recalled Judge activities. Her greatest accomplishment however is getting my friend, Judge Casula, here.

The speakers tonight don't need any kudos from me. Judge Harrell, my friend and neighbor whose influence is felt not only on the Court of Appeals but more importantly in our Homeowners Association, Judge Missouri (or Judge Leasure), Tim Maloney, whose friendship I greatly value and whose professional and political skills I admire. Each has accomplished a great deal in their own careers which is well known. Thank you for being willing to say what you said.

To all my colleagues, the Judges, Administrators and Clerks on all the Courts on which I served, you confidence and your cooperative spirit has inspired me and allowed me to reach my goals and to make the Judiciary in this County and State something we can all be proud of.. Thank you. You've been great and we've had some laughs along the way. Especially you, Chief Judge Loveless who I had the great privilege to clerk for and learn from. What better role model could I have had?

You have heard a great deal about me tonight, some of which even I myself didn't believe. But I have to be honest. I enjoyed it. I've still got a lot of time and my work is not done. In fact, I am busier now than I was a few months ago and I am enjoying life even more. As I listened to the speakers tonight, I really felt like the British Historian and Philosopher Isaiah Berlin on his own retirement when he said, "I have been overestimated all my life. I will not pretend that this has been a source of grave distress. As someone once said to me, it is much nicer to receive more than one's due than one's due and I cannot deny it.

Thank you all again for making tonight and all that possible. Good night.

Other Books by This Author

Black Robe Fever

The Role of the Judge in American Society

The Winding Road

Criminal Courts, Civil Matters, and the Ongoing Quest for Access to Justice

Of Politics & Economics

The School of Hard Knocks and Gentle Persuasion

RAMSES HOUSE PUBLISHING LLC
BALTIMORE, MD

Index

Made in the USA
Columbia, SC
04 August 2023

21220426R00185